i never metaphor
i didn't like

Also by Dr. Mardy Grothe

Viva la Repartee

Oxymoronica

Never Let a Fool Kiss You or a Kiss Fool You

i never metaphor i didn't like

A Comprehensive Compilation of History's
Greatest Analogies, Metaphors, and Similes

Dr. Mardy Grothe

An *Imprint of* HarperCollins*Publishers*

dedication

To my very special grandson

Ryan Matthew Wood,

who at the age of eight
already knows about *chiasmus* and *oxymoronica*
and will soon be learning about
analogies, *metaphors*, and *similes*

Designed by Emily Cavett Taff

Library of Congress Cataloging-in-Publication Data is available upon request.

ISBN: 978-0-06-135813-5

09 10 11 12   OV/RRD   10 9 8 7 6 5 4

contents

introduction

T he sentence you are reading at this very moment is an example of *prose* (the word comes from the Latin *prosa*, meaning "straightforward"). Prose is the language people generally use to transmit information and express ideas. Closely resembling the patterns of everyday speech, prose is the kind of writing typically found in books, newspapers, and magazines. These are examples:

> Prose and poetry are two methods
> people can use to express ideas.

> A committee is a questionable mechanism
> for making decisions or solving problems.

> Adolescence is a time of great turmoil.

Every now and then, though, prose is spiced up and becomes more fanciful:

> **Prose is to poetry as walking is to dancing.**
>
> PAUL VALÉRY

> **A committee is a cul-de-sac down which**
> **ideas are lured and then quietly strangled.**
>
> BARNETT COCKS

Adolescence is a kind of emotional seasickness.

ARTHUR KOESTLER

In the first set of observations, the prose is straightforward but *prosaic*, meaning it lacks imagination and even borders on dull. In the second set, the prose is enhanced by *analogies*, *metaphors*, and *similes*, a trio of extremely valuable tools at the disposal of writers, orators, and poets. With the assistance of these three stylistic devices, ordinary language is elevated, often to an extraordinary degree. This is undoubtedly what the nineteenth-century American journalist and poet William Cullen Bryant had in mind when he wrote:

Eloquence is the poetry of prose.

This book will celebrate history's most spectacular examples of *poetic prose*—all constructed by the use of analogies, metaphors, and similes. Let's begin by meeting the key players.

ANALOGY

From the dawn of civilization, human beings have tried to understand one thing by relating it to something else. This approach—called analogical thinking—has been extremely helpful as people try to make sense out of a world that can often seem confusing or even incomprehensible.

Formally, an *analogy* is an attempt to state a relationship between two things that don't initially appear to have much in common (the word derives from the Greek word *analogia*, formally meaning a "proportionate" relationship between two pairs of things). In what may be the oldest analogy ever recorded, from around 1350 B.C., the Egyptian pharaoh Akhenaton was said to have observed:

**As the moon retains her nature,
though darkness spread itself before her face as a curtain,
so the Soul remains perfect
even in the bosom of the fool.**

In this ancient observation, the pharaoh was drawing an analogy between the moon hidden behind a curtain of darkness and a soul hidden behind a curtain of foolishness. Both continue to exist, he maintains, even when they cannot be seen. For many centuries, analogies have been used to instruct people and to dispense moral lessons. In this case, the ethical principle embedded in the analogy might be expressed this way: don't be too quick to shun or reject people, for behind all foolish or inappropriate actions there exists a perfect soul within.

While analogical thinking goes back to the oldest days of antiquity, people thinking about analogies these days are likely to recall those peculiar and often perplexing constructions that have long been a staple of intelligence tests and scholastic aptitude tests. The format will probably be familiar to you:

illness : life :: (blank) : iron
a. steel   b. blade   c. forge   d. rust

Following a convention going back to ancient times, the analogy is read this way:

"Illness is to life as (blank) is to iron."

The task here is to figure out which one of the four multiple-choice options bears the same relationship to iron as illness does to life. After a moment's thought, the answer is easily reasoned out. Just as illness can threaten or end a life, rust can threaten or destroy iron.

In the fourth century B.C., the Greek philosopher Antisthenes found another aspect of the human experience that was analogous to iron and rust:

As iron is eaten away by rust,
so the envious are consumed by their own passion.

Rather than simply assert that envy is a destructive passion, Antisthenes begins by taking a phenomenon that is well known—the damaging effect of rust on iron—and relates it to something not so familiar—the damaging effect of envy on people. By expressing his thought in an analogy, he made it very easy for people to forge a mental picture of the slow, corrosive process whereby one thing gradually eats away and eventually destroys something else.

People who say "Let me offer an analogy" are trying to explain one thing by relating it to something else. The entry on analogy in *The Concise Oxford Dictionary of Literary Terms* explains it this way:

> *Illustration of an idea by means of a more familiar idea that is*
> *similar or parallel to it, and thus said to be analogous to it.*

Structurally, analogies are often constructed in the *A is to B as C is to D* format:

Reading is to the mind,
what exercise is to the body.
JOSEPH ADDISON

As cold waters to a thirsty soul,
so is good news from a far country.
THE BIBLE—PROVERBS 25:25

As soap is to the body,
tears are to the soul.
YIDDISH PROVERB

What garlic is to salad,
insanity is to art.
AUGUSTUS SAINT-GAUDENS

Sometimes the format is varied slightly, and the intention shifts from the serious to the humorous:

**The murals in restaurants are
on a par with the food in museums.**

PETER DE VRIES

And sometimes an additional explanation is appended after the formal analogy, just to make sure the point is understood:

**Doing business without advertising is like winking at a girl in the dark.
You know what you are doing, but nobody else does.**

STUART H. BRITT

**Al Capone was to crime what J. P. Morgan was to Wall Street,
the first man to exert national influence over his trade.**

ANDREW SINCLAIR

Analogies form the basis for much of the thinking people do about life. When we encounter something new and unfamiliar—or try to make sense out of something that is not well understood—we often benefit from relating it to something else we know well. Sigmund Freud expressed it nicely:

**Analogies, it is true, decide nothing,
but they can make one feel more at home.**

In 2006, seventy-eight-year-old Harry Whittington was accidentally shot in the face by Vice President Dick Cheney in a celebrated hunting accident. When it became apparent that Whittington's wounds were not life threatening—and that he was expected to fully recover—countless jokes from comedians and late-night talk-show hosts filled the airwaves. I'm sure you recall some of them.

Whittington, it was soon learned, was an Austin attorney, a successful real-estate investor, and a long-time member of the Texas Republican party. Early in his career, when LBJ and the Democrats were in control of the Lone Star

State, Whittington was the only Republican serving on the board of the Texas Department of Corrections. As he learned more about the grim reality of incarceration, he made an unsettling discovery. Yes, prisons get criminals off the street, but they do a miserable job of rehabilitation and, ironically, may even stimulate further criminal behavior. He began to express his view this way:

Prisons are to crime what greenhouses are to plants.

In his analogy between prison life and the world of horticulture, Whittington made a compelling point—as greenhouses foster the growth of budding plants, prisons are excellent breeding grounds for future criminal behavior.

Whittington's observation illustrates an important point about analogies—when they are well-crafted, they have a *ring of truth* to them. As a result, analogies have long been considered one of the best ways to communicate profound ideas. Henry David Thoreau was thinking along these lines when he wrote:

All perception of truth is the perception of an analogy.

Analogies have enjoyed a long and honored history in philosophical and political discourse, but they have also been favored by orators, writers, artists, actors, and humorists. When comedic actor Harvey Korman turned seventy-seven in 2004, he was asked if he was using the erectile dysfunction drug Viagra. He replied:

The idea of using Viagra at my age is like erecting a brand-new flag pole in front of a condemned building.

Similarly, out of all the complaints of bloated government spending and the questionable competence of our elected leaders, few can match the inspired analogy of P. J. O'Rourke in his 1991 classic, *Parliament of Whores:*

**Giving money and power to government
is like giving whiskey and car keys to teenage boys.**

Analogical phrasing is only one tool available to people interested in more eloquently expressing their ideas. Another device—and a close cousin to the analogy—is the *metaphor*.

METAPHOR

If an analogy can be formatted as *A is to B as C is to D*, a metaphor is the flat assertion that *A is B*. Even though analogies and metaphors are constructed slightly differently, they share one essential feature—they try to capture a key aspect of one thing by relating it to something else. In one of his many collections of aphorisms, the American writer Mason Cooley wrote:

A skyscraper is a boast in glass and steel.

Notice that Cooley does not suggest that a skyscraper is *like* a boast—which would make it a *simile*—he maintains that it *is* a boast, fulfilling the *A is B* requirement and making it a metaphor. To demonstrate the close relationship between metaphors and analogies, notice how easy it is to transform the observation into an analogy:

A skyscraper is in architecture as a boast is in interpersonal relations.

I came across Cooley's observation some years ago, and now rarely visit a major American city without having it come to mind. This happens routinely with metaphors—the best ones take up permanent residence in our minds.

There is one other thing about the Cooley metaphor that may not be apparent. A skyscraper is a building, not a boast, so the statement is not literally true. All metaphors are violations of logic in the sense that they assert that two different things are the same. In the fascinating world of human discourse, we make allowances for such flights of fancy by calling them *figuratively* true. Like *leaps of faith* in religion, when people believe things that cannot be proved, we make *leaps of logic* when we use metaphors—we say something is true, even when we know it is literally untrue or logically false. This shows up the following observations, which also—it should be noted—help us see familiar things in new ways:

Worry is interest paid on trouble before it falls due.

W. R. INGE

Art is the sex of the imagination.

GEORGE JEAN NATHAN

**America is an enormous frosted cupcake
in the middle of millions of starving people.**

GLORIA STEINEM

In some metaphorical observations, the formal metaphor is not obvious:

Art washes away from the soul the dust of everyday life.

PABLO PICASSO

Here, the formal *A is B* assertion is not explicitly stated. But it is clearly suggested—*art (is a liquid that) washes*. The observation also illustrates the difference between literal and figurative truth. In real life, art cannot wash anything. And a soul doesn't literally accumulate dust. But by imbuing art with the cleansing properties of water, Picasso offers a memorable metaphor. If you examine the observation closely, you can also discern the underlying analogy—*as water is a cleanser for the body, art is a cleanser for the soul*.

All the observations we have just seen are examples of prose, but none are prosaic. Some even rise to the level of eloquence described earlier as the poetry of prose. And they all meet the definition of a *metaphor*, according to the *American Heritage Dictionary:*

> *A figure of speech in which a word or phrase that ordinarily designates one thing is used to designate another, thus making an implicit comparison, as in "a sea of troubles" or "All the world's a stage."*

The word *metaphor* made its first appearance in English in 1533. It derives from two Greek roots: *meta*, meaning "over, beyond" and *pherein*, meaning "to carry, transfer." The root sense of the word is to carry a word over and beyond its original meaning by applying it to something else (Aristotle said a metaphor was giving a thing a name that belonged to something else). And that is exactly what Shakespeare does in his famous passage from *As You Like It*:

> **All the world's a stage,**
> **And all the men and women merely players.**
> **They have their exits and entrances,**
> **And one man in his time plays many parts. . . .**

Shakespeare might have expressed the thought in a formal analogy *(people are to the world as actors are to a stage)*, but he went with a metaphor instead. He goes on to describe people as actors and then—true to the root sense of the word—*carried* the metaphor further by referring to exits, entrances, and the many parts played in a lifetime. In the rest of the passage, he went on to describe the seven ages of man, but he could have pursued the metaphor in many other ways. He might have talked about people being well suited—or miscast—for their roles. He might have contrasted lead actors with those in supporting roles. He might have compared award-winning performances with forgettable ones. Once *world* is metaphorically transformed into *stage*, then all of the attributes of the *target domain* (stage) can be applied back to the original *source domain* (world). Notice how Richard Lederer leaps from one conceptual domain to another in this metaphorical gem from *Get Thee to a Punnery* (1988):

Puns are a three-way circus of words:
words clowning, words teetering on tightropes,
words swinging from tent-tops,
words thrusting their heads into the mouths of lions.

A metaphor is a kind of magical mental changing room—where one thing, for a moment, becomes another, and in that moment is seen in a whole new way. It's like watching a man imitating a woman. We often learn more about the man in the few moments he acts like a woman than we can after years of observing him behave as a man. As soon as something old is seen in a new way, it stimulates a torrent of new thoughts and associations, almost as if a mental floodgate has been lifted. Bernard Malamud put it this way:

I love metaphor.
It provides two loaves where there seems to be one.
Sometimes it throws in a whole load of fish.

Throughout history, certain rare individuals have demonstrated a special ability to discern a relationship between things that initially seem quite alien to each other. The talent was recognized nearly 2,500 years ago by Aristotle, who observed in *Poetics:*

The greatest thing by far is to be a master of metaphor.
This alone cannot be imparted by another;
it is the mark of genius,
for to make good metaphors implies an eye for resemblance.

While I disagree that a command of metaphor cannot be imparted by the right teacher, I agree that there is a certain talent—even a kind of genius—involved in finding something in common between very different domains of life. Robert Frost said it well:

**An idea is a feat of association,
and the height of it is a good metaphor.**

A keen *eye for resemblance*, to use Aristotle's phrase, is a rare gift, but it may also be an essential skill for a person who is trying to express a powerful idea in an original way. And once people make a connection between two different domains, they often take the initial metaphor and tweak it with an additional thought, leaving us with truly memorable observations:

**The world is a book,
and those who do not travel read only one page.**
ST. AUGUSTINE

**Medicine is my lawful wife and literature my mistress;
when I tire of one, I spend the night with the other.**
ANTON CHEKHOV

**Art at its most significant is a Distant Early Warning System
that can always be relied on
to tell the old culture what is beginning to happen to it.**
MARSHALL MCLUHAN

Observations like these—and many, many more to be found later—may help you appreciate another observation from Aristotle, this from his classic *Rhetoric:*

**It is metaphor above all else that gives
clearness, charm, and distinction to the style.**

So far, we've examined analogies and metaphors. But when it comes to making connections between dissimilar things, there's a third major player in the drama.

SIMILE

Webster's New World Dictionary defines *simile* this way:

> *A figure of speech in which one thing is likened to another, dissimilar thing by the use of "like," "as," etc. ("a heart as big as a whale," "her tears flowed like wine").*

Simile and the related word *similar* derive from the Latin *similis*, meaning "like." The word has an even longer history in English than *metaphor*, making its first written appearance in English in 1393 in William Langland's *Piers Plowman*. Similes share with analogies and metaphors the goal of relating one thing to another, but they do it in a slightly different way. Look at these quotations:

> **Books are like imprisoned souls**
> **till someone takes them down from a shelf and frees them.**
> SAMUEL BUTLER

> **Books . . . are like lobster shells,**
> **we surround ourselves with 'em,**
> **then we grow out of 'em and leave 'em behind,**
> **as evidence of our earlier stage of development.**
> DOROTHY L. SAYERS

> **No furniture is so charming as books.**
> SYDNEY SMITH

These observations help us see books—among our most familiar possessions—in new ways. And because of the words *like* and *as*, they are classified as similes.

In many observations, the presence or absence of only one word separates a simile from a metaphor. An ancient Chinese proverb—written when many books were available in smaller editions—once offered the lovely idea that a book was like a portable garden we could take with us in our travels. The proverb, as usually presented, is a perfect simile, but by deleting one word it is transformed from one figure of speech into another:

> *Simile:* A book *is like* a garden carried in the pocket.
> *Metaphor:* A book *is* a garden carried in the pocket.

In a simile, there is an *explicit* comparison—one thing is said to be *like* something else. In a metaphor, there is no comparison because the two things are treated as identical (an *implicit* comparison, it is often said). Similes are similar to—but distinctly different from—metaphors, and they can be equally impressive:

> **Writers, like teeth, are divided into incisors and grinders.**
> WALTER BAGEHOT

> **Justice is like a train that's nearly always late.**
> YEVGENY YEVTUSHENKO

While some people make a big deal out of the difference between similes and metaphors, there is a great deal of truth in a joke that has long been popular among teachers of English:

> **A simile is like a metaphor.**

In his 1955 book on style, the poet and critic F. L. Lucas put it this way:

"The simile sets two ideas side by side; in the metaphor they become super-imposed." Here's a quick structural overview:

> *An analogy says that A is to B as C is to D.*
> *A metaphor says that A is B, or substitutes B for A.*
> *A simile says that A is like B.*

In addition to *like* or *as*, several other words and expressions indicate the presence of a simile. A common one is *than*, as in "faster than a speeding bullet" or "sharper than a serpent's tooth," as in this classic line from Shakespeare's *King Lear*:

> **How sharper than a serpent's tooth**
> **It is to have a thankless child.**

Here are some more expressions that signal the use of a simile:

is similar to	*may be compared to*	*is akin to*
is comparable to	*puts one in mind of*	*is a kind of*
as though	*can be likened to*	*is the same as*
is not unlike	*is not dissimilar to*	*may be seen as*

In the world of figurative language, similes have long taken a back seat to the more glamorous metaphor. Aristotle preferred metaphors over similes, and language snobs have slavishly followed his example for centuries. But what similes lack in prestige they make up for in frequency. Here is just a sampling of similes that are a staple of everyday speech:

busy as a bee	*hard as a rock*	*thin as a rail*
dry as a bone	*sharper than a tack*	*happy as a clam*
selling like hotcakes	*fit as a fiddle*	*proud as a peacock*
stubborn as a mule	*soft as a pillow*	*cuter than a button*

light as a feather	*smooth as silk*	*higher than a kite*
slow as molasses	*spread like wildfire*	*shaking like a leaf*
sly as a fox	*smart as a whip*	*fresh as a daisy*

Expressions like these are often the first things that come to mind when people are asked to provide a simile. And while they may have been quite original when first employed, they've now become *clichés*. It is likely that these stale, trite, and hackneyed expressions are responsible for diminishing the reputation of similes in the minds of so many people.

Similes do not have to be bland and uninspired, however, and in the hands of gifted writers they can be raised to the level of an art form. John Updike once wrote:

Critics are like pigs at the pastry cart.

The observation illustrates one of the things I love most about metaphorical language. When imaginatively conceived they're like beautiful *word paintings*. In Updike's observation, we can easily visualize a pastry cart piled high with a variety of beautifully presented literary delicacies. Gathering around the cart are a group of swine, clearly out of place in a swanky establishment. The pigs—well known for favoring *slop* but willing to eat just about anything—are clearly incapable of appreciating the quality of the treats they're about to devour.

Another unforgettable *word picture* comes from Stephen King. With grand dreams of ultimately becoming a writer, he took a job teaching high school English after graduating from college. He didn't last long. Exhausted after planning lessons and correcting students' papers, he was sapped of any energy he might have devoted to writing. He described the experience vividly:

Teaching school is like
having jumper cables hooked to your brain,
draining all the juice out of you.

While similes are generally contrasted with metaphors, they actually have more in common with analogies. Indeed, when a simile is slightly extended, it has an *A is to B as C is to D* structure that makes it virtually indistinguishable from an analogy. This has resulted in much confusion. For example, in the *American Heritage Dictionary*, Shakespeare's "So are you to my thoughts as food to life" is given as an example of a simile. In my mind, though, I see Shakespeare identifying a proportionate relationship between two sets of things—*you to my thoughts* and *food to life*—and view it as an analogy.

Some similes are deliciously entertaining, as when Norman Mailer compared his regular novels with the ones that had been adapted to the film world:

**Novels are like wives; you don't talk about them.
But movies are different; they're like mistresses, and you can brag a bit.**

Some are highly unusual but oddly compelling. In *The Book on Writing* (2003), Paula La Rocque quotes Roger Angell writing about Barry Bonds:

**Bonds . . . stands in the middle of the Giants' batting order
like an aneurysm.**

Like an aneurysm? Well, think about it for a moment. Whether you love or loathe major league baseball's all-time home-run champ, Angell's simile perfectly describes what I have seen for years when Bonds is at the plate—a player who is about to explode.

Some similes are educational as well as entertaining, making us wish that more teachers would make them a part of the instructional process:

**A dependent clause is like a dependent child:
incapable of standing on its own but able to cause a lot of trouble.**
WILLIAM SAFIRE

Having seen numerous accolades delivered to metaphors, I consider it a treat to see kudos occasionally tossed in the direction of this less heralded figure of speech. In 2006, the popular syndicated columnist James J. Kilpatrick wrote of the simile:

> **It's the most familiar of all literary enbellishments,**
> **in a class with a wedge of lemon or a sprig of parsley.**
> **It can raise a cupcake to the level of a *petit four*.**

Lovely as Kilpatrick's thought is, it would be wrong to view the simile as a mere garnish or an ornament to thought. As all language lovers know, similes can be intellectually nourishing as well as tasty. And when similes and metaphors are seamlessly interwoven—as they often are—we are treated to language that is enlivened and ideas that are brought to life:

> **Society is like a stew.**
> **If you don't stir it up every once in a while,**
> **then a layer of scum floats to the top.**
> EDWARD ABBEY

> **We can think of history as a kind of layer cake**
> **in which a number of different layers run side by side through time,**
> **each with a dynamic of its own, and yet each from time to time**
> **profoundly penetrating and interacting with others.**
> KENNETH E. BOULDING

> **Men resemble great deserted palaces:**
> **the owner occupies only a few rooms**
> **and has closed-off wings where he never ventures.**
> FRANÇOIS MAURIAC

We could go on and on about these three superstars of figurative language, and even explore some of their close relatives—like *personification, allegory, fable,* and *parable*—but it's time to bring this introductory chapter to a close. Before we do, let's review where we've come so far. We began by talking about how the prose we read and hear on a regular basis is stale, dull, and uninspired. However, when writers and orators consciously employ a variety of linguistic tools that have been well known for three thousand years, prose can be elevated to such a degree it rivals the grace and beauty of poetry. Of the many stylistic devices that are available, we have focused on the Big Three—analogies, metaphors, and similes.

The rest of the book is a compilation of nearly two thousand quotations, all formed by the use of analogies, metaphors, and similes. The book is organized into topics—like *politics, sports, sex,* and *love*—but I've decided to give each chapter a metaphorical title.

Some titles—like "Sports Is the Toy Department of Life"—clearly indicate the subject of the chapter. Other titles are not so obvious. The very next chapter—the most personal in the book—is titled "An Ice-Axe for the Frozen Sea Within." The meaning of the title will become clear to you shortly, but I don't think it is an exaggeration to say that the metaphor—from Franz Kafka—may forever alter the way you look at your book-reading efforts. The table of contents at the beginning of the book provides all the chapter titles as well as the subject area of each one.

In each chapter, I'll begin by introducing the subject in a way that I hope will whet your interest. After a few foundation-laying pages, I'll present a wide variety of quotations that fit within the theme of the chapter. In every chapter except one—which I'll explain when you get there—the quotations will be arranged alphabetically by author. If you want to locate observations from a particular person, consult the Author Index.

Throughout the book, you will occasionally find brief *commentary* after a quotation. In general, this will be my attempt to explain an observation, tell you something about the author, or provide some other information to enhance your appreciation of the quotation.

This book is aimed at readers who have a deep interest in seeing language used in creative ways. It should also appeal to readers with a professional interest in language and the effective presentation of ideas: writers, poets, journalists, speakers, preachers, speechwriters, and teachers, especially those who teach writing, poetry, and public speaking.

In his 1625 classic *Essays*, the great English man of letters Francis Bacon wrote:

> **Some books are to be tasted, others to be swallowed,**
> **and some few to be chewed and digested.**

I'm not exactly sure where this book belongs in Bacon's scheme of things, but I do know one thing for sure about how to approach this book. *Go slowly.* Like a museum curator putting together a special art exhibition, I have attempted to compile some of history's greatest *word paintings*. So, just as you would be ill advised to rush through an art museum, it would be a mistake to speed-read your way through this book. Take the time to savor the observations and to admire the skill that was required to create them.

Professionally, I've been a psychologist for over thirty years. Personally, I'm a voracious reader and a serious quotation collector. Just as some people collect coins, or stamps, or butterflies, I collect quotations. I've been doing it for more than four decades, and I now have hundreds of thousands of specimens in my personal collection.

This is my fourth book in the *word and language* arena and like the previous ones, it has been a labor of love. But the process of writing a book is always more fun at the beginning and middle stages than at the end. For the past six weeks, with a production deadline staring me in the face, the project has consumed my life. Winston Churchill described the process best, and he did it metaphorically:

> **Writing a book is an adventure.**
> **To begin with, it is a toy and an amusement;**
> **then it becomes a mistress,**

**and then it becomes a master, and then a tyrant.
The last phase is that just as you are about to be reconciled to your
servitude, you kill the monster, and fling him out to the public.**

Before I fling this monster in your direction, let me add one more thing. While I've been committed to accuracy, I'm sure I've made some mistakes. If you discover any errors or would simply like to offer some feedback, please write me in care of the publisher or e-mail me at DrMGrothe@aol.com.

I've also launched a Web site where you can delve into the topic a bit deeper or sign up for my free weekly e-newsletter ("Dr. Mardy's Quotes of the Week"). Come up and visit sometime: www.DrMardy.com.

chapter 1

An Ice-Axe For the Frozen Sea Within

It was early winter, 1962, and I was in the middle of my junior year at the University of North Dakota. A charismatic American president with a grand vision had been in office for nearly two years, and a movement for racial equality, led by an eloquent Southern preacher with an equally grand vision, was beginning to take root all over the country.

I was not tuned into these developments, though, for my priorities lay elsewhere. I was president of my fraternity, vice-president of the student senate, a member of the prestigious Blue Key service fraternity, and an officer of Golden Feather, a highly selective pep club that had the enviable task of selecting cheerleaders for the school's athletic teams. I was, to use a popular expression of the era, a *Big Man on Campus* (BMOC). From the outside, I seemed to be leading a full and exciting life. On the inside, I felt cold and empty.

To the extent I had thought it out—which, in truth, was not very much—I had hoped my extracurricular activities would bring me happiness and satisfaction. But instead of feeling good about my accomplishments and better about myself, I was discovering that the path I'd been walking down was not taking me to a place where I wanted to go.

I'm not exactly sure what precipitated the decision, but somewhere in the middle of the school year, I impulsively—and, in hindsight, ungracefully—resigned from almost all the groups that up to that point had been so important to me. My fraternity brothers and quite a few other people viewed my decision as a personal rejection, and for a time I was *persona non grata* with many former friends. Feeling alone and afraid, I took a small room in the basement of an off-campus apartment and began a program of intense reading and reflection. With the help of several people who agreed to serve as guides, I began reading as much as I could from a dozen or so writers, including Henry David Thoreau, Ralph Waldo Emerson, and a newcomer on the intellectual scene, the 1960 winner of the Nobel Prize, Albert Camus.

Reading *Walden* for the first time, I was struck by the parallel between my recent personal choices and Thoreau's decision to "live deliberately" and "to front only the essential facts of life." I resonated deeply to his essential goal:

I wanted to live deep and suck out all the marrow of life.

Life, of course, doesn't have marrow; bones do. But Thoreau was writing figuratively, not literally. And by crafting his words in this way, he created an unforgettable image. Reading Thoreau for the first time, I felt as if I had made a new friend.

I embarked on my reading program with enthusiasm, but it was far from a systematic effort. Like the proverbial child in a candy store, I jumped from one treat to another, sampling something from one writer, and then another, and then another. Early in my efforts, an observation from Albert Camus almost seemed to leap off the pages:

One recognizes one's course by discovering the paths that stray from it.

The words had an unexpected impact, softening some of the self-criticism I had been feeling for making what seemed like poor choices. But perhaps I hadn't been so foolish after all. Maybe Camus was right—we best discover what is right for us only after chasing what is wrong. In *Sand and Foam*, Kahlil Gibran expressed the thought in a slightly different way:

One may not reach the dawn save by the path of the night.

A short while later, returning to the writings of Thoreau, I was struck by an 1853 entry he made in his journal:

Dwell as near as possible to the channel in which your life flows.

By relating human lives to the course of a river, Thoreau was suggesting we follow our natural inclinations. Yes, Shakespeare had said pretty much the same thing in "To thine own self be true," but that line had already become a cliché. The Thoreau observation, on the other hand, seemed new and special. As his words reverberated in my mind, it was becoming clear that I had indeed made a mistake—but recalling the earlier Camus observation, an honest mistake—by trying to walk down a path better designed for another.

A short while later, I felt a similar emotional stirring when I came across an observation attributed to Ralph Waldo Emerson:

Do not go where the path may lead,
go instead where there is no path and leave a trail.

And then again, when—for the first time—I came across this classic passage from Robert Frost's 1916 poem *The Road Not Taken*:

Two roads diverged in a wood, and I—
I took the one less traveled by,
And that has made all the difference.

The ideas embedded in these observations seemed so important and profound that I jotted them down on those 3 × 5 index cards that were used back
then for library research. Once they were recorded, I thumb-tacked the cards
on the walls of my room. As the weeks passed I found myself going back to
the quotations again and again for reinforcement and re-inspiration.

As my reading program progressed, I continued this simple recording
ritual. After a few months, my dingy little basement room came alive, looking almost as if it had been plastered with a special kind of quotation wall-
paper. Thoreau was well represented on my Wall of Quotes:

> **We are all sculptors and painters,**
> **and our material is our own flesh and bones.**

> **Be a Columbus to whole new continents and worlds within you,**
> **opening new channels, not of trade, but of thought.**

As was Ralph Waldo Emerson:

> **Hitch your wagon to a star.**

> **The profoundest thought or passion sleeps as in a mine,**
> **until an equal mind and heart finds and publishes it.**

and Albert Camus:

> **There is no sun without shadow,**
> **and it is essential to know the night.**

> **In the depth of winter, I finally learned that**
> **within me there lay an invincible summer.**

As much as any quotation on my wall, this last observation from Camus described what had been happening to me. My investment in a reflective reading program was paying unexpectedly large—and largely unexpected—dividends. A few months earlier, I was in the depths of a dark winter. Now, however, I was beginning to break through to a deeper level of understanding about myself and what I needed to do with my life.

Years later, I would come across an observation that captured what I had been experiencing. In a 1904 letter to a friend, Franz Kafka asked a provocative rhetorical—and metaphorical—question: "If the book we are reading does not wake us, as with a fist hammering on our skull, why then do we read it?" And then he answered the question this way:

A book should serve as an ice-axe to break the frozen sea within us.

For the remainder of my college years, I read voraciously. My grades suffered, as did many personal relationships, but I was self-medicating with a drug that appeared to hold great promise. Unlike the street drugs that were beginning to become popular, the substance I was using was legal, free for the taking, and capable of unrivaled mind-expanding effects. Another metaphorical observation, this one from Rudyard Kipling—and also discovered many years later—expressed it perfectly:

Words are, of course, the most powerful drug used by mankind.

It's now been more than four decades since I graduated from college, and I'm still addicted—although these days I simply describe myself as an avid quotation collector. In the same way other people collect coins, or stamps, or butterflies, I collect quotations. It is a passion that will continue for the remainder of my life.

At the end of my college years, I dismantled my Wall of Quotes and secured them in a manila folder that I labeled *Words to Live By*. As the years passed, the folder became so bloated with new discoveries that I had to use large rubber bands to keep everything together. After a decade or so, the folder and its contents became so tattered and worn that I transferred all the quotations into a computer file designated by the initials *WTLB*. Since then, my regimen has been pretty much the same. Whenever I find a particularly inspiring quotation in a book or article, I make a notation in the margin. Later, when I've finished the reading, I record those observations in the *WTLB* file on my computer.

All the specimens in my *Words to Live By* file have inspired or challenged me in some important way. And while many of the quotations are examples of other favorite literary devices—like chiasmus and paradox—a significant number of them, just like the quotations that have appeared so far in this chapter, are analogies, metaphors, and similes. In the remainder of the chapter, I've selected many more that have helped me become a better person; perhaps they will be of some benefit to you as well.

> I don't want to get to the end of my life
> and find that I have lived just the length of it.
> I want to have lived the width of it as well.
>
> DIANE ACKERMAN

> Not to engage in the pursuit of ideas is to live like ants instead of like men.
>
> MORTIMER ADLER

> Words are the physicians of a mind diseased.
>
> AESCHYLUS

> Without passion, man is a mere latent force and possibility, like the flint
> which awaits the shock of the iron before it can give forth its spark.
>
> HENRI-FRÉDÉRIC AMIEL

Passion is a good thing only as long as we realize that too much of a good thing is bad. Ben Franklin advised: "If passion drives, let reason hold the reins."

Such as are your habitual thoughts,
such also will be the character of your mind;
for the soul is dyed by the color of the thoughts.

MARCUS AURELIUS

If a man be gracious and courteous to strangers,
it shows he is a citizen of the world,
and that his heart is no island cut off from other islands,
but a continent that joins to them.

FRANCIS BACON

This topographical metaphor, from Bacon's *Essays* (1597), may have inspired one of literature's most famous passages, John Donne's 1624 "No man is an island" sentiment.

In diving to the bottom of pleasure we bring up more gravel than pearls.

HONORÉ DE BALZAC

Thomas Jefferson observed similarly: "Do not bite the bait of pleasure till you know there is no hook beneath it."

You never know till you try to reach them how accessible men are;
but you must approach each man by the right door.

HENRY WARD BEECHER

If you board the wrong train,
it is no use running along the corridor in the other direction.

DIETRICH BONHOEFFER

Authority without wisdom is like a heavy axe without an edge,
fitter to bruise than polish.

ANNE BRADSTREET

If we had no winter, the spring would not be so pleasant:
if we did not sometimes taste of adversity,
prosperity would not be so welcome.

ANNE BRADSTREET

These two observations come from *Meditations Divine and Moral* (1664), the only prose work from Anne Bradstreet, the first published poet (of either gender) in the American colonies. She wrote the book for her son Simon, writing in the dedication: "You once desired me to leave something for you in writing that you might look upon when you should see me no more." Even though *Meditations* was written nearly 350 years ago, it can be read with great pleasure and much benefit today.

Light tomorrow with today.

ELIZABETH BARRETT BROWNING

Where the heart lies, let the brain lie also.

ROBERT BROWNING

Growth itself contains the germ of happiness.

PEARL S. BUCK

Holding on to anger is like grasping a hot coal
with the intent of throwing it at someone else;
you are the one who gets burned.

SIDDHARTHA GAUTAMA BUDDHA

When a person is down in the world,
an ounce of help is better than a pound of preaching.

EDWARD BULWER-LYTTON

The rule in carving holds good as to criticism;
never cut with a knife what you can cut with a spoon.

CHARLES BUXTON

We must be willing to get rid of the life we've planned,
so as to have the life that is waiting for us.
The old skin has to be shed before the new one can come.

JOSEPH CAMPBELL

What we become depends on what we read
after all of the professors have finished with us.
The greatest university of all is a collection of books.

THOMAS CARLYLE

Never seem wiser, nor more learned, than the people you are with.
Wear your learning like your watch, in a private pocket;
do not pull it out and strike it merely to show you have one.

LORD CHESTERFIELD *(Philip Dormer Stanhope)*

Every difficulty slurred over will be a ghost to disturb your repose later on.

FREDERIC CHOPIN

It is better to wear out than to rust out.
There will be time enough for repose in the grave.

RICHARD CUMBERLAND

This observation—likening human life to a machine—has a contemporary feel but goes back over three centuries. Cumberland was a seventeenth-century English theologian. The saying was attributed to him in a 1786 sermon by a fellow Anglican clergyman, George Horne. Theodore Roosevelt reprised the sentiment in an 1898 speech: "Let us live in the harness, striving mightily; let us rather run the risk of wearing out than rusting out."

Chase after the truth like all hell and you'll free yourself,
even though you never touch its coat-tails.

CLARENCE DARROW

A man should live with his superiors as he does with his fire;
not too near, lest he burn; not too far off, lest he freeze.

DIOGENES

In the fourth century B.C., the Greek philosopher Diogenes advocated a life of self-sufficiency and the repudiation of human luxuries. Here he offers history's oldest and best advice on "managing your boss."

Without goals, and plans to reach them,
you are like a ship that has set sail with no destination.

FITZHUGH DODSON

We should take care not to make the intellect our god;
it has, of course, powerful muscles, but no personality.

ALBERT EINSTEIN

The Promised Land always lies on the other side of a Wilderness.

HAVELOCK ELLIS

Make your own bible.
Select and collect all the words and sentences that
in all your reading have been to you like the blast of triumph.

RALPH WALDO EMERSON

Never feel self-pity, the most destructive emotion there is.
How awful to be caught up in the terrible squirrel cage of self.

MILLICENT FENWICK

Acting without thinking is like shooting without aiming.

B. C. FORBES

He who knows no hardships will know no hardihood.
He who faces no calamity will need no courage.
Mysterious though it is, the characteristics in human nature
which we love best grow in a soil with a strong mixture of troubles.

HARRY EMERSON FOSDICK

Just as a cautious businessman avoids investing all his capital in one concern,
so wisdom would probably admonish us also
not to anticipate all our happiness from one quarter alone.

SIGMUND FREUD

If thou hast Knowledge,
let others light their Candle at thine.

THOMAS FULLER, M.D.

Dr. Thomas Fuller—not to be confused with the seventeenth-century English historian by the same name—was a London physician and preacher. He put together two early and important quotation anthologies, the 1731 *Introductio ad Prudentiam*, and a year later *Gnomologia*. This is the original version of a saying that is commonly attributed to both Margaret Fuller and Winston Churchill: "If you have knowledge, let others light their candles at it." Recalling the earlier Diogenes thought about superiors, Fuller also offered this: "I do not recommend to thee the Familiarity of great Men; it's a fire that often scorches."

One does not discover new continents
without consenting to lose sight of the shore for a very long time.

ANDRÉ GIDE

We are our own devils; we drive ourselves out of our Edens.

JOHANN WOLFGANG VON GOETHE

Goethe was writing in the late 1700s, when most people believed the devil was a real entity, capable of seizing control and causing us to do evil things, just as Satan convinced Eve to taste of the forbidden apple. In the 1970s, comedian Flip Wilson parodied this view with his signature line, "The devil made me do it."

Happiness is as a butterfly which,
when pursued, is always beyond our grasp,
but which if you will sit down quietly, may alight upon you.

NATHANIEL HAWTHORNE

I find the great thing in this world is not so much where we stand,
as in what direction we are moving.
To reach the port of heaven, we must sail sometimes with the wind
and sometimes against it—
but we must sail, and not drift, nor lie at anchor.

OLIVER WENDELL HOLMES, SR.

Our acts make or mar us; we are the children of our own deeds.

VICTOR HUGO

Once you wake up thought in a man,
you can never put it to sleep again.

ZORA NEALE HURSTON

An inexhaustible good nature is one of the most precious gifts of heaven,
spreading itself like oil over the troubled sea of thought,
and keeping the mind smooth and equable in the roughest weather.

WASHINGTON IRVING

In matters of principle, stand like a rock;
in matters of taste, swim with the current.

THOMAS JEFFERSON

As far as we can discern, the sole purpose of human existence
is to kindle a light in the darkness of mere being.

CARL JUNG

Let the mind be a thoroughfare for all thoughts.

JOHN KEATS

A mind, like a home, is furnished by its owner,
so if one's life is cold and bare he can blame none but himself.

LOUIS L'AMOUR

Peter Ustinov offered a similar thought: "Once we are destined to live
out our lives in the prison of our mind, our duty is to furnish it well."

One cannot violate the promptings of one's nature
without having that nature recoil upon itself.

JACK LONDON

I would rather be ashes than dust!
I would rather that my spark should burn out in a brilliant blaze
than it should be stifled by dry-rot.
I would rather be a superb meteor,
every atom of me in magnificent glow,
than a sleepy and permanent planet.
The proper function of man is to live, not to exist.

JACK LONDON, *his "credo,"*
said two months before his death

Never mind trifles.
In this world a man must either be anvil or hammer.

HENRY WADSWORTH LONGFELLOW

These words, inspired by a 1764 Voltaire observation, come from a character in "The Story of Brother Bernardus," in Longfellow's 1839 *Hyperion*. By likening the lives of people to the tools of a blacksmith, he suggests that human beings can strike with force on the world around them or stand firm under the force of the blows they receive.

Who speaks the truth stabs Falsehood to the heart.

JAMES RUSSELL LOWELL

Do not think of knocking out another person's brains
because he differs in opinion from you.
It would be as rational to knock yourself on the head
because you differ from yourself ten years ago.

HORACE MANN

For this is the journey that men make: to find themselves.
If they fail in this, it doesn't much matter what else they find . . .
and when the tickets are collected at the end of the ride,
they are tossed into a bin marked "Failure."
But if a man happens to find himself . . . then he has found a mansion
which he can inhabit with dignity all the days of his life.

JAMES MICHENER

Man's task is to make of himself a work of art.

HENRY MILLER

Let him who would write heroic poems make his life a heroic poem.

JOHN MILTON

We must embrace pain and burn it as fuel for our journey.

KENJI MIYAZAWA

It is good to rub and polish our brain against that of others.

MICHEL DE MONTAIGNE

Montaigne did his writing in a circular room he constructed in the tower of his family chateau. His *solitarium*, as he called it, contained his books and writing table. He outdid my Wall of Quotes with his Beam of Quotes. On the roof-beams of his room, he hand-carved approximately fifty inspirational quotations, such as Terence's "I am a man; nothing human is alien to me."

**It's a good thing to turn your mind upside down now and then,
like an hour-glass, to let the particles run the other way.**

CHRISTOPHER MORLEY

When one has much to put into them, a day has a hundred pockets.

FRIEDRICH NIETZSCHE

**A strong and well-constituted man digests his experiences
(deeds and misdeeds all included) just as he digests his meats,
even when he has some tough morsels to swallow.**

FRIEDRICH NIETZSCHE

**And the day came when the risk it took to remain tight inside the bud
was more painful than the risk it took to blossom.**

ANAÏS NIN

**A man's duty . . . is to find out where the truth is, or if he cannot, at least
to take the best possible human doctrine and the hardest to disprove,
and to ride on this like a raft over the waters of life.**

PLATO

Remember, you are just an extra in everyone else's play.
FRANKLIN DELANO ROOSEVELT

It is only in marriage with the world that our ideals can bear fruit;
divorced from it, they remain barren.
BERTRAND RUSSELL

Sometimes our light goes out but is blown again into flame
by an encounter with another human being.
Each of us owes deepest thanks to those who have rekindled this inner light.
ALBERT SCHWEITZER

In the late 1700s, the German man of letters Johann Gottfried von Herder
offered a related thought: "Without inspiration, the best powers of the mind
remain dormant; there is a fuel in us which needs to be ignited with sparks."

Constant kindness can accomplish much.
As the sun makes ice melt,
kindness causes misunderstanding, mistrust, and hostility to evaporate.
ALBERT SCHWEITZER

Reading is a means of thinking with another person's mind;
it forces you to stretch your own.
CHARLES SCRIBNER, JR.

This is the true joy in life,
the being used for a purpose recognized by yourself as a mighty one;
the being thoroughly worn out before you are thrown on the scrap heap;
the being a force of Nature instead of a feverish selfish little clod
of ailments and grievances complaining that the world
will not devote itself to making you happy.
GEORGE BERNARD SHAW

I dread success.
To have succeeded is to have finished one's business on earth,
like the male spider, who is killed by the female
the moment he has succeeded in his courtship.
I like a state of continual *becoming*, with a goal in front and one behind.

GEORGE BERNARD SHAW

Don't judge each day by the harvest you reap, but by the seeds you plant.

ROBERT LOUIS STEVENSON

To keep a lamp burning we have to keep putting oil in it.

MOTHER TERESA

A mind all logic is like a knife all blade.
It makes the hand bleed that uses it.

RABINDRANATH TAGORE

He who has more learning than good deeds
is like a tree with many branches but weak roots;
the first great storm will throw it to the ground.
He whose good works are greater than his knowledge
is like a tree with fewer branches but with strong and spreading roots,
a tree which all the winds of heaven cannot uproot.

THE TALMUD

If a man does not keep pace with his companions,
perhaps it is because he hears a different drummer.
Let him step to the music which he hears, however measured or far away.

HENRY DAVID THOREAU

This passage from *Walden* resulted in the metaphor about *marching to the beat of a different drummer*, one of history's most popular sayings, and a reminder to be tolerant of those who shun the crowded path and go their own way.

> **So behave that the odor of your actions may enhance the general sweetness of the atmosphere.**
> HENRY DAVID THOREAU

> **Follow the grain in your own wood.**
> HOWARD THURMAN

> **We can't reach old age by another man's road.**
> MARK TWAIN

Twain wrote this in a piece he composed for his seventieth birthday celebration at Manhattan's Delmonico's restaurant in 1905.

> **Shun idleness. It is a rust that attaches itself to the most brilliant metals.**
> VOLTAIRE

> **We must cultivate our garden.**
> VOLTAIRE

These words come at the end of Voltaire's 1760 classic, *Candide*. Replying to a remark from Dr. Pangloss, Candide is referring to his vegetable garden, but he was also speaking metaphorically. In my years as a marriage counselor, I often reminded clients that *a relationship is like a garden*. And when we cultivate gardens, two things are necessary—nutrients must be added and weeds must be picked.

> **Feeling gratitude and not expressing it is like wrapping a present and not giving it.**
> WILLIAM ARTHUR WARD

On her final day on the *Today Show* in 2006, Katie Couric used this quotation—without crediting the author—to sum up her feelings toward co-host Matt Lauer and the others she had worked with during her fifteen years on the show.

> **But beware you be not swallowed up in books!**
> **An ounce of love is worth a pound of knowledge.**
>
> JOHN WESLEY,
> *in a 1768 letter to his brother Joseph*

> **There are two ways of spreading light:**
> **to be the candle, or the mirror that reflects it.**
>
> EDITH WHARTON

> **A man's rootage is more important than his leafage.**
>
> WOODROW WILSON

> **Born originals, how comes it to pass that we die copies?**
>
> EDWARD YOUNG

This extraordinary line comes from Young's *Conjectures on Original Compositions* (1759). After reading it for the first time, I formulated a new motto: "You were born an original, so don't die a copy." A century after Young wrote his words, Alexis de Tocqueville carried the metaphor further: "History is a gallery of pictures in which there are few originals and many copies."

> **However vague they are, dreams have a way of concealing themselves**
> **and leave us no peace until they are translated into reality,**
> **like seeds germinating underground,**
> **sure to sprout in their search for the sunlight.**
>
> LIN YUTANG

chapter 2

Reserved Seats at a
Banquet of Consequences

In 121 A.D., the man the world has come to know as Marcus Aurelius was born into one of the most powerful families in the Roman Empire. The young Marcus was so precocious that he aroused the attention of the emperor Hadrian. He was soon on a fast track to Roman leadership and, at age ten, was being educated by Rome's best thinkers. By age eleven, the ruler-in-training was describing himself as a follower of the Stoic philosopher Epictetus.

Shortly after becoming emperor at age forty, Marcus was the realization of a dream Plato once had—that a philosopher-king would one day rule the empire. Over the next two decades, though, his record didn't quite live up to the hype. Ever since, historians have tried to reconcile his high-minded principles with his actual accomplishments.

In the last ten years of his reign, Marcus kept a personal journal in which he recorded his personal reflections. The diary, never intended for publication, was discovered after his death at age fifty-nine and was eventually published under the simple title *Meditations*. It went on to become one of antiquity's most influential books. As a result of *Meditations*, more is known about the inner thoughts of this one Roman emperor than all the other emperors combined.

During Bill Clinton's first presidential campaign, he was asked to name one book—other than the Bible—that had helped him most. When he cited the *Meditations of Marcus Aurelius*, it sparked my interest. As I began to peruse the book, one observation got my attention:

> **The art of living is more like that of wrestling than of dancing;**
> **the main thing is to stand firm and be ready for an unforeseen attack.**

In this observation, we see what may be a shift in Marcus's thinking as he has grown older. At an earlier stage of life, the privileged young man might easily have taken the view that life was like dancing—an affair where things go well if one only learns the necessary steps and keeps in time with the music. As emperor, though, he reigned over a country that was threatened by barbarians outside the gate and many political enemies within. The mature Aurelius replaced a dancing metaphor with a wrestling one.

The *Meditations of Marcus Aurelius*, even in translations that go back a century, have a distinctly modern feel. Dipping into almost any page of the work, one finds observations that would not be out of place in a modern self-help manual, such as "Our life is what our thoughts make it." There are also many metaphorical observations:

> **What is not good for the hive is not good for the bee.**

> **Be like the promontory against which the waves continually break;**
> **it stands firm and tames the fury of the water around it.**

When reflecting on the human condition, philosophically inclined people have always been drawn to metaphorical thinking. Notice what happens when Leo Tolstoy likens the human capacity for self-delusion to a mathematical fraction:

**A man is like a fraction whose numerator is what he is
and whose denominator is what he thinks of himself.
The larger the denominator, the smaller the fraction.**

For anybody with a basic understanding of mathematics, this is a brilliant way of describing something we all know but have trouble putting into words—the more people inflate themselves, the smaller they become.

Also writing on the subject of man and the phenomenon of self-evaluation, Oliver Wendell Holmes, Sr., wrote in his 1891 book *Over the Teacups*:

**A man is a kind of inverted thermometer, the bulb uppermost,
and the column of self-valuation is all the time going up and down.**

Like so many good metaphors, this one is hard to get out of one's mind once it is first read. The bulb, it should be clear, is a person's head, and the different temperature readings reflect the varying self-concept assessments, which change—often markedly—from day to day and season to season. It was Ralph Waldo Emerson, though, who offered the most inspired metaphorical thought on the subject of temperatures and human beings:

We boil at different degrees.

Metaphorical language has also proved invaluable in helping people cope with tragedies. In 1945, a New Jersey couple on the periphery of Albert Einstein's life experienced one of the great human sorrows—the death of their child. More than four decades earlier, in 1902, the twenty-two-year-old Einstein had experienced the same loss. At the time, while working as a clerk in a Swiss patent office, he was informed by his girlfriend and eventual wife, Mileva, that she was pregnant. The prospect of an illegitimate child was not likely to enhance the young man's career prospects, so the couple decided to register with an adoption agency. Shortly after the birth, though, the baby died of scarlet fever. The event left the new parents deeply shaken.

Einstein's 1945 note to the grieving parents suggests a deep familiarity with the emotions they were likely to be experiencing:

> **When the expected course of everyday life is interrupted,**
> **we realize that we are like shipwrecked people**
> **trying to keep their balance on a miserable plank in the open sea,**
> **having forgotten where they came from**
> **and not knowing whither they are drifting.**

Einstein had a lot on his plate in those days, so he might have simply penned a brief note of condolence. But he took the time to craft a message that reflected the emotional state of people who've suffered a great loss— the helpless feeling of being adrift.

When people try to communicate deeply personal experiences, it can be difficult. After all, such experiences are—well—deeply personal. In a 1960 article in the *Ladies' Home Journal*, opera singer Marian Anderson described what life was like for a black woman in a white world. Two decades earlier, the internationally acclaimed contralto had been denied permission to sing in Washington's Constitution Hall. Undeterred, she decided to give an outdoor concert at the Lincoln Memorial. More than 75,000 people showed up, providing support for Anderson and showing contempt for the racist policy that had tried to silence her. In the article, she chose a fascinating way to describe racial prejudice:

> **Sometimes, it's like a hair across your cheek.**
> **You can't see it, you can't find it with your fingers,**
> **but you keep brushing at it because the feel of it is irritating.**

In this personal and poignant reflection, Anderson found a beautiful way to describe one of the uglier aspects of life. It was also a perfect way for the singer to connect her experience with the *Journal's* mainly female readers, all of whom could relate to the analogy of a hair across the face.

Prejudice—whether based on religion, race, gender, class, or anything else—is one of the most troublesome weeds in the garden of human life and will in all likelihood never be completely eliminated. The essential nature of the affliction—and the difficulty involved in overcoming it—was captured in a passage in Charlotte Brontë's 1847 classic, *Jane Eyre:*

Prejudices, it is well known, are most difficult to eradicate from the heart whose soil has never been loosened or fertilized by education; they grow there, firm as weeds among stones.

Another great theme in human history has been the short-sighted pursuit of practices that are not in our long-term best interest. Whether it has to do with smoking, eating, drinking, or a wide variety of other behaviors, countless people live every day as if the principle of accountability did not apply to them. Norman Cousins, aware of this flaw in the human character, wrote, "Wisdom consists of the anticipation of consequences." And then he added:

A human being fashions his consequences as surely as he fashions his goods or his dwelling. Nothing that he says, thinks, or does is without consequences.

Writing a century before Cousins, Robert Louis Stevenson—as adept at penning pithy aphorisms as he was at writing adventure stories—said it even better:

Everybody, soon or late, sits down to a banquet of consequences.

Throughout history, analogies, metaphors, and similes have been extremely helpful when people have tried to describe life's drama and adventure, its joy and tragedy, and even its dark and seamy side. In the remainder of the chapter, let's continue our figurative foray into the human condition.

When suffering knocks at your door and you say there is no seat for him,
he tells you not to worry because he has brought his own stool.

CHINUA ACHEBE

The effect of power and publicity on all men is the aggravation of self,
a sort of tumor that ends by killing the victim's sympathies.

HENRY BROOKS ADAMS

Self-pity in its early stages is as snug as a feather mattress.
Only when it hardens does it become uncomfortable.

MAYA ANGELOU

Vocations which we wanted to pursue, and didn't,
bleed, like colors, on the whole of our existence.

HONORÉ DE BALZAC

The world's battlefields have been in the heart chiefly;
more heroism has been displayed in the household and the closet,
than on the most memorable battlefields in history.

HENRY WARD BEECHER

Adversity has the same effect on a man
that severe training has on the pugilist:
it reduces him to his fighting weight.

JOSH BILLINGS
(Henry Wheeler Shaw)

In the 1860s, Shaw adopted the pen name Josh Billings and became famous for his cracker-barrel philosophy and aphorisms written in a pho-
netic dialect (he called them "affurisms"). Mark Twain was a fan, and
once even compared Billings to Ben Franklin. In an 1851 speech, William
Cullen Bryant said similarly: "Difficulty . . . is the nurse of greatness—a

harsh nurse, who roughly rocks her foster-children into strength and athletic proportion."

> Mountains appear more lofty the nearer they are approached,
> but great men resemble them not in this particular.
>
> MARGUERITE BLESSINGTON

> Living at risk is jumping off the cliff
> and building your wings on the way down.
>
> RAY BRADBURY

> Prejudice is the psoriasis of the human condition:
> it's unsightly and it never completely vanishes,
> but with a little care we can keep it under control.
>
> RICK BAYAN

> Every person's work, whether it be literature or music or pictures
> or architecture or anything else, is always a portrait of that person.
>
> SAMUEL BUTLER

> If facts are the seeds that later produce knowledge and wisdom,
> then the emotions . . . are the fertile soil in which the seeds must grow.
>
> RACHEL CARSON

> No fathers or mothers think their own children ugly;
> and this self-deceit is yet stronger with respect to the offspring of the mind.
>
> MIGUEL DE CERVANTES

> A man is not necessarily intelligent because he has plenty of ideas,
> any more than he is a good general because he has plenty of soldiers.
>
> NICOLAS CHAMFORT

Alcohol is like love: the first kiss is magic,
the second is intimate, the third is routine.
After that you just take the girl's clothes off.

RAYMOND CHANDLER

Young men are apt to think themselves wise enough,
as drunken men are apt to think themselves sober enough.

LORD CHESTERFIELD *(Philip Dormer Stanhope)*

We are all serving a life-sentence in the dungeon of self.

CYRIL CONNOLLY

Men deal with life as children with their play,
Who first misuse, then cast their toys away.

WILLIAM COWPER

There are some people who leave impressions
not so lasting as the imprint of an oar upon the water.

KATE CHOPIN

Criticism may not be agreeable, but it is necessary.
It fulfills the same function as pain in the human body.
It calls attention to an unhealthy state of things.

WINSTON CHURCHILL

To most men, experience is like the stern lights of a ship,
which illumine only the track it has passed.

SAMUEL TAYLOR COLERIDGE

In a related observation, W. R. Inge wrote, "Experience is a good teacher, but her fees are very high."

Common men pass treasures by;
they respond to the spectacle of nature
as guests at a banquet who are neither hungry nor thirsty.
EUGÈNE DELACROIX

What is man, when you come to think upon him,
but a minutely set, ingenious machine for turning,
with infinite artfulness, the red wine of Shiraz into urine?
ISAK DINESEN *(Karen Blixen)*

Along the same lines, Christopher Morley once penned this thought: "A human being: an ingenious assembly of portable plumbing."

Trying to predict the future is like
trying to drive down a country road at night with no lights
while looking out the back window.
PETER DRUCKER

There is a great deal of unmapped country within us
which would have to be taken into account
in an explanation of our gusts and storms.
GEORGE ELIOT

This comes from Eliot's 1876 novel *Daniel Deronda*. Blaise Pascal communicated the same notion more than two centuries earlier when he wrote, "The heart has reasons that the reason knows not of." The point of both observations is that the motivation behind much of our behavior—especially our occasional outbursts and eruptions—is beyond our conscious awareness.

There are men too superior to be seen except by the few,
as there are notes too high for the scale of most ears.
RALPH WALDO EMERSON

Also writing about great men (and women), Kahlil Gibran wrote, "The lights of stars that were extinguished ages ago still reach us. So it is with great men who died centuries ago, but still reach us with the radiations of their personalities."

The fundamental principle of human action—
the law that is to political economy what the law of gravitation is to physics—
is that men seek to gratify their desires with the least exertion.

HENRY GEORGE

God has placed in each soul an apostle to lead us upon the illumined path.
Yet many seek life from without, unaware that is within them.

KAHLIL GIBRAN

Men are apt to mistake the strength of their feeling
for the strength of their argument.
The heated mind resents the chill touch and relentless scrutiny of logic.

WILLIAM E. GLADSTONE

A reputation once broken may possibly be repaired,
but the world will always keep their eyes on the spot where the crack was.

JOSEPH HALL

Men heap together the mistakes of their lives,
and create a monster they call Destiny.

JOHN OLIVER HOBBES
(pen name of Pearl Richards Craigie)

There are thoughts which are prayers.
There are moments when, whatever the posture of the body,
the soul is on its knees.

VICTOR HUGO

The richest genius, like the most fertile soil,
when uncultivated, shoots up into the rankest weeds.

DAVID HUME

There are years that ask questions and years that answer.

ZORA NEALE HURSTON

To a person uninstructed in natural history,
his country or seaside stroll is a walk through a gallery
filled with wonderful works of art,
nine-tenths of which have their faces turned to the wall.

THOMAS H. HUXLEY

Viewing nature as an art gallery with ninety percent of the paintings turned to the wall starkly describes the average person's ignorance of the natural world.

The chess-board is the world;
the pieces are the phenomena of the universe;
the rules of the game are what we call the laws of Nature.
The player on the other side is hidden from us.
We know that his play is always fair, just, and patient.
But also we know, to our cost, that he never overlooks a mistake,
or makes the smallest allowance for ignorance.

THOMAS H. HUXLEY

A tart temper never mellows with age, and a sharp tongue
is the only edged tool that grows keener with constant use.

WASHINGTON IRVING

Most people live . . . in a very restricted circle of their potential being.
They make very small use of their possible consciousness,

and of their soul's resources in general,
much like a man who, out of his whole bodily organism,
should get into a habit of using and moving only his little finger.

WILLIAM JAMES

A man who uses a great many words to express his meaning
is like a bad marksman who, instead of aiming a single stone at an object,
takes up a handful and throws at it in hopes he may hit.

SAMUEL JOHNSON

Your morals are like roads through the Alps.
They make these hairpin turns all the time.

ERICA JONG

There is always some frivolity in excellent minds;
they have wings to rise, but also stray.

JOSEPH JOUBERT

Great talents are the most lovely
and often the most dangerous fruits on the tree of humanity.
They hang upon the most slender twigs that are easily snapped off.

CARL JUNG

Trying to help an oppressed person
is like trying to put your arm around somebody with a sunburn.

FLORYNCE KENNEDY

There are many people who reach their conclusions about life like schoolboys;
they cheat their master by copying the answer out of a book
without having worked out the sum for themselves.

SØREN KIERKEGAARD

Adversity draws men together
and produces beauty and harmony in life's relationships,
just as the cold of winter produces ice flowers on the window panes,
which vanish with the warmth.

SØREN KIERKEGAARD

In another memorable window pane metaphor, Elisabeth Kübler-Ross wrote: "People are like stained-glass windows. They sparkle and shine when the sun is out, but when the darkness sets in, their true beauty is revealed only if there is a light from within."

In my youth I regarded the universe as an open book,
printed in the language of equations,
whereas now it appears to me as a text written in invisible ink,
of which in our rare moments of grace we are able to decipher a small segment.

ARTHUR KOESTLER

No snowflake in an avalanche ever feels responsible.

STANISLAW LEC

Every stink that fights the ventilator thinks it is Don Quixote.

STANISLAW LEC

This world is a great sculptor's shop.
We are the statues and there is a rumor going round the shop
that some of us are some day going to come to life.

C. S. LEWIS

For happiness one needs security,
but joy can spring like a flower even from the cliffs of despair.

ANNE MORROW LINDBERGH

Whenever nature leaves a hole in a person's mind,
she generally plasters it over with a thick coat of self-conceit.
HENRY WADSWORTH LONGFELLOW

The highest intellects, like the tops of mountains,
are the first to catch and to reflect the dawn.
THOMAS BABINGTON MACAULAY

The desire for success lubricates secret prostitutions in the soul.
NORMAN MAILER

Ignorance breeds monsters to fill up the vacancies of the soul
that are unoccupied by the verities of knowledge.
HORACE MANN

Nature may abhor a vacuum, but according to Mann, ignorance loves them. Also thinking about the monsters bred by ignorance, Goethe wrote, "There is nothing more frightful than ignorance in action."

Every age has a keyhole to which its eye is pasted.
MARY MCCARTHY

The human mind treats a new idea the same way
the body treats a strange protein; it rejects it.
PETER B. MEDAWAR

The childhood shows the man,
As morning shows the day.
JOHN MILTON

This comes from *Paradise Regained* (1671). The basic notion is that early indicators are great predictors of what is to come. William Wordsworth made the same point in a famous line in his 1807 poem "My Heart Leaps Up": "The child is father of the man."

What was once called the objective world is a sort of Rorschach ink blot, into which each culture, each system of science and religion, each type of personality, reads a meaning only remotely derived from the shape and color of the blot itself.

LEWIS MUMFORD

Most truths are so naked that people feel sorry for them and cover them up, at least a little bit.

EDWARD R. MURROW

The naked truth, a metaphor for plain and unadorned truth, originated in an ancient Roman fable. Truth and Falsehood went for a swim. Falsehood emerged from the water first, dressed in Truth's clothes, and departed. Truth refused to wear the clothing Falsehood had left behind, preferring to go naked instead. The expression has been used countless times by writers, ancient and modern, but one of my favorites comes from Ann Landers, who wrote, "The naked truth is better than the best-dressed lie."

The self is merely the lens through which we see others and the world.

ANAÏS NIN

Nin is also widely quoted as saying, "We don't see things as they are; we see things as we are."

There are people who so arrange their lives that they feed themselves only on side dishes.

JOSÉ ORTEGA Y GASSET

Living is like working out one long addition sum,
and if you make a mistake in the first two totals
you will never find the right answer.

CESARE PAVESE

He that uses many words for explaining any subject, doth,
like the cuttlefish, hide himself for the most part in his own ink.

JOHN RAY

In other words, lengthy explanations are often a smoke screen that people hide behind. This observation from Ray, a seventeenth-century English naturalist with a great fondness for proverbs, may have inspired one of George Orwell's best-known lines: "The great enemy of clear language is insincerity. When there is a gap between one's real and one's declared aims, one turns as it were instinctively to long words and exhausted idioms, like a cuttlefish squirting out ink."

The world is . . . a kind of spiritual kindergarten, where millions
of bewildered infants are trying to spell God with the wrong blocks.

EDWIN ARLINGTON ROBINSON

Every man, wherever he goes, is encompassed by a cloud of
comforting convictions, which move with him like flies on a summer day.

BERTRAND RUSSELL

There are books in which the footnotes or comments scrawled by
some reader's hand in the margin are more interesting than the text.
The world is one of these books.

GEORGE SANTAYANA

In the country of pain we are each alone.
MAY SARTON

The point is that we can never truly understand the pain of another person. On the same subject, William Cullen Bryant wrote, "Pain dies quickly, and lets her weary prisoners go; the fiercest agonies have shortest reign." And on pain's brief reign, Katherine Mansfield wrote, "As in the physical world, so in the spiritual world, pain does not last forever."

We are not unlike a particularly hardy crustacean . . . .
With each passage from one stage of human growth to the next
we, too, must shed a protective structure.
We are left exposed and vulnerable—but also yeasty and embryonic again,
capable of stretching in ways we hadn't known before.
GAIL SHEEHY,
on human beings & lobsters

Society attacks early, when the individual is helpless.
B. F. SKINNER

To suppose, as we all suppose,
that we could be rich and not behave as the rich behave,
is like supposing that we could drink all day and keep absolutely sober.
LOGAN PEARSALL SMITH

Human beings cling to their delicious tyrannies,
and to their exquisite nonsense, like a drunkard to his bottle,
and go on until death stares them in the face.
SYDNEY SMITH

Smith, an English clergyman in the early nineteenth century, was a popular essayist and lecturer. He inspired the phrase "You can't put a square peg

in a round hole" in an extended metaphorical passage that may be found at
www.DrMardy.com.

**It is a common experience that a problem difficult at night
is resolved in the morning after the committee of sleep has worked on it.**
JOHN STEINBECK

**It is with narrow-souled people as with narrow-necked bottles:
the less they have in them, the more noise they make in pouring it out.**
JONATHAN SWIFT

This was likely based on a famous analogy from Plato: "As empty vessels make the loudest sound, so they that have the least wit are the greatest
babblers."

**Although men are accused for not knowing their own weakness,
yet, perhaps, as few know their own strength.
It is in men as in soils, where sometimes
there is a vein of gold which the owner knows not of.**
JONATHAN SWIFT

**As the internal-combustion engine runs on gasoline,
so the person runs on self-esteem:
if he is full of it, he is good for the long run;
if he is partly filled, he will soon need to be refueled;
and if he is empty, he will come to a stop.**
THOMAS SZASZ

**The world is a looking-glass
and gives back to every man the reflection of his own face.**
WILLIAM MAKEPEACE THACKERAY

This is from *Vanity Fair* (1847–48). The passage continues: "Frown at it, and it will in turn look sourly upon you; laugh at it and with it, and it is a jolly kind companion; and so let all young persons take their choice."

**For every ten people who are clipping at the branches of evil,
you're lucky to find one who's hacking at the roots.**
HENRY DAVID THOREAU

**Everyone is a moon,
and has a dark side which he never shows to anybody.**
MARK TWAIN

This is from *Following the Equator* (1897). More recently, Faith Baldwin wrote: "We, too, the children of the earth, have our moon phases all through any year; the darkness, the delivery from darkness, the waxing and waning."

**One may have a blazing hearth in one's soul
and yet no one ever comes to sit by it.
Passersby see only a wisp of smoke from the chimney
and continue on the way.**
VINCENT VAN GOGH

**A flaw in the human character
is that everybody wants to build and nobody wants to do maintenance.**
KURT VONNEGUT, JR.

I have one share in corporate Earth, and I am nervous about the management.
E. B. WHITE

Marshall McLuhan said similarly, "There are no passengers on spaceship earth. We are all crew." And earlier, R. Buckminster Fuller wrote,

"The most important thing about Spacecraft Earth—an instruction book didn't come with it."

On the outskirts of every agony sits some observant fellow who points.

VIRGINIA WOOLF

I sit astride life like a bad rider on a horse.
I only owe it to the horse's good nature
that I am not thrown off at this very moment.

LUDWIG WITTGENSTEIN

chapter 3

Humor Is the
Shock Absorber of Life

One of the vexing problems facing American leaders after the Japanese surrender in 1945 was what to do with Emperor Hirohito and his family. After lengthy—and apparently heated—discussions at the White House, it was decided that the emperor would not be tried for war crimes. But what exactly should be done with him and the rest of the Imperial Household? The details were left in the hands of General Douglas MacArthur, who was given free rein to make such decisions. MacArthur believed that a key to Japan's future was the proper education of the emperor's twelve-year-old son, Crown Prince Akihito.

MacArthur did something that would never happen today—he arranged for a virtually unknown American teacher to take the young prince under her wing. The tutor was Elizabeth Gray Vining, a Philadelphia widow with no children and no obvious credentials for the job. The forty-three-year-old Quaker woman had never visited Japan, spoke no Japanese, and came only with a strong recommendation from the American Friends Service Committee.

The tutor quickly won the trust of her young charge—even playing Monopoly with him during study breaks—and went on to play a pivotal role in his life. When she left Japan four years later, her pupil had flourished. He was fluent in English, was proficient in French and German, and showed a keen interest in Western ideas about individual freedom. In 1959, when Akihito became the first crown prince in Japanese history to marry a commoner, the only Westerner to attend the wedding was his beloved Mrs. Vining. On every birthday until she died in 1999—at age ninety-seven—she received a bouquet of flowers from her former pupil, delivered by limousine from the Japanese Embassy. When Emperor Hirohito died in 1989, Akihito ascended to the throne, a position he occupies to this day.

What does all this have to do with the chapter you're reading? Well, as it turns out, the Japanese emperor and I have something in common—we both learned something special from Mrs. Vining. In her 1960 book *Return to Japan*, she wrote:

> The word humor, according to the Oxford Dictionary, originally meant moisture or juice and only fairly recently, that is to say from the 17th century, came to mean that quality of action, speech, or writing which excites amusement, or the faculty of perceiving what is ludicrous or amusing. As anyone who has experienced the lubricating effect of even a small joke . . . humor still has an element of juice. It keeps life from drying up, gives it freshness and flavor.

In the first part of this passage, Vining correctly points out that the English word *humor* derives from a Latin word that means "fluid, moisture." That root word is *umor*, which somewhere along the line added the letter *h* and gave us words like *humor* and *humidity*. The word originally conveyed the sense of "bodily fluids," as in the ancient concept of *bodily humors*. In ancient Greece, physicians believed that the precise composition of four bodily fluids—blood, black bile, yellow bile, and phlegm—determined a person's temperament.

In the second part of the passage, Vining gracefully moves from the literal to the metaphorical realm by suggesting that the juice of humor can help to make life fresh and flavorful. When I first came upon her observation, I recalled something that Oliver Wendell Holmes, Sr., recommended in his 1891 book *Over the Teacups*:

> **Take a music-bath once or twice a week for a few seasons,
> and you will find that it is to the soul what the water-bath is to the body.**

If music baths can be cleansing, it can also be argued that periodic humor baths are a good way to wash away some of the grime of life. Over the years, this beneficial aspect of humor has been well recognized, and many have expressed the view metaphorically:

> **Humor is a social lubricant that helps us get over some of the bad spots.**
> STEVE ALLEN

> **Humor is just another defense against the universe.**
> MEL BROOKS

> **Laughter is a tranquilizer with no side effects.**
> ARNOLD H. GLASGOW

> **Humor is the shock absorber of life; it helps us take the blows.**
> PEGGY NOONAN

> **What soap is to the body, laughter is to the soul.**
> YIDDISH PROVERB

> **The human race has one really effective weapon, and that is laughter.**
> MARK TWAIN

Many people have come to believe that humor—especially if it provokes hearty laughter—isn't simply a life enhancer but is also a life preserver, and maybe even a life prolonger. The most famous exponent of this view is undoubtedly Norman Cousins, the long-time *Saturday Review* editor and legendary peace activist. In the 1970s, Cousins was diagnosed with a painful and life-threatening illness. In his 1979 book *Anatomy of an Illness as Perceived by the Patient,* he described how he stumbled upon a letter that a consulting physician had written to his doctor. After reading the words "I'm afraid we're going to lose Norman," Cousins figured he had nothing to lose and began to take more control over his own treatment. He began viewing Marx Brothers' movies and *Candid Camera* videos, discovering that "ten minutes of genuine belly laughter had an anesthetic effect that would give me at least two hours of pain-free sleep."

While continuing to work closely with his physicians, Cousins checked himself out of the hospital and into a nearby hotel, saying it was a place where he could "laugh twice as hard at half the price." He slowly began to improve—greatly surprising his doctors—and he began to view laughter as sedentary aerobic exercise. All of this was occurring at the height of a worldwide running craze, and Cousins described the medical benefits of humor in a timely metaphor:

Laughter is internal jogging.

Anatomy of an Illness became an extremely influential book, stimulating intense interest in the mind–body connection and extensive research on the role of humor in medical treatment. Cousins, with no formal medical training, even went on to become an adjunct professor at UCLA's school of medicine. In 1990, he died at age seventy-five, twenty-one years after the publication of his classic book.

In addition to the medical benefits, wit and humor are also believed to be great philosophical aides in our journey through life. Mark Van Doren wrote:

> **Wit is the only wall**
> **Between us and the dark.**

According to comic genius Victor Borge, there are also important interpersonal benefits:

> **Laughter is the shortest distance between two people.**

And J. B. Priestley even extended the benefits to the larger society:

> **Comedy, we may say, is society protecting itself—with a smile.**

On the basis of everything said so far, one might easily conclude that humor is a good thing. And while that is true, it is also true that too much of a good thing is a bad thing. In history's best argument for moderation in the arena of wit, William Hazlitt wrote:

> **Wit is the salt of conversation, not the food.**

This is a lovely reminder that wit should be dished out in the correct portions. Too little seasoning, and the food is insipid; too much, and it becomes inedible. Noël Coward also employed a culinary metaphor to make the same point:

> **Wit is like caviar—it should be served in small portions,**
> **and not spread about like marmalade.**

Recalling Mark Twain's earlier remark, it is well accepted that wit can be a weapon, and a dangerous one as well. But when a weapon backfires, it leaves the intended victim unharmed, and it damages—sometimes seriously—the one wielding the weapon. The English writer and historian Geoffrey Bocca described the phenomenon this way:

**Wit is a treacherous dart.
It is perhaps the only weapon with which it is possible
to stab oneself in one's own back.**

History is filled with examples of people whose failed attempts at wit have come back to haunt them. The most dramatic example in recent years was the "nappy-headed hoes" remark that shock jock Don Imus made about the Rutgers University women's basketball team in the spring of 2007. Despite his numerous apologies and his excuse that he was "a good man who had done a bad thing," Imus was fired by both CBS and MSNBC within a week.

Like Norman Cousins, who preferred the Marx Brothers and *Candid Camera* videos, I also have my favorites when a humor bath is required. I'm especially fond of stand-up comedians, who often build entire portions of their routines around a metaphor and then milk the routine until the laughs stop. A perfect example is this riff from Jerry Seinfeld:

**Why is commitment such a big problem for a man?
I think that for some reason when a man is driving down
that freeway of love, the woman he's with is like an exit.
But he doesn't want to get off there. He wants to keep driving.
And the woman is like, "Look, gas, food, lodging, that's our exit,
that's everything we need to be happy. Get off here, now!"
But the man is focusing on the sign underneath that says,
"Next exit 27 miles," and he thinks, "I can make it."
Sometimes he can, sometimes he can't.
Sometimes, the car ends up on the side of the road,
hood up and smoke pouring out of the engine.
He's sitting on the curb all alone,
"I guess I didn't realize how many miles I was racking up."**

One of the great pleasures of life is the unexpected appearance of something genuinely funny or particularly witty. A while back, I got one of those forwarded e-mails that have become so popular in recent years. I generally delete them almost automatically, but this one was titled "Men are like computers," so I figured I'd take a look. I'm glad I did, as it went on to read:

Computers are like Men . . .
. . . **In order to get their attention, you have to turn them on.**
. . . **They're supposed to help you solve problems, but half the time they are the problem.**
. . . **They have a lot of data, but are still clueless.**
. . . **As soon as you commit to one, you realize that if you had waited a little longer you could have had a better model.**
. . . **They hear what you say, but not what you mean.**

Computers are like Women . . .
. . . **No one but the Creator understands their internal logic.**
. . . **The native language they use to communicate with other computers is incomprehensible to everyone else.**
. . . **Even your smallest mistakes are stored in long-term memory for later retrieval.**
. . . **As soon as you make a commitment to one, you find yourself spending half your paycheck on accessories for it.**
. . . **You do the same thing for years, and suddenly it's wrong.**

In the rest of the chapter, you'll find a wide variety of additional quotations on a wide variety of subjects. As you peruse these many examples of wit and humor, keep in mind the words of Italian filmmaker Lina Wertmüller: "Laughter is the Vaseline that makes the ideas penetrate better."

I love deadlines.
I love the whooshing noise they make as they go by.
DOUGLAS ADAMS

**A bikini is like a barbed-wire fence.
It protects the property without disturbing the view.**

JOEY ADAMS

Aaron Levenstein, longtime professor at Baruch College, is also well known for a bikini metaphor: "Statistics are like a bikini. What they reveal is suggestive, but what they conceal is vital."

**I don't like nature. It's big plants eating little plants,
small fish being eaten by big fish, big animals eating each other.
It's like an enormous restaurant.**

WOODY ALLEN

**The opera is like a husband with a foreign title—
expensive to support, hard to understand,
and therefore a supreme social challenge.**

CLEVELAND AMORY

My face looks like a wedding cake left out in the rain.

W. H. AUDEN

Auden had a heavily wrinkled face that he accepted with good humor. But it was the subject of many fascinating observations by others. Lord David Cecil said of Auden's face, "Were a fly to attempt to walk across it, it would break its leg." And after the artist David Hockney did a drawing of Auden, he said, "I kept thinking, if his face was that wrinkled, what did his balls look like?"

The goal of all inanimate objects is to resist man and ultimately defeat him.

RUSSELL BAKER

Personification, a type of metaphorical thinking, attributes human qualities—like hatred or revenge—to animals, plants, ideas and concepts, and even inanimate objects. It's an integral part of humor, as Baker demonstrates in this quip about man versus machine.

> **Dogs need to sniff the ground;**
> **It's how they keep abreast of current events.**
> **The ground is a giant dog newspaper, containing all kinds**
> **of late-breaking news items, which, if they are especially urgent,**
> **are often continued in the next yard.**
>
> DAVE BARRY

> **A gourmet who thinks of calories**
> **is like a tart who looks at her watch.**
>
> JAMES BEARD

> **MTV is to music as KFC is to chicken.**
>
> LEWIS BLACK

> **Reading someone else's newspaper**
> **is like sleeping with someone else's wife.**
>
> MALCOLM BRADBURY

He added: "Nothing seems to be precisely in the right place, and when you find what you are looking for, it is not clear then how to respond to it."

> **An after-dinner speech should be like a lady's dress—**
> **long enough to cover the subject and short enough to be interesting.**
>
> R. A. "RAB" BUTLER

> **Like a camel, I can go without a drink for seven days—**
> **and have on several horrible occasions.**
>
> HERB CAEN

What Billie Holiday is to jazz,
what Mae West is to tits . . .
what Seconal is to sleeping pills,
what King Kong is to penises,
Truman Capote is to the great god Thespis!

TRUMAN CAPOTE, *on himself as an actor*

Capote's efforts at self-promotion were legendary, and often hilarious. Thespis, a Greek poet in the sixth century B.C., is considered the world's first actor. At a time when all stage productions were choral affairs, he was the first person to deliver spoken lines. He lives on in the word *thespian*, an eponym for an actor.

I want to get married but I look at husbands the same way I look at tattoos.
I want one, but I can't decide what I want,
and I don't want to be stuck with something
I'd grow to hate and have surgically removed.

MARGARET CHO

Smoking cigars is like falling in love:
first you are attracted to its shape;
you stay with it for its flavor;
and you must always remember never, never let the flame go out.

WINSTON CHURCHILL

A dead bird does not leave its nest.

WINSTON CHURCHILL

This was the elderly Churchill's reply when he was once told that his fly was open. For most of his life, the Grand Old Man of English politics was on the lookout for witty replies. Many of his best, like this one, were self-deprecating.

Cleaning your house
While your kids are still growing
Is like shoveling the walk
Before it stops snowing.

PHYLLIS DILLER

Working as a journalist is exactly like being a wallflower at an orgy.

NORA EPHRON

This was Ephron's way of pointing out that working journalists get close to the action without actually participating in it.

A plumber's idea of Cleopatra.

W. C. FIELDS, *on Mae West*

Telling a teenager the facts of life is like giving a fish a bath.

ARNOLD H. GLASGOW

Mothers, food, love, and career: the four major guilt groups.

CATHY GUISEWITE

Girls are like pianos.
When they're not upright, they're grand.

BENNY HILL

Humor is a rubber sword—
it allows you to make a point without drawing blood.

MARY HIRSCH

I've been attacked by Rush Limbaugh on the air,
an experience somewhat akin to being gummed by a newt.

MOLLY IVINS

This remark is impressive at two levels. First, being gummed by any toothless animal—much less a newt—isn't very dangerous. And second, it was a clever way for Ivins to take a back-handed jab at another foe: Newt Gingrich.

**Don't sit in a restaurant by the tank
where they keep the lobsters—it's very depressing.
Lobsters always have that look of, "Any word from the governor?"**

RICHARD JENI

If you haven't struck oil in the first three minutes, *stop boring*!

GEORGE JESSEL

In the mid-1900s, Jessel was America's most popular after-dinner speaker. By relating speech-making to oil drilling—and playfully punning on both meanings of the word *boring*—he provides great advice to anyone who is asked to "say a few words." John Updike made a similar point when he likened boring adults to boring insects: "A healthy adult male bore consumes each year one and a half times his own weight in other people's patience."

**In any world menu,
Canada must be considered the vichyssoise of nations—
it's cold, half-French, and difficult to stir.**

J. STUART KEATE

**I feel about airplanes the way I feel about diets.
It seems to me that they are wonderful things for other people to go on.**

JEAN KERR

**People . . . have often been likened to snowflakes.
This analogy is meant to suggest that each is unique—no two alike.
This is quite patently not the case.**

People . . . are quite simply a dime a dozen.
And, I hasten to add, their only similarity to snowflakes
resides in their invariable and lamentable tendency to turn,
after a few warm days, to slush.

FRAN LEBOWITZ

He looked at me as if I were a side dish he hadn't ordered.

RING LARDNER

Lardner penned many memorable lines on the *looks* people give one another: "They gave each other a smile with a future in it" and "He gave her a look that you could pour on a waffle." Also on the subject of looks, there is this classic line from Raymond Chandler: "She gave me a smile I could feel in my hip pocket."

Thoughts, like fleas, jump from man to man.
But they don't bite everybody.

STANISLAW LEC

Here's something I've never understood;
how come men have nipples?
What's the point? They're like plastic fruit.

CAROL LEIFER

I never did like working out—
it bears the same relationship to real sport
as masturbation does to real sex.

DAVID LODGE

Lodge may have been inspired by Karl Marx's famous analogical observation on the impotence of philosophy: "Philosophy stands in the same relation to the study of the actual world as masturbation to sexual love."

Hickeys are like PG-13 movies.
You think they're pretty hot stuff after being limited to G and PG,
but you never bother with them once you're seriously into R.

JUDY MARKEY

A car is useless in New York, essential everywhere else.
The same with good manners.

MIGNON MCLAUGHLIN

The point is that that neither manners nor cars are necessary to get around New York. The rudeness of New Yorkers, while often not apparent to residents, is one of the first things noticed by visitors. Roy Blount, Jr., offered a similar thought when he compared Southerners with New Yorkers: "Being humorous in the South is like being . . . argumentative in New York . . . you're in trouble if you aren't." If one were to express his thought in an analogy, it might go like this: "A sense of humor is to Southerners what a chip on the shoulder is to New Yorkers."

We must respect the other fellow's religion,
but only in the sense and to the extent that we respect his theory
that his wife is beautiful and his children smart.

H. L. MENCKEN

English humor resembles the Loch Ness monster
in that both are famous but there is
a strong suspicion that neither exists.

GEORGE MIKES

The suggestion here is that English humor, because of its dry and droll quality, is often viewed as not particularly funny by Americans and others around the world.

We are all but sailboats on the river of life, and money is the wind.
With enough money, you can get blown anywhere.
DENNIS MILLER

In this witty *double-entendre* observation, Miller is only partially talking about being blown by the wind.

For a purely untrustworthy human organ,
the memory is right in there with the penis.
P. J. O'ROURKE

Making fun of born-again Christians
is like hunting dairy cows with a high-powered rifle and scope.
P. J. O'ROURKE

O'Rourke's point is that born-again Christians are such an easy target that it's not particularly impressive to make wisecracks about them.

TV evangelists are the pro wrestlers of religion.
RICK OVERTON

There's a helluva distance between wisecracking and wit.
Wit has truth in it; wisecracking is simply calisthenics with words.
DOROTHY PARKER

Awards are like hemorrhoids; in the end, every asshole gets one.
FREDERIC RAPHAEL

Raphael, a novelist and screenwriter, has written screenplays for many films, including Stanley Kubrick's 1999 film *Eyes Wide Shut*. He has won several awards, including an Oscar for *Darling* in 1965. I believe his remark was more of an attempt at self-deprecatory humor than a critical remark about awards. The basic sentiment has become extremely popular, surfacing in almost every discussion of prizes and awards. In 1999, British actress Maureen Lipman said it more delicately: "Awards are like piles. Sooner or later, every bum gets one."

I can't get past the fact that food is coming out of my wife's breasts. What was once . . . an entertainment center has now become a juice bar.

PAUL REISER, *on breastfeeding*

If you're black, you got to look at America a little bit different. You got to look at America like the uncle who paid for you to go to college, but who molested you.

CHRIS ROCK

The struggling for knowledge hath a pleasure in it like that of wrestling with a fine woman.

GEORGE SAVILE *(Lord Halifax)*

Lord Halifax, writing in 1690, was likely the first person in history to find an analogy between such disparate activities. His point is that both pursuits involve considerable struggle, but the pleasure associated with each is so great that the struggle is worth it.

People are always wanting me to smoke with them or drink beers with them or to hook me up with chicks. It's like I'm the Spuds MacKenzie of humans.

PAULY SHORE

Spuds Mackenzie, a bull terrier, became an overnight star after appearing in a Bud Lite beer commercial during the 1987 Super Bowl. A true party animal, the fun-loving dog also generated much publicity when it was revealed that *he* was actually a *she*.

It's silly for a woman to go to a male gynecologist.
It's like going to an auto mechanic who never owned a car.

CARRIE SNOW

The United States is like the guy at the party
who gives cocaine to everybody and still nobody likes him.

JIM SAMUELS

A two-year-old is like having a blender,
but you don't have a top for it.

JERRY SEINFELD

Experience: a comb life gives you after you lose your hair.

JUDITH STERN

As soon as you say "I do,"
you'll discover that marriage is like a car.
Both of you might be sitting in the front seat, but only one of you is driving.
And most marriages are more like a motorcycle than a car.
Somebody has to sit in the back, and you have to yell just to be heard.

WANDA SYKES

American students are like American colleges—
each has half-dulled faculties.

JAMES THURBER

I think of it as a kind of Hamburger Helper for the boudoir.

LILY TOMLIN, *speaking of a vibrator*

Wit is the sudden marriage of ideas which, before their union,
were not perceived to have any relation.

MARK TWAIN

Our lives are like soap operas.
We can go for months and not tune into them;
then six months later we look in
and the same stuff is going on.

JANE WAGNER

Analyzing humor is like dissecting a frog.
Few people are interested and the frog dies of it.

E. B. WHITE

The world is a stage, but the play is badly cast.

OSCAR WILDE

Here, Wilde cleverly piggy-backs on the famous passage from *As You Like It*.

The English country gentleman galloping after a fox—
the unspeakable in full pursuit of the uneatable.

OSCAR WILDE

Nonalcoholic beer is kind of like a Nerf vibrator.
It's not really going to work.

ROBIN WILLIAMS

Spring is nature's way of saying, "Let's party!"

ROBIN WILLIAMS

Williams once said of himself, "My comedy is like emotional hang-gliding." His remark about spring may have inspired another seasonal observation, this one from Robert Byrne: "Winter is nature's way of saying, 'Up yours!'"

**The lunches of fifty-seven years
had caused his chest to slip down into the mezzanine floor.**

P. G. WODEHOUSE

The works of Wodehouse—a true master of metaphor—were sprinkled with numerous figurative gems, many on the subject of being overweight. Here are two more:

"(He) was a tubby little chap who looked as if he had been poured into his clothes and had forgotten to say 'when!'"

"She fitted into my biggest armchair as if it had been built round her by someone who knew they were wearing armchairs tight around the hips that season."

College: a fountain of knowledge where all go to drink.

HENNY YOUNGMAN

chapter 4

The Lights May Be on,
but Nobody's Home

On March 7, 1850, Daniel Webster of Massachusetts rose from his seat in the Senate to make what he thought would be the speech of his career. He talked for three and a half hours in support of Kentucky Senator Henry Clay's "Compromise of 1850," arguing that it was pointless to oppose slavery in the Southern states, or even to argue against its extension into the new territories in the American Southwest. Webster took the view that plantation owners were entitled to safeguard their property, and even went so far as to advocate a rigorous enforcement of the recently passed fugitive slave statutes.

News of the speech was quickly telegraphed back to Massachusetts, a hotbed of abolitionist sentiment. Most people in the region were stunned, leading one commentator to say—metaphorically—that the speech had slammed into New England with the fury of a hurricane. Many Bay State luminaries made impassioned attacks on Webster. Horace Mann called the speech "a vile catastrophe." John Quincy Adams described "the gigantic intellect, the envious temper, the ravenous ambition, and the rotten heart of Daniel Webster." And Ralph Waldo Emerson, the most famous New Englander of the time, wrote:

> **The word *liberty* in the mouth of Mr. Webster
> sounds like the word *love* in the mouth of a courtesan.**

After Emerson shared the analogy with a few friends, it quickly began to be whispered throughout New England. As often happens, the quotation got simplified as it was passed along, and most people were just as likely to hear it this way:

> **The word *liberty* in the mouth of Mr. Webster
> is like the word *love* in the mouth of a whore.**

The impact was dramatic. With his political base in shambles, Webster resigned three months later. Almost immediately, historians began to refer to "the speech that lost a Senate seat." What they generally fail to mention, however, is the role that a few critical and insulting remarks—and one spectacular analogy—played in the process.

Disparaging remarks are such a staple of life that we hear them every day without recognizing that so many of them are metaphorical. As a child, I routinely heard people question the sanity of others by saying things like *he's got a screw loose* or *she has bats in the belfry*. And over the years an entire class of idiomatic expressions—all metaphorical—have been created to describe a deficiency of intelligence:

> **He doesn't have all his marbles.**

> **She's not playing with a full deck.**

> **He's one brick short of a load.**

> **She's a few grapes short of a bunch.**

The elevator doesn't go all the way to the top.

The stairs don't go all the way up to the attic.

The lights are on, but there's nobody home.

The political arena has been filled with memorable metaphorical insults. In 1897, Theodore Roosevelt, a thirty-nine-year-old assistant secretary of the Navy, was itching for the United States to rid the Western hemisphere of European colonialism, particularly Spain's involvement in Cuba. The hawkish Roosevelt believed a powerful show of force was required, but President William McKinley favored a diplomatic approach to the problem. In a rare display of candor from a junior official in any presidential administration, Roosevelt said of McKinley:

He shows all the backbone of a chocolate éclair.

In April 1898, shortly after the sinking of the U.S. battleship *Maine* in Havana harbor, Congress declared war on Spain. It was a once-in-a-lifetime opportunity for Roosevelt, who quickly resigned his post and eagerly volunteered for action. Within weeks, Lieutenant Colonel Roosevelt transformed a collection of college athletes, cowboys, policemen, and miners into a fighting group that went on to achieve lasting glory as the Rough Riders. Roosevelt was lionized in the American press, and his status as a war hero guaranteed a successful political future. In 1900, despite his many qualms about McKinley, Roosevelt was persuaded to become the vice-presidential running mate. They won the election, of course, and after McKinley's assassination in 1901, Roosevelt became the twenty-sixth president of the United States, the youngest man, at age forty-two, to serve in the office.

As president, Roosevelt continued to use metaphors about *backbone* and *spine*, believing they were great shorthand terms for courage (or the lack of it). In another example, he said of Supreme Court Justice Oliver Wendell Holmes, Jr.:

I could carve out of a banana
a justice with more backbone than that.

The theatrical and entertainment world is filled with magnificent metaphorical insults. Many come from critics, whose reviews have contained some real gems:

She was good at playing abstracted confusion
in the same way a midget is good at being short.
CLIVE JAMES, *on Marilyn Monroe*

He played the King as though under the momentary apprehension
that someone else was about to play the Ace.
EUGENE FIELD, *reviewing*
Creston Clarke as King Lear

Her voice sounded like an eagle being goosed.
RALPH NOVAK, *on Yoko Ono*

Reading Proust is like bathing in someone else's dirty water.
ALEXANDER WOOLLCOTT,
on Marcel Proust

Sometimes the recipients of reviews have fired back in similar ways, as when the American playwright David Mamet described two influential critics this way:

Frank Rich and John Simon are
the syphilis and gonorrhea of the theater.

Metaphorical insults are generally directed at people, but every now and then, we come across examples of what might be called impersonal invective:

Like two skeletons copulating on a corrugated tin roof.

THOMAS BEECHAM,
on the harpsichord

**A war between architecture and painting
in which both come out badly maimed.**

JOHN CANADY,
on the Guggenheim Museum

A monstrous carbuncle on the face of a much-loved and elegant friend.

PRINCE CHARLES, *on a proposed
addition to London's National Gallery*

Analogies and metaphors can be used to deliver compliments as well as insults. Garrison Keillor once said that Alfred Kinsey was to sex what Columbus was to geography. In his 2001 *Jazz* documentary, filmmaker Ken Burns said of Louis "Satchmo" Armstrong:

**Armstrong is to music what Einstein is to physics
and the Wright Brothers are to travel.**

And Nunnally Johnson offered this tribute to Marilyn Monroe:

**She is a phenomenon of nature,
like Niagara Falls or the Grand Canyon.
You can't talk to it. It can't talk to you.
All you can do is stand back and be awed by it.**

Sometimes the compliments have a double-edged quality, as when John Mason Brown said of Dorothy Parker:

To those she did not like, she was a stiletto made of sugar.

More metaphorical compliments can be found in other chapters of the book, but in the remainder of this chapter you will find only examples of words being used as weapons—and all will be expressed metaphorically.

A beautiful palace without central heating.
ANONYMOUS, *on Clare Booth Luce*

According to Luce's biographer, Sylvia Jukes Morris, this was a popular saying about Luce. If you know a great beauty—or a handsome man—who lacks warmth and sensitivity, you won't find a better metaphorical insult.

A one-man slum.
ANONYMOUS, *on Heywood Broun*

Broun was a rotund man who was notorious for his disheveled appearance. He was once described this way, and it followed him for the rest of his life.

The glittering structure of her cultivation sits on her novels like a rather showy icing that detracts from the cake beneath.
LOUIS AUCHINCLOSS, *on Edith Wharton*

America is an adorable woman chewing tobacco.
FRÉDÉRIC-AUGUSTE BARTHOLDI

Bartholdi was a nineteenth-century French sculptor who loved America but was turned off by its citizens' disgusting personal habits, especially tobacco chewing. His most famous work, a statue he titled Liberty Enlightening the World, was a mouthful for everyday Americans, who since 1886 have informally referred to it by the name it has today: the Statue of Liberty. Another European aesthete who loved Americans but detested tobacco chewing—and the spitting associated with it—was Oscar Wilde. The practice inspired his famous metaphorical remark, "America is one long expectoration."

His mind had one compartment for right and one for wrong, but no middle chamber where the two could commingle.
HOWARD K. BEALE, *on Andrew Jackson*

This is an extaordinary description of a black-and-white thinker by a respected twentieth-century historian who wrote insightfully about many American leaders. Jackson, like so many either-or thinkers, was also stubborn—a characteristic also captured by Beale: "He could bear insult, personal danger, obloquy; but he could not yield his point."

Her singing reminds me of a cart coming downhill with the brake on.
THOMAS BEECHAM, *on an unidentified soprano in* Die Walkyre

She has a face that belongs to the sea and the wind, with large rocking-horse nostrils, and teeth that you just know bite an apple every day.
CECIL BEATON, *on Katharine Hepburn*

Getting kicked out of the American Bar Association is like getting kicked out of the Book-of-the-Month Club.
MELVIN BELLI

This was Belli's clever way of saying "no big deal" to American Bar Association president Walter Craig, who suggested that Belli's membership in the ABA might be revoked when Belli made intemperate and unprofessional remarks after his client Jack Ruby was convicted of murdering Lee Harvey Oswald. Belli, the flamboyant "king of torts," had described the Dallas trial as "the biggest kangaroo-court disgrace in the history of American law."

His mind was like a Roquefort cheese,
so ripe that it was palpably falling to pieces.

VAN WYCK BROOKS, *on Ford Madox Ford*

Ricardo Montalban is to improvisational acting
what Mount Rushmore is to animation.

JOHN CASSAVETES

Why refer to an actor as *wooden* or *stiff* when you can say something like this?

He occasionally stumbled over the truth,
but hastily picked himself up and hurried on as if nothing had happened.

WINSTON CHURCHILL,
on Stanley Baldwin

He is the only bull that brings his own china shop with him.

WINSTON CHURCHILL,
on John Foster Dulles

This is a clever alteration of *bull in a china shop*, which means being clumsy or reckless in situations that call for grace or delicacy. Churchill used it to describe the performance of U. S. Secretary of State Dulles in the post-World War II years.

Listening to the Fifth Symphony of Ralph Vaughan Williams
is like staring at a cow for forty-five minutes.

AARON COPLAND

Toward the end of her life she looked like a hungry insect
magnified a million times—a praying mantis that had forgotten how to pray.

QUENTIN CRISP, *on Joan Crawford*

**He festooned the dung heap on which he had placed himself with sonnets
as people grow honeysuckle around outdoor privies.**
QUENTIN CRISP, *on Oscar Wilde*

A day away from Tallulah is like a month in the country.
HOWARD DIETZ, *on Tallulah Bankhead*

He was like a cock who thought the sun had risen to hear him crow.
GEORGE ELIOT, *in* Adam Bede *(1859)*

This is how the line is usually presented, but the full original passage is
even more interesting. As Mr. and Mrs. Irwine discuss Mrs. Poyser, he says:
"Her tongue is like a new-set razor. She's quite original in her talk, too; one
of those untaught wits that help to stock a country with proverbs. I told you
that capital thing I heard her say about Craig—that he was like a cock, who
thought the sun had risen to hear him crow. Now, that's an Aesop's fable in
a sentence."

***The Love Machine* is a far better book than *Valley (of the Dolls)* . . .
It is still, to be sure, not exactly a literary work.
But in its own little sub-category . . .
it shines, like a rhinestone in a trash can.**
NORA EPHRON, *on Jacqueline
Susann's* The Love Machine (1969)

**He looks like the guy in a science-fiction movie
who is the first to see the Creature.**
DAVID FRYE, *on President Gerald Ford*

**He's like a man who sits on a stove
and then complains that his backside is burning.**
W. S. GILBERT, *on partner Arthur Sullivan*

Despite their remarkable creative partnership, Gilbert and Sullivan had a rocky personal relationship. Gilbert made this comment after Sullivan had complained that Gilbert's skill as a librettist didn't match his as a composer.

Bambi with testosterone.

OWEN GLEIBERMAN, *on Prince*

This appeared in *Entertainment Weekly* in 1990. In 1986, Boy George said of Prince: "He looks like a dwarf who's been dipped in a bucket of pubic hair."

He cast off his friends, as a huntsman his pack,
For he knew when he pleas'd he could whistle them back.

OLIVER GOLDSMITH,
on David Garrick

He talks so fast that listening to him is like
trying to read *Playboy* magazine with your wife turning the pages.

BARRY GOLDWATER,
on Hubert H. Humphrey

Freud is the father of psychoanalysis. It had no mother.

GERMAINE GREER

This, from Greer's 1971 *The Female Eunuch*, is one of the twentieth century's most sophisticated insults. Feminists long quarreled with Freud, believing that psychoanalysis was a giant edifice built around a male-dominated view of the world. But it wasn't until this observation that a female voice grasped the concept that the most effective counterattack was not with anger but with wit.

A very weak-minded fellow I am afraid, and, like the feather pillow, bears the marks of the last person who has sat on him.

EARL DOUGLAS HAIG,
on Edward Stanley (Lord Derby)

His speech was rather like being savaged by a dead sheep.

DENIS HEALY, *on Sir Geoffrey Howe*

Healy said this in a House of Commons debate in 1978. In his 1989 memoir he said the comment "was an adaptation of Churchill's remark that an attack by Attlee was 'like being savaged by a pet lamb.'" Nobody else recalls Churchill's remark (although he once did describe Attlee as "a sheep in sheep's clothing").

**If ignorance ever goes to $40 a barrel,
I want drilling rights on George Bush's head.**

JIM HIGHTOWER,
on George H. W. Bush, in 1988

That man's ears make him look like a taxi-cab with both doors open.

HOWARD HUGHES, *on Clark Gable*

He was to ordinary male chauvinist pigs what Moby Dick was to whales.

ROBERT HUGHES, *on Pablo Picasso*

A grenade with the pin pulled.

JOHN HUSTON,
on the volatile Charles Bronson

**The trouble with Senator Long is that
he is suffering from halitosis of the intellect.**

HAROLD L. ICKES, *on Senator Huey P. Long*

Ickes was FDR's Secretary of the Interior. His best-known quip came in 1939, just after the thirty-seven-year-old Thomas Dewey announced his intention to become the Republican presidential nominee: "Dewey has thrown his diaper into the ring."

Calling George Bush shallow is like calling a dwarf short.
MOLLY IVINS

Ivins said this about the elder Bush in 1990, but she wouldn't have quibbled with anyone who applied it to George W. Bush. In 1999, she wrote about him: "If you think his daddy had trouble with 'the vision thing,' wait'll you meet this one."

Arnold Schwarzenegger looks like a condom full of walnuts.
CLIVE JAMES

As a work of art, it has the same status as
a long conversation between two not very bright drunks.
CLIVE JAMES, *on Judith Krantz's*
Princess Daisy (1980)

The poet of junk food and pop culture.
SHEILA JOHNSTON, *on Steven Spielberg*

The biggest bug in the manure pile.
ELIA KAZAN,
on Harry Cohn and Hollywood

This little flower, this delicate little beauty, this cream puff . . .
He is simply a shiver looking for a spine to run up.
PAUL KEATING,
on Australian politician John Hewson

The Christian Coalition has no more to do with Christianity than the Elks Club has to do with large animals with antlers.

GARRISON KEILLOR

The Canadian comedian Robin Tyler offered a related analogy: "Fundamentalists are to Christianity what paint-by-numbers is to art."

She looked as though butter wouldn't melt in her mouth— or anywhere else.

ELSA LANCHESTER, *on Maureen O'Hara*

A cold bitch might be used today, but Lanchester excelled in the art of analogy. If her full meaning is not apparent, *or anywhere else* suggests frigidity.

Jimmy Carter as president is like Truman Capote marrying Dolly Parton. The job is too big for him.

RICH LITTLE

The idea of a job being too big for someone has never been better described. Don Rickles was thinking similarly when he said, "Eddie Fisher married to Elizabeth Taylor is like me trying to wash the Empire State Building with a bar of soap."

He looks just like the little man on the wedding cake.

ALICE ROOSEVELT LONGWORTH,
on Thomas E. Dewey

Mrs. Longworth, the colorful daughter of Theodore Roosevelt, became such a fixture in our nation's capital in the mid-1900s that she was called "Wash-ington's other monument." She made this remark during the 1948 presidential race, when Dewey was heavily favored to defeat Harry S Truman.

Once the remark was made, many voters couldn't get the image out of their minds—Dewey, with his pencil-thin mustache and formal demeanor, did look as stiff as the groom figures seen on wedding cakes. How many votes did it cost Dewey? Enough to give Truman the surprise victory, which he celebrated by hoisting a *Chicago Tribune* with the famously wrong headline: DEWEY DEFEATS TRUMAN.

> **Though I yield to no one in my admiration for Mr. Coolidge,**
> **I do wish he did not look as if he had been weaned on a pickle.**
> ALICE ROOSEVELT LONGWORTH,
> *on Calvin Coolidge*

Mrs. L. heard this remark from her doctor, and even though she went to great lengths to credit him, the saying is almost always attributed to her.

> **His imagination resembled the wings of an ostrich.**
> **It enabled him to run, though not to soar.**
> THOMAS BABINGTON MACAULAY,
> *on John Dryden*

Macaulay added: "When he attempted the highest flights, he became ridiculous; but while he remained on a lower region, he outstripped all competitors."

> **You know, the French remind me a little bit**
> **of an aging actress of the 1940s who was still trying**
> **to dine out on her looks but doesn't have the face for it.**
> JOHN McCAIN

When France failed to support the 2003 invasion of Iraq, many American politicians fired rhetorical shots at our former ally. Another insulting analogy came from Jed Babbin, a former deputy undersecretary of defense in the first Bush administration. Appearing on MSNBC's *Hardball* in January 2003, he said, "You know, frankly, going to war without France is like going deer hunting without an accordion. You just leave a lot of useless noisy baggage behind."

She is closer to organized prostitution than anything else.

MORRISSEY, *on Madonna*

A pile of shit in a silk stocking.

NAPOLEON BONAPARTE,
on Charles-Maurice de Talleyrand

The triumph of sugar over diabetes.

GEORGE JEAN NATHAN,
on James M. Barrie

The Englishman has all the qualities of a poker except its occasional warmth.

DANIEL O'CONNELL

The lighthouse in a sea of absurdity.

FRIEDRICH NIETZSCHE,
on Victor Hugo

The air currents of the world never ventilated his mind.

WALTER H. PAGE,
on Woodrow Wilson

Page, an early Wilson supporter, was rewarded with an appointment as ambassador to Great Britain in 1913. He became disenchanted with Wilson's policy of neutrality in the early years of World War I. While he was pleased when the United States entered the war in 1917, he never again supported Wilson. The line perfectly describes many contemporary Americans who have taken love of country a little too far. They fold up the American flag and wrap it around their eyes like a blindfold, making them virtually immune to international influence.

A vacuum with nipples.

OTTO PREMINGER, *on Marilyn Monroe*

Also speaking about Monroe, Billy Wilder said: "The question is whether Marilyn is a person at all or one of the greatest Dupont products ever invented. She has breasts like granite and a brain like Swiss cheese, full of holes."

He is a man of splendid abilities, but utterly corrupt. He shines and stinks like rotten mackerel by moonlight.

JOHN RANDOLPH, *on Edward Livingston*

Many books and Web sites continue to mistakenly report that Henry Clay was the target of this legendary metaphorical insult. John F. Kennedy even got it wrong in his 1957 book *Profiles in Courage* (where he described the line as "the most memorable and malignant sentence in the history of personal abuse"). Randolph, who was hailed by William Safire as the recognized "master of American political invective," said it about Edward Livingston, a former New York City mayor who had been elected to Congress. In 1998, Bill Weld, the ex-federal prosecutor and former governor of Massachusetts, titled his first novel *Mackerel by Moonlight*. Appropriately, it was a tale of political corruption.

He is to acting what Liberace was to pumping iron.

REX REED, *on Sylvester Stallone*

Most of the time, Brando sounds like he has a mouth full of wet toilet paper.

REX REED, *on Marlon Brando*

If a swamp alligator could talk, it would sound like Tennessee Williams.

REX REED

I was particularly stunned by the casting of Cruise, who is no more my Vampire Lestat than Edward G. Robinson is Rhett Butler.

ANNE RICE, *on Tom Cruise*

Rice said this in 1993, shortly after the announcement that Cruise would play the Vampire Lestat in a film adaptation of her 1974 novel, *Interview With a Vampire*. After screening the film a year later, Rice was so captivated by Cruise's performance that she recanted her position in a full-page ad she took out in the trade newspaper *Variety*. In a later interview, she replaced her insulting analogy with a complimentary one: "I like to believe Tom's Lestat will be remembered the way Olivier's Hamlet is remembered."

Poor George, he can't help it. He was born with a silver foot in his mouth.

ANN RICHARDS, *on George H. W. Bush*

In 1988, three years before becoming Texas governor, Richards delivered this line in an address at the Democratic National Convention. The remark, an alteration of the metaphor about being born with a silver spoon in one's mouth, was a two-fisted jab—referring to Bush's elocution difficulties as well as his privileged background. On this latter point, Democrats in Texas were fond of saying about Bush: "He was born on third base and thought he got there by hitting a triple."

Beethoven always sounds to me like the upsetting of a bag of nails, with here and there an also dropped hammer.

JOHN RUSKIN

Dealing with network executives is like being nibbled to death by ducks.

ERIC SEVAREID

Miss Streisand looks like a cross between an aardvark and an albino rat surmounted by a platinum-coated horse bun.

JOHN SIMON, *on Barbra Streisand*

Miss Garland's figure resembles
the giant-economy-size tube of toothpaste in girls' bathrooms:
squeezed intemperately at all points, it acquires a shape
that defies definition by the most resourceful solid geometrician.

JOHN SIMON, *on Judy Garland*

Diana Rigg is built like a brick mausoleum
with insufficient flying buttresses.

JOHN SIMON, *on Rigg's*
nude scene in Abelard and Heloise

Rigg is best-known for playing Mrs. Peel in the 1960s TV series *The Avengers*. Simon's remark became popular in part because of its similarity to a simile American men have long used to describe buxom women: *built like a brick shithouse*.

He not only overflowed with learning, but stood in the slop.

SYDNEY SMITH,
on Thomas Babington Macaulay

Nixon, Ford, Carter, Reagan—a Mount Rushmore of incompetence.

DAVID STEINBERG

His mind was like a soup dish, wide and shallow;
it could hold a small amount of nearly anything,
but the slightest jarring spilled the soup into somebody's lap.

IRVING STONE, *on William Jennings Bryan*

Reading him is like wading through glue.

ALFRED, LORD TENNYSON, *on Ben Jonson*

A louse in the locks of literature.

ALFRED, LORD TENNYSON,
on critic Churton Collins

**The bosom friend of senators and congressmen
was about as daring as an early Shirley Temple movie.**

JAMES THURBER, *on Will Rogers*

**A solemn, unsmiling, sanctimonious old iceberg
that looked like he was waiting for a vacancy in the Trinity.**

MARK TWAIN, *on an
unidentified cruise ship passenger*

Twain wrote this about a passenger who, in the middle of an 1867 Atlantic Ocean crossing, asked the captain if the ship was going to come to a halt on Sundays.

**His ignorance covered the whole earth like a blanket,
and there was hardly a hole in it anywhere.**

MARK TWAIN, *on Charles L. Webster*

Twain formed his own publishing company in 1885 and appointed Charles L. Webster, his nephew by marriage, as president. Twain never had much respect for Webster and forced him out of the company three years later. The complete passage in which I found this observation is a metaphorical *tour de force*. It may even have stimulated the popular expression about *engaging in a battle of wits with an unarmed person*. The full passage can be found at: www.DrMardy.com.

Donald Trump's hair is to coiffure what Ashton Kutcher is to dramatic acting.
TONY VITALE

Froth at the top, dregs at bottom, but the middle excellent.
VOLTAIRE, *describing the English nation*

Audrey Hepburn is the patron saint of anorexics.
ORSON WELLES

The unpleasant sound Bush is emitting as he traipses from one conservative gathering to another is a thin, tinny *arf*—the sound of a lap dog.
GEORGE F. WILL, *on George W. Bush*

Former president George H. W. Bush was also the recipient of an insulting dog analogy. In the late 1980s, Mike Royko wrote, "He has the look about him of someone who might sit up and yip for a Dog Yummie."

Little Truman had a voice so high it could only be detected by a bat.
TENNESSEE WILLIAMS, *on Truman Capote*

Williams was referring to Capote's high-pitched voice. On Capote's writing ability, Katherine Anne Porter was not as generous, calling him "the pimple on the face of American literature."

With a pig's eyes that never look up,
with a pig's snout that loves muck,
with a pig's brain that knows only the sty,
and a pig's squeal that cries only when he is hurt,
he sometimes opens his pig's mouth, tusked and ugly,
and lets out the voice of God,
railing at the whitewash that covers the manure about his habitat.
WILLIAM ALLEN WHITE, *on H. L. Mencken*

An improbable creature, like a human giraffe,
sniffing down his nostrils at mortals beneath his gaze.

RICHARD WILSON *(Lord Moran)*,
on Charles de Gaulle

Mrs. Patrick Campbell is an aged British battleship sinking rapidly
and firing every available gun on her rescuers.

ALEXANDER WOOLLCOTT

A hyena in syrup.

YEVGENY YEVTUSHENKO,
on Barbara Walters

This extraordinary insult first surfaced in a 1972 *Time* magazine article
on Walters. The piece cleverly described her this way: "Barbara is alter-
nately breathy and brittle, cool and aggressive. Her technique is a model, to
some observers, of what makes an interview great; to others, of what makes
an interview grate." The legendary Russian poet found her grating.

chapter 5

Enclosing Wild Ideas
Within a Wall of Words

On May 25, 1843, Ralph Waldo Emerson wrote in his journal:

The sky is the daily bread of the eyes.

One can almost imagine the scene. It is a bright May New England day. Emerson is rambling through the woods just outside his home town of Concord. With a book in one hand and his ever-present journal tucked safely away in a coat pocket, he leans against a tree, thinking about a passage he has just read or contemplating an idea that has recently occurred to him. Glancing upward, he slowly examines the vastness of the heavens above. Suddenly, an analogy flashes into his mind—as eating food nourishes the body, looking at the sky nourishes the soul.

Emerson the thinker might have been pleased with the analogy, and he might have wondered if the connection had ever occurred to anyone else. More than once he had an insight that seemed original, only to discover later that a legendary thinker had beaten him to the punch (he once said, oxymoronically, "Some of my best thoughts have been stolen by the ancients").

Emerson the writer, however, may have decided to tinker with the thought, hoping to better express it. Whether the final version came to him immediately, or after several drafts and revisions, the observation that Emerson finally recorded in his journal—*the sky is the daily bread of the eyes*—is a remarkable metaphor, and arguably the best words ever written on something we see every day but usually take for granted. It may even be regarded as the definitive observation on the subject.

In a usage note on the word *definitive* in the *American Heritage Dictionary*, the editors write:

> *Definitive generally refers specifically to a judgment or description that serves as a standard or reference point for others, as in . . . the definitive biography of Nelson (i.e., the biography that sets the standard against which all other accounts of Nelson's life must be measured).*

As there are definitive biographies, there are definitive quotations—observations that are so exceptionally well phrased they *set the bar* for all other observations on the same subjects. Emerson's *sky* metaphor deserves such a distinction. And many definitive quotations on a variety of other subjects are also metaphors.

There is even a definitive metaphorical quote on the topic of *definitions*. Before we look at it, though, here's the formal meaning, again from the *American Heritage Dictionary*:

> *Definition. A statement of the meaning of a word, phrase, or term, as in a dictionary definition.*

It's an adequate description, yes. But like so many dictionary definitions, it's not particularly exciting. To word and language lovers, though, there is nothing unexciting about dictionary definitions. But it was not until I found an observation in the 1912 *Notebooks* of the English writer Samuel Butler that I found a metaphorical description that perfectly described the drama of the lexicographer's task:

A definition is the enclosing
a wilderness of idea within a wall of words.

This is a remarkable observation, conjuring up a delightfully vivid image of lexicographers as cowboys or frontier settlers, corralling wild ideas inside the confines of a series of carefully constructed words. No previous observation on the subject of definitions even comes close, making this the definitive one. That is, Butler's metaphorical observation may be considered the standard by which all other similar observations on the subject of definitions must be measured.

On many subjects, it's difficult to select a single definitive quote. For example, I have long believed that the best observation ever made on the subject of architecture was an 1829 observation by Johann Wolfgang von Goethe:

I call architecture frozen music.

If one could freeze music, and then shape it into a form, it would seem appropriate to view it as a kind of architecture. Over the years, I've come across several additional architecture metaphors, and none could rival Goethe's spectacular creation. Then I came across this observation from Constantin Brancusi:

Architecture is inhabited sculpture.

Here, the legendary sculptor asserts that architecture *is* sculpture, and a kind of sculpture inhabited by people. Nobody had ever before described sculpture in this way, but when one examines the many striking office buildings that have been built in recent years, the observation is perfectly apt. Which of the two observations is the *definitive* one? You be the judge.

You can also cast your vote for one of three observations on *faith*. They're all wonderfully phrased, and they come from three of my favorite writers. For me, selecting only one involved the pain of rejecting two, and I just didn't have the heart to do it.

**Faith is an oasis in the heart
which will never be reached by the caravan of thinking.**
KAHLIL GIBRAN

Faith is taking the first step even when you don't see the whole staircase.
MARTIN LUTHER KING, JR.

Faith is the bird that feels the light and sings while the dawn is still dark.
RABINDRANATH TAGORE

You can also weigh in on two metaphors on *fame*. They come from two of history's most graceful and stylish writers, and so far are in a dead heat:

Fame is a pearl many dive for and only a few bring up.
LOUISA MAY ALCOTT

Fame is a fickle food upon a shifting plate.
EMILY DICKINSON

Many definitive metaphors are brief and pithy, as when an anonymous wag once described a *cubicle* as "a padded cell without a door." Or when Clifton Fadiman referred to *cheese* as "milk's leap toward immortality." Others are slightly longer, like this spectacular observation from Canadian writer Mark Abley's delightful 2003 book, *Spoken Here: Travels Among Threatened Languages:*

**Modern English is the Wal-Mart of languages:
convenient, huge, hard to avoid, superficially friendly,
and devouring all rivals in its eagerness to expand.**

A variety of metaphorical observations on the English language have made it into my personal quotation collection, including William Safire's terrific remark that "English is a stretch language; one size fits all." As good as the others are, though, they can't match Abley's inspired observation. What it lacks in brevity it makes up in wit and originality. And, because it attempts to illuminate one thing—*English*—by relating it to something that, at first glance, couldn't seem more dissimilar—*Wal-Mart*—it is a perfect metaphor.

In the remainder of the chapter, I will present more metaphorical observations that, in my opinion, set the standard for all other observations on the subjects examined. Unlike other chapters in the book, the quotations here will not be arranged alphabetically by author, but by the central subject of the quote. We'll begin with *action* and end with *zeal*. Think of this chapter as a brief A-to-Z dictionary of definitive metaphorical quotations.

A man's action is only a picture book of his creed.

RALPH WALDO EMERSON

The adjective is the banana peel of the parts of speech.

CLIFTON FADIMAN

This comes from a 1956 *Reader's Digest* article titled "Beware the Awful Adjective." Used wisely, Fadiman argued, adjectives enliven and enhance language. But when used badly, they cause a multitude of slip-ups. Quotation anthologist James Simpson hailed this as one of the "best quotes of 1956."

Adventure is the champagne of life.

G. K. CHESTERTON

All affectation is the vain and ridiculous attempt
of poverty to appear rich.

JOHANN KASPAR LAVATAR

Unsolicited advice is the junk mail of life.

BERN WILLIAMS

Anger is a wind which blows out the lamp of the mind.

ROBERT G. INGERSOLL

Anxiety is the dizziness of freedom.

SØREN KIERKEGAARD

The aphorism is a personal observation inflated into a universal truth,
a private posing as a general.

STEFAN KANFER

An apology is the superglue of life. It can repair just about anything.

LYNN JOHNSTON

Autumn is a second spring, when every leaf is a flower.

ALBERT CAMUS

A bagel is a doughnut with the sin removed.

GEORGE ROSENBAUM

Our birthdays are feathers in the broad wing of time.

JEAN PAUL RICHTER

Business is a combination of war and sport.

ANDRÉ MAUROIS

The cat is a dilettante in fur.

THÉOPHILE GAUTHIER

Chance is the pseudonym of God when he did not want to sign.

THÉOPHILE GAUTHIER

Chaos is the score upon which reality is written.

HENRY MILLER

Charm is a glow within a woman that casts a most becoming light on others.

JOHN MASON BROWN

Coincidences are spiritual puns.

G. K. CHESTERTON

The dew of compassion is a tear.

LORD BYRON

Compromise makes a good umbrella, but a poor roof.

JAMES RUSSELL LOWELL

Conscience reigns but it does not govern.

PAUL VALÉRY

Courage is the ladder on which all the other virtues mount.

CLARE BOOTH LUCE

I also like this one from Mignon McLaughlin: "Courage can't see around corners, but goes around them anyway."

The dance is a poem of which each movement is a word.

MATA HARI

Mata Hari was the stage name of a Dutch exotic dancer whose scantily clad dance routines and openly promiscuous life style captivated Parisian society in the early 1900s. She was found guilty—on flimsy evidence—of espionage and executed by a French firing squad in 1917. After Greta Garbo brought her story to the big screen in the 1931 film *Mata Hari*, she became known as a classic *femme fatale*, and her name became an eponym for a beautiful female double agent. Another memorable metaphorical observation on dancing came from George Bernard Shaw, who called it "a perpendicular expression of a horizontal desire."

Despair is vinegar from the wine of hope.

AUSTIN O'MALLEY

The point is that people wouldn't feel despair unless they first felt hope. And just as bad wine turns into vinegar, dashed hopes often turn into despair.

Doctrine is nothing but the skin of truth set up and stuffed.

HENRY WARD BEECHER

The dog . . . is the god of frolic.

HENRY WARD BEECHER

Doodling is the brooding of the mind.

SAUL STEINBERG

A discovery is said to be an accident meeting a prepared mind.

ALBERT SZENT-GYORGYI

The allusion here is to a famous remark from Louis Pasteur, who said in 1854: "Where observation is concerned, chance favors only the prepared mind."

The dress is a vase which the body follows.

PIERRE CARDIN

Egotism is the anesthetic that dulls the pain of stupidity.

FRANK LEAHY

Euphemisms are unpleasant truths wearing diplomatic cologne.

QUENTIN CRISP

This is a remarkable observation in its own right, but the full passage in which it appeared is even more impressive: "Euphemisms are not . . . useless verbiage for that which can and should be said bluntly; they are like secret agents on a delicate mission, they must airily pass by a stinking mess with barely so much as a nod of the head, make their point of constructive criticism and continue on in calm forbearance. *Euphemisms are unpleasant truths wearing diplomatic cologne.*"

An exaggeration is a truth that has lost its temper.

KAHLIL GIBRAN

Failure is the condiment that gives success its flavor.

TRUMAN CAPOTE

Fame is the perfume of heroic deeds.

SOCRATES

Feedback is the breakfast of champions.

KEN BLANCHARD & SPENCER JOHNSON

The flower is the poetry of reproduction.

JEAN GIRAUDOUX

A close contender here was Luther Burbank's "A flower is an educated weed." On uneducated weeds, Ralph Waldo Emerson observed, "What is a weed? A plant whose virtues have not yet been discovered." And on weeds in general, Ella Wheeler Wilcox wrote simply, "A weed is but an unloved flower."

Freedom is the oxygen of the soul.

MOSHE DAYAN

Genius is a promontory jutting out into the infinite.

VICTOR HUGO

Global warming might be a fever the earth is running in an attempt to ward off a deadly infection known as *homo sapiens*.

RICK BAYAN

God is a metaphor for that which transcends all levels of intellectual thought. It's as simple as that.

JOSEPH CAMPBELL

Goodness is the only investment that never fails.

HENRY DAVID THOREAU

Gratitude is the heart's memory.

FRENCH PROVERB

Habit is a cable; we weave a thread of it each day, and at last we cannot break it.

HORACE MANN

Happiness makes up in height for what it lacks in length.

ROBERT FROST

This was the title of a 1942 poem that figuratively captured the allure of happiness. Ralph Waldo Emerson is often credited with another classic on the subject, but so far I have been unable to find the original observation in any of his published works: "Happiness is a perfume you cannot pour on others without getting a few drops on yourself."

Honesty is the first chapter of the book of wisdom.

THOMAS JEFFERSON

A house is a machine for living in.

LE CORBUSIER

A hunch is creativity trying to tell you something.

FRANK CAPRA

Ignorance is the night of the mind.

CONFUCIUS

Imagination is intelligence with an erection.

VICTOR HUGO

This is the only R-rated observation to be found in this chapter, and some may find it inappropriate. But even if you do, you must admit that it stimulates quite an image. A more socially acceptable—and also exceptional— observation comes from Joseph Joubert: "Imagination is the eye of the soul."

Inspiration could be called inhaling the memory of an act never experienced.

NED ROREM

Jazz is the music of the body.

ANAÏS NIN

Journalism is literature in a hurry.
MATTHEW ARNOLD

Justice is truth in action.
BENJAMIN DISRAELI

Is not a kiss the very autograph of love?
HENRY THEOPHILUS FINCK

This observation comes from Finck's 1887 book *Romantic Love and Personal Beauty*. Finck, a nineteenth-century music critic who was also interested in philosophy and the classics, may have inspired a famous Mae West line: "A man's kiss is his signature." There have been many other wonderful kiss observations, but another potentially definitive one is this classic from Edmond Rostand's *Cyrano de Bergerac*: "'Tis a secret told to the mouth instead of to the ear."

Laughter is the sun that drives winter from the human face.
VICTOR HUGO

Letters are expectation packed in an envelope.
SHANA ALEXANDER

A line is a dot that went for a walk.
PAUL KLEE

Memory is a crazed woman that hoards colored rags and throws away food.
AUSTIN O'MALLEY

The point is that we forget the essential and remember—often with great clarity—the tantalizing trivia. Other deserving candidates on this subject include:

"Our memories are card indexes consulted and then put back in disorder, by authorities whom we do not control." *Cyril Connolly*

"Memory is the personal journalism of the soul." *Richard Schickel*

The mind, of course, is just what the brain does for a living.

SHARON BEGLEY

Moral indignation is jealousy with a halo.

H. G. WELLS

Music is the wine that fills the cup of silence.

ROBERT FRIPP

Nostalgia is a seductive liar.

GEORGE BALL

**Opportunity is missed by most people
because it is dressed in overalls and looks like work.**

THOMAS ALVA EDISON

Henry J. Kaiser said similarly: "Trouble is only opportunity in work clothes."

**Passion makes the best observations
and the most wretched conclusions.**

JEAN PAUL RICHTER

Another favorite, from Ralph Waldo Emerson, is this: "Passion, though a bad regulator, is a powerful spring."

The past is a foreign country; they do things differently there.

L. P. HARTLEY

On the same subject, Maxim Gorky wrote in *The Lower Depths* (1903): "In the carriages of the past you can't go anywhere."

Peanut butter is *paté* for children.

BRIGITTE BARDOT

The piano is a monster that screams when you touch its teeth.

ANDRÉS SEGOVIA

Popularity? It's glory's small change.

VICTOR HUGO

Poverty is the mother of crime.

MARCUS AURELIUS

A prayer, in its simplest definition,
is merely a wish turned heavenward.

PHILLIPS BROOKS

Procrastination is the thief of time.

EDWARD YOUNG

A promise is an IOU.

ROBERT HALF

A proverb is anonymous human history compressed to the size of a seed.

STEFAN KANFER

If I were personally to define religion,
I would say that it is a bandage that man has invented
to protect a soul made bloody by circumstance.

THEODORE DREISER

Research is the process of going up alleys to see if they are blind.

MARSTON BATES

A riot is at bottom the language of the unheard.

MARTIN LUTHER KING, JR.

Rock and roll is the hamburger that ate the world.

PETER YORK

Scientists are peeping toms at the keyhole of eternity.

ARTHUR KOESTLER

Skepticism is the chastity of the intellect.

GEORGE SANTAYANA

The point is that we should apply the admonition about keeping one's chastity to our mental as well as our physical life. That is, we should retain our skepticism as long as possible and avoid giving it up too early—or too easily—to a seductive idea.

Slang is language that takes off its coat, spits on its hands, and goes to work.

CARL SANDBURG

Tact is after all a kind of mind-reading.

SARAH ORNE JEWETT

**Tears are the safety valve of the heart
when too much pressure is laid on it.**

ALBERT SMITH

That great, growling engine of change—technology.

ALVIN TOFFLER

Thought is the seed of action.
RALPH WALDO EMERSON

Time is a dressmaker specializing in alterations.
FAITH BALDWIN

Toleration is the best religion.
VICTOR HUGO

Truth is error burned up.
NORMAN O. BROWN

Some other close contenders in this category include the following:
"The color of truth is gray." *André Gide*
"Truth is a fruit which should not be plucked until it is ripe." *Voltaire*
"The best mind-altering drug is truth." *Jane Wagner* (for Lily Tomlin)

Twilight: A time of pause when nature changes her guard.
HOWARD THURMAN

Virtual reality is just air guitar writ large.
ROBERT J. SAWYER

Virtue is the beauty of the soul.
SOCRATES

The voice is a second face.
GERARD BAUER

Vulgarity is the garlic in the salad of charm.
CYRIL CONNOLLY

Wine is bottled poetry.

ROBERT LOUIS STEVENSON

A word is a bud attempting to become a twig.

GASTON BACHELARD

**Zeal is a volcano, on the peak of which
the grass of indecisiveness does not grow.**

KAHLIL GIBRAN

chapter 6

Life Is the Art of Drawing Without an Eraser

In 1977, six years before he was awarded the Nobel Prize for literature, the British writer William Golding was invited to speak to a group of Anglophiles in Lille, France. In his address, he said:

> **Consider a man riding a bicycle.**
> **Whoever he is, we can say three things about him.**
> **We know he got on the bicycle and started to move.**
> **We know that at some point he will stop and get off.**
> **Most important of all, we know that**
> **if at any point between the beginning and the end of his journey**
> **he stops moving and does not get off the bicycle, he will fall off it.**
> **That is a metaphor for the journey through life of any living thing.**

Golding had been groomed by his parents to become a scientist, but in his second year at Oxford he got the literature bug and abandoned thoughts of a scientific career. Things started off nicely. A year before he graduated in 1935, he came out with a small volume of verse, making him a published author at age twenty-three.

After graduation, he worked for several years at a series of odd jobs while writing in his spare time, but nothing of importance emerged. In 1940, he joined the Royal Navy and spent the next six years witnessing a host of life-altering sights, including the sinking of the *Bismarck* and the Normandy invasion.

After the war, Golding's view of the world was transformed, and any prior illusions he had held about civilization were gone forever (years later, he would say he had come to the view that "man produces evil as a bee produces honey"). While teaching during the day, he began working at night on a dark, allegorical tale about a group of boys who become stranded on a desert island and slowly degenerate from civilized English schoolboys to savage and vicious brutes. He titled the work *Lord of the Flies*, a literal translation of the Hebrew word for *Beelzebub*. In the novel, it is also the name the boys give to a fly-ridden pig's skull they have mounted on a stake.

Golding began submitting his manuscript to publishers, only to have it rejected twenty-one times, often in the most unmerciful way. One said it was an "absurd and uninteresting fantasy." Another called it, "Rubbish and dull. Pointless." The negative reception might have caused a less determined person to give up. But, to return to Golding's earlier metaphor, the forty-three-year old writer stayed on the bicycle and kept pedaling—all the way into literary history.

In all metaphorical language, people try to explain one thing—often an abstract concept like *life*—by relating it to something else. Once a link is established, then all the attributes of the second domain—like *riding a bicycle*—can be applied back to the original domain. Golding could have selected any aspect of bicycling—like dodging potholes or breaking away from the pack—but he went with the idea of simply keeping a bike in motion as his metaphor for life's journey. Albert Einstein did the same thing when he observed:

Life is like riding a bicycle.
To keep your balance you must keep moving.

When one is trying to help people get a better understanding of something as ethereal as the nature of life, a bicycle metaphor has especially broad appeal. After all, almost everyone has had the experience of riding one, and most people can extrapolate backward from the concrete experience to the abstract idea. The legendary cartoonist Charles M. Schulz had his character Charlie Brown use a bicycle metaphor to lay out yet another great truth of human existence—that most of us don't even come close to living up to our potential. In his trademark way, Schulz had Charlie say it in a witty rather than a preachy way:

Life is like a ten-speed bicycle.
Most of us have gears we never use.

When people are asked to provide examples of a life metaphor, they commonly say things like *life is a beach*, or *life is a bowl of cherries* (from a popular 1930s song), or perhaps *life is a cabaret* (from the 1966 musical and 1972 film). Or maybe they will offer a simile like *life is like a box of chocolates; you never know what you're gonna get* (popularized by the 1994 film *Forrest Gump*). And while these are all perfectly fine examples of metaphorical phrasing, they don't come close to capturing the power of a metaphor to capture essential aspects of human life.

The Scottish writer James M. Barrie is best remembered as the author of *Peter Pan*, one of the most successful plays of all time, but he also wrote highly regarded satires, essays, and novels. One of his early efforts was *The Little Minister*, an 1891 novel that was turned into an 1897 play (and in 1934 adapted into a film version that featured an impressive performance by the young Katharine Hepburn). The original novel contains a line that made a deep impression on me when I first came upon it many decades ago:

**The life of every man is a diary in which he means to write one story,
and writes another, and his humblest hour is when he compares
the volume as it is with what he vowed to make it.**

After first reading this in my mid-twenties, I began thinking about my
father. I know from a few early conversations that a number of his youthful dreams were never to materialize in his adult years. My dad was a good
man, but he always had a sadness in his eyes. And he was an alcoholic from
as early as I can remember. I didn't have the maturity—at the time—to understand it all, but a decade or so later an observation attributed to George
Bernard Shaw helped put it all in perspective:

Alcohol is the anesthesia by which we endure the operation of life.

When I first read Barrie's diary metaphor, I viewed it as a profound
thought expressed beautifully, and I immediately filed it away in a compartment in my brain. I also recorded it on an index card and placed it in a manila
folder I had titled *Words to Live By*. Over the years, I returned to the observation many times as I reflected on my own journey.

As the decades have passed, I've come across many other wonderful metaphors
for life—and the best ones have never failed to give me pause for reflection:

**Life is a hospital in which every patient
is possessed by the desire of changing his bed.
One would prefer to suffer near the fire,
and another is certain he would get well if he were by the window.**

CHARLES BAUDELAIRE

**Life is like a library owned by an author.
In it are a few books which he wrote himself,
but most of them were written for him.**

HARRY EMERSON FOSDICK

Life . . . is painting a picture, not doing a sum.

OLIVER WENDELL HOLMES, JR.

Life is like a game of cards.
The hand that is dealt you represents determinism;
the way you play it is free will.

JAWAHARLAL NEHRU

Life is no "brief candle" to me.
It is a sort of splendid torch which I have got hold of for the moment,
and I want to make it burn as brightly as possible
before handing it on to future generations.

GEORGE BERNARD SHAW

Some came from unexpected sources, like the Charlie Brown quote earlier. Another pleasant surprise came from a person named Brian Dyson. I'd never heard of him, but the image he painted was so vivid—and the sentiment so powerful—I was shocked to discover he was, at the time, CEO of Coca-Cola:

Imagine life as a game in which you are juggling some five balls in the air.
You name them—work, family, health, friends, and spirit,
and you're keeping all of these in the air.
You will soon understand that work is a rubber ball.
If you drop it, it will bounce back.
But the other four balls—family, health, friends, and spirit—are made of glass.
If you drop one of these,
they will be irrevocably scuffed, marked, nicked, damaged, or even shattered.
They will never be the same.
You must understand that and strive for balance in your life.

Still others came from people I had long admired, like John W. Gardner, the noted American educator and President Kennedy's secretary of health, education, and welfare. Gardner, a provocative thinker and a beautiful writer, authored several inspiring works, including a 1961 book—titled *Excellence*—that I still take off the shelf from time to time. He once wrote:

Life is the art of drawing without an eraser.

This observation reminds us that the mistakes we make in life cannot be erased away or treated as if they never happened. Mistakes, along with triumphs, are part of our permanent record—like a transcript from the school of life. Part of the art of living is to recognize that we must learn from the mistakes we will inevitably make, and incorporate that learning into the steps we take as we move forward. It's often called *failing forward*.

In the remainder of the chapter, you will find over a hundred observations in which life is likened to such things as a banquet, a college, a mansion, an onion, a violin (and other musical instruments), a superhighway, a painting, a game of chess, and even a roll of toilet paper. No other book in history, to the best of my knowledge, has ever assembled in one chapter more analogies and metaphors on this topic. I hope the compilation will help you gain a deeper appreciation of your life, or help you explain some lessons of life to others.

Life is my college. May I graduate well and earn some honors!
LOUISA MAY ALCOTT

Life is a dream for the wise, a game for the fool,
a comedy for the rich, a tragedy for the poor.
SHOLOM ALEICHEM

Life loves to be taken by the lapel and told,
"I am with you kid. Let's go!"
MAYA ANGELOU

**Life is like a taxi ride; the meter keeps on ticking,
whether you're getting anywhere, or just standing still.**

ANONYMOUS

The point of this saying, which goes back to at least the early years of
the twentieth century, is clear: life goes on whether you do something with
it, or not. A *taximeter* (notice that it is one word) is a device that calculates
fares on the basis of distance traveled and total travel time. The device goes
back to ancient Rome, and increasingly sophisticated forms have been used
ever since. In the 1800s, they were attached to a horse-driven two-wheeled
carriage known as a *cabriolet*. The word *taxicab* is a shortened version of
taximeter cabriolet.

It is best to rise from life as from a banquet, neither thirsty nor drunken.

ARISTOTLE

Aristotle was an advocate of the *golden mean*, the desirable middle course
between two ineffective extremes. Here he makes an argument for moderation. The implication is clear—drink enough of life so that, at the end, you
won't be thirsting for more; but not so much that you will stagger in a stupor
into your grave.

Life is a journey, but don't worry, you'll find a parking spot at the end.

ISAAC ASIMOV

**Life is always walking up to us and saying, "Come on in, the living's fine,"
and what do we do? Back off and take its picture.**

RUSSELL BAKER

**Someone told me life is a water wheel. It turns. The trick is to
hold your nose when you're under and not get dizzy when you're up.**

JAMES BALDWIN

This passage from *Nobody Knows My Name* (1961) is a nice reminder that we shouldn't get too happy when things go well, or too upset when they don't.

> **Such is life. It is no cleaner than a kitchen;**
> **and if you mean to cook your dinner, you must expect to soil your hands;**
> **the real art is in getting them clean again.**
>
> HONORÉ DE BALZAC

> **Life is a long lesson in humility.**
>
> JAMES M. BARRIE

> **Life is rather like a tin of sardines.**
> **We're all of us looking for the key.**
>
> ALAN BENNETT

> **Life consists not in holding good cards but in playing those you hold well.**
>
> JOSH BILLINGS *(Henry Wheeler Shaw)*

> **Life is a grindstone, and whether it grinds a man down**
> **or polishes him up depends on what he is made of.**
>
> JOSH BILLINGS *(Henry Wheeler Shaw)*

This observation has been attributed to many others, most notably Jacob M. Braude of *The Speaker's Library* fame. The most clever alteration of the saying comes from Fred Allen: "The world is a grindstone and life is your nose."

> **Life is much more manageable when thought of as a scavenger hunt**
> **as opposed to a surprise party.**
>
> JIMMY BUFFETT

Life itself is the proper binge.

JULIA CHILD

That is, there is no shortage of improper things to binge on, but only one proper one—life itself.

**Life is like playing a violin solo in public
and learning the instrument as one goes on.**

SAMUEL BUTLER

Life is like music, it must be composed by ear, feeling, and instinct, not by rule.

SAMUEL BUTLER

**Life is like arriving late for a movie, having to figure out what was going on
without bothering everybody with a lot of questions,
and then being unexpectedly called away before you find out how it ends.**

JOSEPH CAMPBELL

Life is a moderately good play with a badly written third act.

TRUMAN CAPOTE

**Life is like a beautiful flirt, whom we love and to whom, finally,
we grant every condition she imposes as long as she doesn't leave us.**

GIOVANNI GIACOMO CASANOVA

Life is a tragedy when seen in close up, but a comedy in long shot.

CHARLES CHAPLIN

**Life is a maze in which we take the wrong turning
before we have learnt to walk.**

CYRIL CONNOLLY

Life is an incurable disease.
ABRAHAM COWLEY

Cowley, who wrote this in the seventeenth century, may have inspired a popular twentieth-century spin-off: "Life is a sexually transmitted disease." British psychiatrist R. D. Laing put a neat twist on that saying when he wrote: "Life is a sexually transmitted disease and there is a one-hundred percent mortality rate."

Life is a sum of all your choices.
ALBERT CAMUS

Life is a crowded superhighway with bewildering cloverleaf exits on which a man is liable to find himself speeding back in the direction he came.
PETER DE VRIES

De Vries also observed succinctly: "Life is a zoo in a jungle."

Life is a great tapestry.
The individual is only an insignificant thread in an immense and miraculous pattern.
ALBERT EINSTEIN

All life is an experiment.
The more experiments you make, the better.
RALPH WALDO EMERSON

Emerson wrote this in his journal in 1842. The physician and runner George Sheehan recently echoed the theme: "Life is the great experiment. Each of us is an experiment of one—observer and subject—making choices, living with them, recording the effects."

Life is a game played on us while we are playing other games.

EVAN ESAR

For most men, life is a search for the proper manila envelope
in which to get themselves filed.

CLIFTON FADIMAN

The Game of Chess is not merely an idle amusement . . .
for life is a kind of Chess, in which we have often points to gain,
and competitors or adversaries to contend with.

BENJAMIN FRANKLIN

Many have likened life to a game of chess, but it is helpful to remember that life is not a game—at least not literally. This is what Isaac Asimov meant when he said, "In life, unlike chess, the game continues after checkmate."

When Life does not find a singer to sing her heart
she produces a philosopher to speak her mind.

KAHLIL GIBRAN

Gibran suggests here that the *heart of life* is best expressed in music and song. But when that is not possible, people turn to words and language. Philosophers who write about life, then, don't *sing her heart* but rather *speak her mind*.

Life is a verb, not a noun.

CHARLOTTE PERKINS GILMAN,
written in 1904

In life, as in football, you won't go far
unless you know where the goalposts are.

ARNOLD H. GLASGOW

Lewis Grizzard carried the metaphor further: "The game of life is a lot like football. You have to tackle your problems, block your fears, and score your points when you get the opportunity."

> **Life has been compared to a race,**
> **but the allusion improves by observing that the most swift**
> **are usually the least manageable and the most likely**
> **to stray from the course.**
>
> OLIVER GOLDSMITH

> **Life is a quarry,**
> **out of which we are to mold and chisel and complete a character.**
>
> JOHANN WOLFGANG VON GOETHE

> **Life is the childhood of our immortality.**
>
> JOHANN WOLFGANG VON GOETHE

If you believe in life after death, as Goethe did, your current life becomes the childhood of your immortal life.

> **Life is a journey that must be traveled**
> **no matter how bad the roads and accommodations.**
>
> OLIVER GOLDSMITH

> **Life is like a dog-sled team.**
> **If you ain't the lead dog, the scenery never changes.**
>
> LEWIS GRIZZARD

> **Life is made up of constant calls to action,**
> **and we seldom have time for more than hastily contrived answers.**
>
> LEARNED HAND

Life is like a blanket too short. You pull it up and your toes rebel,
you yank it down and shivers meander about your shoulder;
but cheerful folks manage to draw their knees up
and pass a very comfortable night.

MARION HOWARD

Fortunately, analysis is not the only way to resolve inner conflicts.
Life itself still remains a very effective therapist.

KAREN HORNEY

Horney (HORE-nye), a twentieth-century psychoanalyst, added: "Life
as a therapist is ruthless; circumstances that are helpful to one neurotic may
crush another."

Hold fast to dreams
For if dreams die
Life is a broken-winged bird
That cannot fly.
Hold fast to dreams
For when dreams go
Life is a barren field
Frozen with snow.

LANGSTON HUGHES,
from the poem "Dreams"

A chain is no stronger than its weakest link, and life is after all a chain.

WILLIAM JAMES

Life is a pill which none of us can bear to swallow without gilding.

SAMUEL JOHNSON

The basic idea here is that bitter things must be made palatable if people are to accept them. *Gilt* is a thin layer of gold or something simulating gold, and *gilding* is the process of applying gilt to a surface. The process gives a superficially attractive appearance to everyday materials, like wood, metal, or cloth. Now we might say, "Life is a bitter pill that must be sugar-coated before people will swallow it."

Life is a great big canvas,
and you should throw all the paint on it you can.
DANNY KAYE

I compare human life to a large mansion of many apartments,
two of which I can only describe,
the doors of the rest being as yet shut upon me.
JOHN KEATS

Life is a banquet,
and most poor sons-of-bitches are starving to death.
JEROME LAWRENCE & ROBERT E. LEE

This comes from the 1957 play *Auntie Mame*, adapted from Patrick Dennis's 1955 novel. The line, which was delivered in an unforgettable way by Rosalind Russell in the role of Mame, does not appear in the book. In the 1958 film, the line was sanitized to "most poor suckers are starving to death." It became a signature line for Russell, who titled her 1977 autobiography *Life is a Banquet.*

Life for most of us is full of steep stairs to go puffing up
and later, of shaky stairs to totter down;
and very early in the history of stairs
must have come the invention of banisters.
LOUIS KRONENBERGER

Kronenberger also wrote: "The trouble with us in America isn't that the poetry of life has turned to prose, but that it has turned to advertising copy."

I would rather think of life as a good book.
The further you get into it,
the more it begins to come together and make sense.

HAROLD S. KUSHNER

Life is like a sewer.
What you get out of it depends on what you put into it.

TOM LEHRER

Life is so largely controlled by chance
that its conduct can be but a perpetual improvisation.

W. SOMERSET MAUGHAM

Life is the garment we continually alter but which never seems to fit,
and we must make our adjustments as we go.

DAVID MCCORD

In life, as in restaurants, we swallow
a lot of indigestible stuff just because it comes with the dinner.

MIGNON MCLAUGHLIN

This is from *The Neurotic's Notebook* (1960). In *The Second Neurotic's Notebook* (1966), McLaughlin wrote, "Life is a mixed blessing, which we vainly try to unmix."

Life is a dead-end street.

H. L. MENCKEN

Life is a foreign language; all men mispronounce it.

CHRISTOPHER MORLEY

Life is like a very short visit to a toy shop between birth and death.

DESMOND MORRIS

**Life is the only art that we are required
to practice without preparation,
and without being allowed the preliminary trials,
the failures and botches, that are essential for training.**

LEWIS MUMFORD

**Human life is but a series of footnotes
to a vast, obscure, unfinished manuscript.**

VLADIMIR NABOKOV

This comes from Nabokov's 1962 novel *Pale Fire*, where he also writes, "Our existence is but a brief crack of light between two eternities of darkness."

Life is for each man a solitary cell whose walls are mirrors.

EUGENE O'NEILL

**Life is a series of collisions with the future;
it is not a sum of what we have been but what we yearn to be.**

JOSÉ ORTEGA Y GASSET

Life always spills over the rim of every cup.

BORIS PASTERNAK

Life is pain and the enjoyment of love is an anesthetic.

CESARE PAVESE

Life is like a cobweb, not an organization chart.

H. ROSS PEROT

Life is little more than a loan shark:
it exacts a very high rate of interest for the few pleasures it concedes.

LUIGI PIRANDELLO

Life is full of internal dramas, instantaneous and sensational,
played to an audience of one.

ANTHONY POWELL

Life is the game that must be played.

EDWIN ARLINGTON ROBINSON

I've learned that life is like a roll of toilet paper,
the closer you get to the end, the faster it goes.

ANDY ROONEY

Eating, loving, singing, and digesting are, in truth,
the four acts of the comic opera known as life,
and they pass like the bubbles of a bottle of champagne.
Whoever lets them break without having enjoyed them is a complete fool.

GIOACHINO ANTONIO ROSSINI

I long ago came to the conclusion that all life is six to five against.

DAMON RUNYON

This comes from Runyon's 1934 short story "A Nice Price." The line may have inspired Tom Stoppard, who wrote in *Rosencrantz and Guildenstern are Dead* (1967): "Life is a gamble at terrible odds—if it was a bet, you wouldn't take it."

Life is a magic vase filled to the brim,
so made that you cannot dip from it nor draw from it;
but it overflows into the hand that drops treasures into it.
Drop in malice and it overflows hate; drop in charity and it overflows love.

JOHN RUSKIN

Lives are like rivers;
eventually they go where they must, not where we want them to.

RICHARD RUSSO

This comes at the beginning of the 2005 HBO film *Empire Falls*. Russo wrote the screenplay as well as the 2001 novel, but the line does not appear in the book.

Life is like an onion:
You peel it off one layer at a time, and sometimes you weep.

CARL SANDBURG

This is the way you will find this quotation in numerous books and scores of Web sites. So far, though, I have not found it in any of Sandburg's writings. The closest I've seen comes from his 1948 novel *Remembrance Rock*. In a chapter titled "Life Is an Onion You Peel," a character quotes his grandmother as saying, "Life is an onion—you peel it year by year and sometimes cry."

The scenes of our life are like pictures done in rough mosaic.
Looked at close-up they produce no effect.
There is nothing beautiful to be found in them,
unless you stand some distance off.

ARTHUR SCHOPENHAUER

This warning about the folly of focusing on the details of life comes from an 1851 essay. The admonition is to step back, see the big picture, and put things into perspective.

Life is a shit sandwich and every day you take another bite.

JOE SCHMIDT

Schmidt, a linebacker for the Detroit Lions from 1953 to 1965, may not have authored this saying, but he helped popularize it. The point is that life is an unpleasant affair that must be endured, like eating a sandwich made of feces. In recent years, the concept has been extended to the business world, as in "I was forced to eat a shit sandwich." Here it describes a critical remark sandwiched between two positive comments. Jonathan Winters offered this variation: "Life is a shit sandwich. But if you've got enough bread, you don't taste the shit."

In the book of life, the answers aren't in the back.

CHARLES M. SCHULZ,
Charlie Brown speaking

Life is like a play: it's not the length,
but the excellence of the acting that matters.

SENECA,
in Letters to Lucilius

The web of our life is of a mingled yarn, good and ill together.

WILLIAM SHAKESPEARE,
in All's Well That Ends Well

You cannot learn to skate without being ridiculous . . . .
The ice of life is slippery.

GEORGE BERNARD SHAW

Life is a disease; and the only difference between one man and another
is the stage of the disease at which he lives.

GEORGE BERNARD SHAW

Life is like a cash register, in that every account, every thought,
every deed, like every sale, is registered and recorded.

FULTON J. SHEEN

There are chapters in every life which are seldom read.

CAROL SHIELDS

Life is a tragedy wherein we sit as spectators for awhile
and then act our part in it.

JONATHAN SWIFT

Life is like an overlong drama through which we sit
being nagged by the vague memories of having read the reviews.

JOHN UPDIKE

Life is thick sown with thorns,
and I know no other remedy than to pass quickly through them.
The longer we dwell on our misfortunes,
the greater is their power to harm us.

VOLTAIRE

Life is a game of whist. From unseen sources
The cards are shuffled, and the hands are dealt.
I do not like the way the cards are shuffled,
But yet I like the game and want to play.

EUGENE F. WARE

Life is always a tightrope or a feather bed. Give me the tightrope.

EDITH WHARTON

**Life is a process of burning oneself out
and time is the fire that burns you.**

TENNESSEE WILLIAMS

Williams said this in a 1958 interview. In his 1953 novel *Camino Real*, he had a character offer another thought on the subject: "Life is an unanswered question, but let's still believe in the dignity and importance of the question."

**Life is a lot like a marathon.
If you can finish a marathon, you can do anything you want.**

OPRAH WINFREY

Life is so like a little strip of pavement over an abyss.

VIRGINIA WOOLF

It's a powerful image—and a stark reminder that we're safe only if we can stay on the thin stretch of pavement. The abyss is always there, just beyond the edge.

Life is a rainbow which also includes black.

YEVGENY YEVTUSHENKO

chapter 7

A Relationship
Is Like a Shark

Antoine de Saint-Exupéry was one of twentieth-century Europe's most fascinating figures. Born in 1900 to aristocratic parents who had fallen on hard times, he attended Jesuit schools in Switzerland and France. A poor student as well as a discipline problem, he was drifting through adolescence when he became fascinated with the new world of flight. In 1921, he joined the French Army, and a year later he was commissioned as a pilot in the nation's newly established Air Force. When he finished military service in 1926, he became a commercial pilot, initially flying airmail routes from France to Morocco and West Africa, and eventually to South America. He was also a test pilot for Air France, where his fearlessness made him a legend in his profession.

These days, Saint-Exupéry is best remembered as a writer. In the decades before World War II, he authored several books that celebrated the fancy of flight and the bravery of aviators. After the fall of France in 1940, he fled to the United States, where he produced his two most famous books, *Letter to a Hostage*, a call for French resistance to the Nazis, and the wildly successful *The Little Prince*, a child's fable for adults. Shortly after both books were published in 1943, he joined the allied forces in North Africa and was presumably killed when his plane crashed at sea in 1944. Saint-Exupéry was a stylish and imaginative writer, penning many spectacular observations. One of my favorites appeared in his 1942 book *Flight to Arras*:

Man is a knot, a web, a mesh into which relationships are tied.

This is a triple threat of a metaphor, immediately provoking a host of visual images and a flurry of associations. The first is about people *tying the knot*, a popular metaphor for marriage. In ancient times, however, it was an actual practice—a priest or family patriarch would symbolize the marital union by tying together the garments of the bride and groom. We can easily pursue the metaphor further:

> Like the knot of a shoelace or rope around a cargo container,
> relationships can be well tied or poorly tied. When tied skill-
> fully and effectively, knots as well as relationships somehow
> hold together, even through periods of turbulence. But when
> they are tied carelessly—or poorly by people who lack the
> essential skills—even the most precious cargo is not secure.

We could take the same approach with the *web* and *mesh* metaphors. Reflecting on the interpersonal world, a *web of relationships* seems an appropriate way to describe one of life's most persistent realities—we are most deeply affected by people who are close to us, but are often keenly aware of things that happen to those on the outskirts of our lives. While *mesh* is a word that is used infrequently, almost everyone is familiar with what happens when the gears of a machine—or the personalities of two people—don't mesh. And in my mind, the popular psychological concept of being *enmeshed* always evokes the image of a fish snared in the mesh of a fishing net (technically, the term means being entangled or hopelessly caught up in a relationship or other vexing situation).

When people create metaphors, they find similarities between things that, on the surface, are dissimilar. A good metaphor is like a bridge that links two territories that have been separated by a body of water or a deep canyon. Once the bridge is connected, people can travel freely back and forth. In her 1982 book *Anatomy of Freedom*, Robin Morgan expressed it this way:

> **Metaphor is the energy charge that leaps between images,**
> **revealing their connections.**

While many relationship metaphors are serious, others are comedic. In the 1977 film *Annie Hall*, Alvy Singer (Woody Allen) says to Annie (Diane Keaton):

> **A relationship, I think, is like a shark. You know?**
> **It has to constantly move forward or it dies.**
> **And I think what we got on our hands is a dead shark.**

The line never fails to elicit a laugh, no matter how many times the film is viewed. But it also never fails to provoke a thought, cleverly reminding us that relationships which stand still often fail to survive.

Of all human relationships, those between men and women have probably received the most attention—and they have definitely inspired the most memorable observations. One of the most famous is this analogy:

> **A woman needs a man like a fish needs a bicycle.**

The point, of course, is that women don't need men at all. The saying is usually attributed to Gloria Steinem, and sometimes to lawyer Florynce Kennedy, both of whom used it frequently in the 1970s. The *feminist slogan*, as it is often called, has always been familiar to baby-boomers, but it was brought to a whole new generation when it showed up in the 1991 U2 song *Tryin' to Throw Your Arms Around the World*. While Steinem and Kennedy have gone to great lengths to deny authorship, attributions to them continue to the present day. Steinem once even wrote a letter to *Time* magazine to identify the woman who first said it: an Australian writer, filmmaker, and former politician named Irina Dunn.

As the news of Dunn's authorship has become better known, a fascinating story about the saying's provenance has also emerged. While studying English Literature at Sydney University more than thirty years ago, Dunn came across a book by a nineteenth-century freethinker that contained these words:

A man needs god like a fish needs a bicycle.

Dunn was so impressed with the analogy that she felt a slight rewording of it could serve as a perfect counter-argument to women who believed they needed a man to lead a complete life. The first appearance of her version came in the form of graffiti she scrawled on the walls of two women's restrooms in Sydney—one at a university theater and the other at a popular student drinking establishment. Regarding the slogan's humble origins, Dunn later told a reporter, "I only wrote it in those two spots, and it spread around the world." Like the fellow who invented the happy face image in the 1960s, Dunn never copyrighted the saying, so up until now she has been only rarely credited as the author of the line. But her story is a wonderful example of how a well-crafted analogy can take on a life of its own and capture the imagination of millions. A decade or so after her line became a staple of feminist thought, it also inspired a number of clever spin-offs, including this from an unknown American male:

A man needs a woman like a neck needs a pain.

Friendship is another type of human relationship that has proved amenable to metaphorical description. In *Lives of the Eminent Philosophers*, written in the third century, Diogenes Laertius wrote of the Greek philosopher Aristotle:

> **To the query, "What is a friend?"**
> **his reply was "A single soul dwelling in two bodies."**

Aristotle couldn't have known it, but around the same time on the other side of the known world, the Chinese sage Mencius said virtually the same thing: "Friendship is one mind in two bodies." It's an illustration of the adage that great minds often do think alike, and it's also evidence that great minds often turn to figurative language when describing life's most important realities. The Aristotle and Mencius observations are among the most famous words ever written on friendship, but they are hardly the only eloquent words on the topic, or the only metaphorical ones:

> **A faithful friend is the medicine of life.**
> APOCRYPHA
> —*Ecclesiasticus 6:16*

> **Friendship is Love without his wings!**
> LORD BYRON

> **A friend is, as it were, a second self.**
> CICERO

> **Friendship is a sheltering tree.**
> SAMUEL TAYLOR COLERIDGE

> **A friend is a present you give yourself.**
> ROBERT LOUIS STEVENSON

All human beings are caught up in a wide array of relationships, and all of them have been the subject of analogical and metaphorical observations. In the three chapters following this one, we will delve deeper into the subjects of *love, marriage & family life*, and *sex*. But in the remainder of this chapter, we will focus our attention on what people have had to say about relationships in general, the nature of friendship, romantic relationships, and the many fascinating things that men and women have said about each other.

Jealousy in romance is like salt in food.
A little can enhance the savor, but too much can spoil the pleasure
and, under certain circumstances, can be life-threatening.

MAYA ANGELOU

This comes from *Wouldn't Take Nothing for My Journey Now* (1993). In a 1922 book, *Little Essays of Love and Virtue*, British psychologist Havelock Ellis warned couples about "the demon of jealousy, that dragon which slays love under the pretense of keeping it alive."

Wishing to be friends is quick work,
but friendship is a slow-ripening fruit.

ARISTOTLE

Almost all of our relationships begin and most of them continue
as forms of mutual exploitation, a mental or physical barter,
to be terminated when one or both parties run out of goods.

W. H. AUDEN

A pseudo-friend is the social equivalent of fast food:
a useful creature who can be called upon to deliver
a tasty illusion of friendship without the expense and bother.

RICK BAYAN

Man without woman would be like playing checkers alone.
JOSH BILLINGS
(Henry Wheeler Shaw)

It has been said that a pretty face is like a passport.
But it's not; it's a visa, and it runs out fast.
JULIE BURCHILL

Don't smother each other. No one can grow in the shade.
LEO BUSCAGLIA

Friendship is like money, easier made than kept.
SAMUEL BUTLER

She understood, as women often do more easily than men,
that the declared meaning of a spoken sentence is only its overcoat,
and the real meaning lies underneath its scarves and buttons.
PETER CAREY

This observation, from Carey's 1989 novel *Oscar and Lucinda*, demonstrates that novelists are generally better than social scientists at describing why men and women have trouble communicating.

The heart of another is a dark forest, always,
no matter how close it has been to one's own.
WILLA CATHER,
in The Professor's House *(1925)*

A woman is like your shadow—
follow her, she flies; fly from her, she follows.
NICOLAS CHAMFORT

This eighteenth-century observation is also a lovely example of *chiasmus*, one of my very favorite rhetorical devices (see www.chiasmus.com).

**A woman watches her body uneasily,
as though it were an unreliable ally in the battle for love.**

LEONARD COHEN

**It is wise to apply the oil of refined politeness
to the mechanisms of friendship.**

COLETTE

Colette was the pen name of a Parisian music-hall dancer who became famous for her plays and novels (*Gigi,* her best-remembered work, was made into a popular 1958 movie starring Leslie Caron). Writing in 1898, African-American writer Frances E. W. Harper penned an equally impressive analogy on the subject: "True politeness is to social life what oil is to machinery, a thing to oil the ruts and grooves of existence."

**The firmest friendships have been formed in mutual adversity,
as iron is most strongly united by the fiercest flame.**

CHARLES CALEB COLTON

This is from Colton's *Lacon* (1820), where he also wrote: "True friendship is like sound health; the value of it is seldom known until it be lost."

**In the sex war, thoughtlessness is the weapon of the male,
vindictiveness of the female.**

CYRIL CONNOLLY

**Women are like tricks by sleight of hand,
Which, to admire, we should not understand.**

WILLIAM CONGREVE

The male is a domestic animal which,
if treated with firmness and kindness,
can be trained to do most things.

JILLY COOPER

The Emotional Bank Account represents
the quality of the relationship you have with others.
It's like a financial bank account in that you can
make "deposits," by proactively doing things that build trust . . .
or "withdrawals," by reactively doing things that decrease the level of trust.

STEVEN R. COVEY

This comes from *The Seven Habits of Highly Effective Families* (1997), a
sequel to the 1990 best-seller, *The Seven Habits of Highly Effective People*,
where Covey introduced the concept of an *emotional bank account*. It's a
powerful metaphor and a helpful reminder that we should strive to make
more deposits and fewer withdrawals.

The happiest moment in any affair takes place
after the loved one has learned to accommodate the lover
and before the maddening personality of either party
has emerged like a jagged rock from the receding tides of lust and curiosity.

QUENTIN CRISP

The woman who too easily and ardently yielded her devotion
will find that its vitality, like a bright fire, soon consumes itself.

ANTOINE DE RIVAROL

A quarrel between friends, when made up,
adds a new tie to friendship, as experience shows that
the callosity formed round a broken bone makes it stronger than before.

ST. FRANCIS DE SALES

Callosity means "the condition of being callused" and refers to the hardened tissue that develops around a fractured bone as it heals. Wallace Stegner made the same point about broken hearts: "Most things break, including hearts. The lessons of life amount not to wisdom, but to scar tissue and callus."

Once a woman has forgiven her man,
she must not reheat his sins for breakfast.

MARLENE DIETRICH

Romance has been elegantly defined as the offspring of fiction and love.

ISAAC D'ISRAELI

This observation, which is commonly misattributed to Benjamin Disraeli, comes from *Curiosities of Literature*, a six-volume study of history and literature by one of England's foremost historians and critics (and also the father of Benjamin Disraeli). Here are two other metaphorical observations on the same subject:

"Romance is the glamour which turns the dust of everyday life into a golden haze." *Elinor Glyn*

"Romance, like alcohol, should be enjoyed, but should not be allowed to become necessary." *Edgar Z. Friedenberg*

A woman who has known but one man
is like a person who has heard only one composer.

ISADORA DUNCAN

Relationships are hard. It's like a full-time job, and we should treat it like one.
If your boyfriend or girlfriend wants to leave you,
they should give you two weeks' notice.
There should be severance pay, and before they leave you,
they should have to find you a temp.

BOB ETTINGER

A man has every season,
while a woman has only the right to spring.

JANE FONDA

Men are like pay phones.
Some of them take your money. Most of them don't work,
and when you find one that does, someone else is on it.

CATHERINE FRANCO

A single man has not nearly the value he would have in a state of union.
He is an incomplete animal. He resembles the odd half of a pair of scissors.

BENJAMIN FRANKLIN

Your friend is your needs answered.
He is your field which you sow with love and reap with thanksgiving.

KAHLIL GIBRAN

The man who discovers a woman's weakness
is like the huntsman in the heat of the day who finds a cool spring.
He wallows in it.

JEAN GIRAUDOUX

Caresses, expressions of one sort or another,
are necessary to the life of the affections, as leaves are to the life of a tree.
If they are wholly restrained, love will die at the roots.

NATHANIEL HAWTHORNE

He was a baked potato—solid . . .
I was a fancy dessert—mocha chip ice cream.

KATHARINE HEPBURN,
comparing herself with Spencer Tracy

A woman . . . should be like a good suspense movie.
The more left to the imagination, the more excitement there is.
This should be her aim—to create suspense.

ALFRED HITCHCOCK

The sound of a kiss is not so loud as that of a cannon,
but its echo lasts a great deal longer.

OLIVER WENDELL HOLMES, SR.

Another spectacular kiss metaphor came in a 1955 observation from Jeanne Bourgeois, the French singer and dancer better known as Mistinguette: "A kiss can be a comma, a question mark, or an exclamation point. That's basic spelling every woman ought to know."

A man . . . should keep his friendship in constant repair.

DR. SAMUEL JOHNSON

The meeting of two personalities is like the contact
of two chemical substances: if there is any reaction, both are transformed.

CARL JUNG

Everything that reminds me of her goes through me like a spear.

JOHN KEATS, *on Fanny Brawne,*
after being spurned

When you get back together with an old boyfriend, it's pathetic.
It's like having a garage sale and buying your own stuff back.

LAURA KIGHTLINGER

Nobody will ever win the battle of the sexes;
there's too much fraternizing with the enemy.

HENRY KISSINGER

Kissinger may have been inspired by a famous seventeenth-century line from George Savile (Lord Halifax): "Love is a passion that hath friends in the garrison." In a 1970 *Esquire* article, Sally Kempton looked at the same phenomenon from the other side of the gender gap: "It is hard to fight an enemy who has outposts in your head."

The relation of man to woman is the flowing of two rivers side by side, sometimes mingling, then separating again, and traveling on.

D. H. LAWRENCE

Absence lessens the minor passions and increases the great ones, as the wind douses a candle and kindles a fire.

FRANÇOIS DE LA ROCHEFOUCAULD

This was La Rochefoucauld's attempt to settle the debate between those who believe "absence makes the heart grow fonder" or "out of sight, out of mind."

Men kick friendship around like a football, but it doesn't seem to crack. Women treat it like glass and it goes to pieces.

ANNE MORROW LINDBERGH

Life without a friend is death without a witness.

ROSE MACAULAY

On the wall of our life together hung a gun waiting to be fired in the final act.

MARY MCCARTHY

McCarthy wrote this about her relationship with *Partisan Review* editor Philip Rahv in her 1992 book *Intellectual Memoirs: New York, 1936–38.* Despite the title, the book is less about her intellectual development than about her sexual adventures.

The worldly relations of men and women often form an equation
that cancels out without warning
when some insignificant factor has been added to either side.

WILLIAM MCFEE

If dating is like shopping,
being engaged is like having a guy put you on lay-a-way.
Like saying, "I know I want it.
I just want to delay taking it home as long as possible."

KRIS MCGAHA

No love, no friendship can cross the path of our destiny
without leaving some mark on it forever.

FRANÇOIS MAURIAC

Women's hearts are like old china, none the worse for a break or two.

W. SOMERSET MAUGHAM

The allurement that women hold out to men
is precisely the allurement that Cape Hatteras holds out to sailors:
they are enormously dangerous and hence enormously fascinating.

H. L. MENCKEN

When women kiss it always reminds one of prize-fighters shaking hands.

H. L. MENCKEN

Finding a man is like finding a job;
it's easier to find one when you already have one.

PAIGE MITCHELL

A face is too slight a foundation for happiness.

MARY WORTLEY MONTAGU

In every man's heart there is a secret nerve
that answers to the vibrations of beauty.

CHRISTOPHER MORLEY

G. K. Chesterton, without formally mentioning beauty, said pretty much the same thing: "There is a road from the eye to the heart that does not go through the intellect."

The quarrels of lovers are like summer storms.
Everything is more beautiful when they have passed.

SUZANNE NECKER

There are two things a real man likes—danger and play;
and he likes women because she is
the most dangerous of playthings.

FRIEDRICH NIETZSCHE

A home-made friend wears longer than one you buy in the market.

AUSTIN O'MALLEY

Never date a woman you can hear ticking.

MARK PATINKIN

This observation, from a *Providence Journal* columnist, is one of the best things ever written on one the most popular metaphors of our time: *the biological time clock*.

A woman is a foreign land,
Of which, though there he settle young,

A man will ne'er quite understand
The customs, politics, and tongue.

COVENTRY PATMORE

Women are like dreams—they are never the way you would like to have them.

LUIGI PIRANDELLO

Let us be grateful to people who make us happy;
they are the charming gardeners who make our souls blossom.

MARCEL PROUST

Giving a man space is like giving a dog a computer:
the chances are he will not use it wisely.

BETTE-JANE RAPHAEL

A man's heart may have a secret sanctuary where only one woman may enter,
but it is full of little anterooms which are seldom vacant.

HELEN ROWLAND, *on men's tendency to stray*

Human relations just are not fixed in their orbits like the planets—
they're more like galaxies, changing all the time,
exploding into light for years, then dying away.

MAY SARTON

Though friendship is not quick to burn,
It is explosive stuff.

MAY SARTON

That common cold of the male psyche, fear of commitment.

RICHARD SCHICKEL

Breaking up is like knocking over a coke machine.
You can't do it in one push.
You've gotta rock it back and forth a few times, and then it goes over.

JERRY SEINFELD

What is a date, really, but a job interview that lasts all night?

JERRY SEINFELD

Seinfeld added: "The only difference is that in not many job interviews is there a chance you'll wind up naked." Comedian Eddie Murphy put it more coarsely, but his metaphor enjoys great popularity among college boys and young adult men: "When you're dating, you're just leasing the pussy with an option to buy."

It is assumed that the woman must wait,
motionless, until she is wooed.
That is how the spider waits for the fly.

GEORGE BERNARD SHAW

Dating is a lot like sports.
You have to practice; you work out; you study the greats.
You hope to make the team, and it hurts to be cut.

SINBAD

The game women play is men.

ADAM SMITH

Going out with a jerky guy
is kind of like having a piece of food caught in your teeth.
All your friends notice it before you do.

LIVIA SQUIRES

Glances are the heavy artillery of the flirt:
everything can be conveyed in a look,
yet that look can always be denied,
for it cannot be quoted word for word.

STENDHAL *(pen name of Marie-Henri Beyle)*

Some looks, however, cannot be denied. One was famously described by the French writer known as Colette: "When she raises her eyelids, it's as if she were taking off all her clothes."

The great majority of men, especially in France,
both desire and possess a fashionable woman,
much in the way one might own a fine horse—
as a luxury befitting a young man.

STENDHAL *(pen name of Marie-Henri Beyle)*

Man is the hunter; woman is his game.

ALFRED, LORD TENNYSON

Friends do not live in harmony, merely, as some say, but in melody.

HENRY DAVID THOREAU

Indeed, we do not really live unless we have friends surrounding us
like a firm wall against the winds of the world.

CHARLES HANSON TOWNE

Talking with a man is like trying to saddle a cow.
You work like hell, but what's the point?

GLADYS UPHAM

The first time you buy a house you think how pretty it is and sign the check.
The second time you look to see if the basement has termites.
It's the same with men.

LUPE VÉLEZ

Be courteous to all, but intimate with few,
and let those few be well tried before you give them your confidence.
True friendship is a plant of slow growth
and must undergo and withstand the shocks of adversity
before it is entitled to the appellation.

GEORGE WASHINGTON

This comes from a 1783 letter. You may be more familiar with another plant metaphor from Washington: "Liberty, when it begins to take root, is a plant of rapid growth." Also on the roots theme, George Eliot wrote in *Daniel Deronda* (1874): "Friendships begin with liking or gratitude—roots that can be pulled up."

Assumptions are the termites of relationships.

HENRY WINKLER

This is a fabulous metaphor from an unexpected source, perfectly describing how assumptions can slowly eat away at the foundation of a relationship. Winkler inserted the line in the middle of a 1995 commencement address he gave at his alma mater, Emerson College in Boston.

What magic there is in a girl's smile. It is the raisin which,
dropped in the yeast of male complacency, induces fermentation.

P. G. WODEHOUSE

chapter 8

Love Is an Exploding Cigar We Willingly Smoke

In his 1995 novel *Corelli's Mandolin*, Louis de Bernieres tells the story of Pelagia Iannis, a young beauty who lives with her physician father on the small Greek island of Cephalonia. When the island is overtaken by Italian troops in the early days of World War II, Dr. Iannis and his daughter are forced to billet the officer in command, Captain Antonio Corelli, in their house. Corelli is a handsome and cultured man who always travels with his prized mandolin. His passion for music is matched by a disdain for military life, which he demonstrates by replying "Heil Puccini" whenever he is offered the Nazi greeting "Heil Hitler." The beautiful Pelagia soon falls for Corelli, even though she is betrothed to a young Greek fisherman who has left to fight in the war. The developing love affair gravely concerns her father, who sits her down one day and says:

Love is a kind of dementia
with very precise and oft-repeated clinical symptoms.

After ticking off some of the "symptoms" that he has observed in the young lovers, Dr. Iannis launches into an extended analogy. I was captivated when I first read the passage, and I hope you will enjoy it as well:

Love is a temporary madness, it erupts like volcanoes and then subsides.
And when it subsides you have to make a decision. You have to work out
whether your roots have so entwined together that it is inconceivable
that you should ever part. Because this is what love is.
Love is not breathlessness, it is not excitement,
it is not the promulgation of promises of eternal passion, it is not
the desire to mate every second minute of the day, it is not lying awake
at night imagining that he is kissing every cranny of your body. . . .
That is just being "in love," which any fool can do.
Love itself is what is left over when being in love has burned away,
and this is both an art and a fortunate accident. Your mother and I had it,
we had roots that grew towards each other underground,
and when all the pretty blossoms had fallen from our branches,
we found that we were one tree and not two.

In the first portion of the passage, Dr. Iannis offers one of history's oldest metaphors: *love is mental illness*. Plato may have been the first to express it:

Love is a grave mental disease.

In *As You Like It*, Shakespeare has Rosalind say it this way: "Love is merely a madness." And over the centuries, many others have echoed the theme:

Love, *n*. A temporary insanity curable by marriage or by removal
of the patient from the influences under which he incurred the disorder.

AMBROSE BIERCE

Love is a pardonable insanity.

NICOLAS CHAMFORT

**Well, love is insanity. The ancient Greeks knew that.
It is the taking over of a rational and lucid mind by delusion . . . .
You lose yourself, you have no power over yourself,
you can't even think straight.**

MARILYN FRENCH

**Romantic love is mental illness. But it's a pleasurable one.
It's a drug. It distorts reality, and that's the point of it.
It would be impossible to fall in love with someone that you really *saw*.**

FRAN LEBOWITZ

Returning to Dr. Iannis's lecture to his daughter, you will notice that he moves from one metaphor—*love is mental illness*—to another: *love is the intertwining of roots*. Out of the ashes of a passionate love, he argues, a deep-rooted and intertwined love often emerges, turning separate individuals into one entity. It's a beautiful passage and a nice reminder that after the fireworks of the early years, the most important dynamics of love are not obvious but go on beneath the surface. In his 1978 book *Thoughts in a Dry Season*, Gerald Brenan said it this way:

**Married love is a stream that, after a certain length of time,
sinks into the earth and flows underground.
Something is there, but one does not know what.
Only the vegetation shows that there is still water.**

In the first century B.C., Ovid was the most popular writer in the Roman Empire. Born into an old and respectable family, the young Ovidius—his formal Latin name—showed early academic promise and was educated by the best teachers of the day. While he showed great potential as an orator, he turned to writing instead, ultimately focusing on love and amorous intrigue. He described the dynamics of love in such a captivating way that his first book, *Amores*, was devoured by the sophisticated and pleasure-seeking society in which he lived. The book was so popular it was followed by what we now call sequels: *The Art of Love*, *The Art of Beauty*, and *Remedies for Love*. Ovid was married three times, finally finding contentment in his third marriage. But his first two marriages were short-lived and not particularly harmonious, giving special relevance to a line that appeared in *The Art of Love*:

Love is a kind of warfare.

Ovid carried the metaphor further when he suggested that the wounds of love are as common as the wounds of war—and just as lethal:

As many as the shells that are on the shore,
so many are the pains of love;
the darts that wound are steeped in much poison.

Ovid was one of the first people in history to say that *love is war,* which rivals *love is mental illness* as the most popular metaphor on the subject. After Ovid, the theme has been pursued by many others:

Love does not begin and end the way we seem to think it does.
Love is a battle, love is a war; love is a growing up.
                                                    JAMES BALDWIN

If it is your time, love will track you down like a cruise missile.
If you say, "No! I don't want it right now,"
that's when you'll get it for sure.
Love will make a way out of no way.
                                                    LYNDA BARRY

**Love and war are the same thing,
and stratagems and policy are as allowable in the one as in the other.**
MIGUEL DE CERVANTES

It is the same in love as in war; a fortress that parleys is half taken.
MARGUERITE DE VALOIS

Love is like war: easy to begin but very hard to stop.
H. L. MENCKEN

In addition to insanity and war, *fire* is another common metaphor for the passion of love. The notion also goes back to ancient times. In the first century B.C. the Roman poet Virgil wrote the *Aeneid*, an epic poem that contains this line:

I feel again a spark of that ancient flame.

That ancient flame—the flame of love—has been a central theme in world literature. In *The Divine Comedy*, written in the early 1300s, Dante used the metaphor to suggest that a great passion can spring from a modest beginning:

A great flame follows a little spark.

In the seventeenth century, an English proverb commonly attributed to English cleric Jeremy Taylor continued the theme and became one of history's most popular observations:

Love is friendship set on fire.

As the centuries passed, scores of writers have continued to compare love to fire. Lord Byron saw love as a kind of celestial fire, calling it "a light from heaven, a spark of that immortal fire." Honoré de Balzac wrote that "Love is like the devil," adding "Whom it has in its clutches it surrounds with flames." And the Chilean poet and 1971 Nobel Prize winner Pablo Neruda expressed it this way:

To feel the love of people whom we love is a fire that feeds our life.

Henry Ward Beecher, one of America's most influential preachers, found the concept helpful in explaining the difference between youthful and mature love:

Young love is a flame;
very pretty, often very hot and fierce, but still only light and flickering.
The love of the older and disciplined heart is as coals,
deep-burning, unquenchable.

While the hot and fierce flame of love blazes gloriously, it too often burns out. The phenomenon has been commonly described in literature, but rarely as simply and starkly as in this 1862 passage from Ivan Turgenev's *Fathers and Sons*:

But within a month it was all over:
the fire had kindled for the last time and had died for ever.

Of all the *love is fire* metaphors in my collection, though, my favorite comes from a woman who is best remembered for her great acting ability and her not-so-great parenting skills. In 1943, actress Joan Crawford was quoted as saying:

Love is a fire.
But whether it is going to warm your hearth
or burn down your house, you can never tell.

So far, we've seen love likened to mental illness, war, and fire. In the rest of the chapter you'll see many more love metaphors. For centuries, as love has been rhapsodized by the romantics, skewered by the cynics, and demonized by the disillusioned, it has been done with an extraordinary array of analogies, metaphors, and similes. Whatever your views on love, you'll find support for your position, and maybe have your thinking stimulated along the way.

Without love our life is . . . a ship without a rudder.

SHOLEM ALEICHEM

Love is a net that catches hearts like a fish

MUHAMMAD ALI

This appeared in a 2004 *Esquire* magazine article titled "What I've Learned." The piece contains many sayings that Ali did not author (like "Wisdom is knowing when you can't be wise") but that he says have guided his life.

Love received and love given comprise the best form of therapy.

GORDON W. ALLPORT

Love as a healing force is a tenet of modern psychology. Karl Menninger put it this way: "Love is a medicine for the sickness of the world; a prescription often given, too rarely taken." Eric Berne added succinctly, "Love is nature's psychotherapy."

Love is like a virus. It can happen to anybody at any time.

MAYA ANGELOU

Love is, above all, the gift of oneself.

JEAN ANOUILH

This is from the novel *Ardèle* (1948), where Anouilh also wrote: "Oh, love is real enough; you will find it someday, but it has one arch-enemy— and that is life."

> **Love has its own instinct, finding the way to the heart,**
> **as the feeblest insect finds the way to its flower,**
> **with a will which nothing can dismay nor turn aside.**
>
> HONORÉ DE BALZAC

Balzac also wrote, "Love may be the fairest gem which Society has filched from Nature."

> **Love is an exploding cigar which we willingly smoke.**
>
> LYNDA BARRY

> **What is irritating about love is that it is a crime that requires an accomplice.**
>
> CHARLES BAUDELAIRE

> **Love is the wine of existence**
>
> HENRY WARD BEECHER

Beecher, the brother of Harriet Beecher Stowe of *Uncle Tom's Cabin* fame, also wrote, "Love cannot endure indifference. It needs to be wanted. Like a lamp, it needs to be fed out of the oil of another's heart, or its flame burns low."

> **Memory is to love what the saucer is to the cup.**
>
> ELIZABETH BOWEN

In this extremely interesting analogy, Bowen suggests that it is the memories of lovers that form the foundation for love.

To fall in love is to create a religion that has a fallible god.

JORGE LUIS BORGES

**When success comes in the door, it seems,
love often goes out the window.**

DR. JOYCE BROTHERS

**Love doesn't drop on you unexpectedly;
you have to give off signals, sort of like an amateur radio operator.**

HELEN GURLEY BROWN

Love is the wild card of existence.

RITA MAE BROWN

**One of the best things about love—
the feeling of being wrapped, like a gift, in understanding.**

ANATOLE BROYARD

**As the cat lapses into savagery by night,
and barbarously explores the dark,
so primal and titanic is a woman with the love-madness.**

GELETT BURGESS

**Once love is purged of vanity,
it resembles a feeble convalescent, hardly able to drag itself about.**

NICOLAS CHAMFORT

**Love is more pleasant than marriage
for the same reason that novels are more amusing than history.**

NICOLAS CHAMFORT

Chamfort's point is that novels are fiction and history is reality—and the fictions surrounding love are more pleasant than the realities surrounding marriage.

In love as in art, good technique helps.
MASON COOLEY

Love is an alliance of friendship and of lust:
if the former predominates, it is a passion exalted and refined;
but if the latter, gross and sensual.
CHARLES CALEB COLTON

Love is a friendship set to music.
E. JOSEPH COSSMAN

Love is not enough. It must be the foundation, the cornerstone—
but not the complete structure. It is much too pliable, too yielding.
BETTE DAVIS

Love never dies of starvation, but often of digestion.
NINON DE LENCLOS

Love is an ocean of emotions, entirely surrounded by expenses.
THOMAS DEWAR

The pain of love is the pain of being alive. It's a perpetual wound.
MAUREEN DUFFY

Love ain't nothin' but sex misspelled.
HARLAN ELLISON

Ellison balanced this cynical observation with a sweet one: "Romantic love is the cloud of perfume through which you pass when you're in a movie theater, and it reminds you of an aunt who hugged you when you were three years old."

**Of all the icy blasts that blow on love,
a request for money is the most chilly and havoc-wreaking.**
GUSTAVE FLAUBERT

Love's tongue is in the eyes.
PHINEAS FLETCHER

This observation captures the role that beauty plays in love. The eyes almost drink in great beauty, much like the tongue savors a great wine. Sometimes, though, the wine that looks so full and hearty turns out to be thin and insipid. Emerson said it all in a famous analogy: "Beauty without grace is the hook without the bait."

**On the banks of the grey torrent of life,
love is the only flower.**
E. M. FORSTER

Love letters are the campaign promises of the heart.
ROBERT FRIEDMAN

**Love is often nothing but a favorable exchange between two people
who get the most of what they can expect,
considering their value on the personality market.**
ERICH FROMM

**Love, like a running brook, is disregarded, taken for granted;
but when the brook freezes over, then people begin to remember
how it was when it ran, and they want it to run again.**
KAHLIL GIBRAN

This comes from a letter Gibran wrote to Mary Haskell, the head of a private girls' school in Boston and a woman Gibran deeply loved. He proposed marriage to her, but she refused, feeling that it was not in *his* best interest to be married. Instead, she devoted her life to encouraging him to develop his talent.

We love because it's the only true adventure.
NIKKI GIOVANNI

Love is a snowmobile racing across the tundra and then suddenly it flips over, pinning you underneath. At night, the ice weasels come.
MATT GROENING

This quotation is usually presented as if it reflected Groening's personal opinion, but it is in reality his darkly comic version of Friedrich Nietzsche's view of love. The quote comes from Groening's pre-*Simpsons* days, when it appeared in his underground comic strip *Life is Hell*. Two other philosophers were featured under the heading *What the Great Philosophers Have Said Vis-à-vis Love*:

"Love is a slippery eel that bites like hell." *Bertrand Russell*

"Love is a perky elf dancing a merry little jig and then suddenly he turns on you with a miniature machine-gun." *Kierkegaard*

Love is a fan club with only two fans.
ADRIAN HENRI

Love fattens on smooth words.
KATHARINE HEPBURN

Love is the master-key that opens the gates of happiness, of hatred, of jealousy, and, most easily of all, the gates of *fear*.
OLIVER WENDELL HOLMES, SR.

I have met on the street a very poor man who was in love.
His hat was old, his coat was out at the elbows,
the water passed through his shoes, and the stars through his soul.

VICTOR HUGO

This is from the 1862 classic *Les Misérables*, where Hugo also wrote, "To love another person is to see the face of God." In yet another memorable metaphor, Hugo wrote, "Life is the flower for which love is the honey."

Love, I find, is like singing.
Everybody can do enough to satisfy themselves,
though it may not impress the neighbors as being very much.

ZORA NEALE HURSTON

Love makes your soul crawl out from its hiding place.

ZORA NEALE HURSTON

Elizabeth Bowen was describing a similar phenomenon when she wrote: "When you love someone, all your saved-up wishes start coming out."

Love is . . .
the perfume of that wondrous flower, the heart.

ROBERT G. INGERSOLL

Love's like the measles—
all the worse when it comes late in life.

DOUGLAS JERROLD,
in an 1859 book

In an 1866 book, Jerome K. Jerome wrote similarly, "Love is like the measles; we all have to go through it. Also like the measles, we take it only once."

I'm not sure at all
If love is salve
Or just
A deeper kind of wound
I do not think it matters.

ERICA JONG

Love didn't grow very well in a place where there was only fear,
just as plants didn't grow very well in a place where it was always dark.

STEPHEN KING

This comes from King's 1978 horror classic *The Stand*, as the character Tom reflects on the absence of love in Las Vegas.

The truest comparison we can make of love is to liken it to a fever.

FRANÇOIS DE LA ROCHEFOUCAULD

La Rochefoucauld was a seventeenth-century nobleman who, until age fifty, was known more for political intrigue than anything else. In 1665, he published *Maximes*, a volume of about five hundred quotable quotes on a host of subjects. History's greatest aphorist, he approached affairs of the heart with a keen metaphorical eye:

"Love, like fire, cannot survive without continual movement, and it ceases to live as soon as it ceases to hope or to fear."

"Love is to the soul of him who loves what the soul is to the body."

"It is with true love as with ghosts; everyone talks of it, but few have seen it."

We love in another's soul whatever of ourselves we can deposit in it;
the greater the deposit, the greater the love.

IRVING LAYTON

Love is like a friendship caught on fire.
In the beginning a flame,
Very pretty, often hot and fierce
But still only light and flickering.
As love grows older, our hearts mature
And our love becomes as coals,
Deep burning and unquenchable.

BRUCE LEE

According to Lee's widow, Lucy Lee Cadwell, Lee wrote this poem for her during their marriage. It first appeared in her 1975 book *Bruce Lee: The Man Only I Knew*. In the poem, Lee was clearly borrowing from both Jeremy Taylor and Henry Ward Beecher, whose observations we saw earlier.

Love doesn't just sit there, like a stone,
it has to be made, like bread; remade all the time, made new.

URSULA K. LE GUIN

Love is like a precious plant.
You can't just accept it and leave it in the cupboard
or just think it's going to get on by itself.
You've got to keep watering it.
You've got to really look after it and nurture it.

JOHN LENNON, *from a 1969 interview*

Anger is the fluid that love bleeds when you cut it.

C. S. LEWIS

He is in love with an Ideal,
A creature of his own imagination,
A child of air; an echo of his heart;

And like a lily on a river floating,
She floats upon the river of his thoughts!
HENRY WADSWORTH LONGFELLOW

As the best wine doth make the sharpest vinegar,
so the deepest love turneth to the deepest hate.
JOHN LYLY

Love is like playing checkers. You have to know which man to move.
JACKIE "MOMS" MABLEY

In the arithmetic of love, one plus one equals everything,
and two minus one equals nothing.
MIGNON MCLAUGHLIN

To be in love is merely to be in a state of perceptual anesthesia—
to mistake an ordinary young man for a Greek god
or an ordinary young woman for a goddess.
H. L. MENCKEN

Mencken, one of America's great curmudgeons, railed at the folly of love for decades. He also wrote that "Love is the delusion that one woman differs from another" and "Love is the triumph of imagination over intelligence."

Love matches, as they are called,
have illusion for their father and need for their mother.
FRIEDRICH NIETZSCHE

Several decades after Nietzsche wrote these words, the Spanish philosopher Miguel de Unamuno continued the theme in his 1913 classic *The Tragic Sense of Life*: "Love is the child of illusion and the parent of disillusion."

Love never dies a natural death.
It dies because we don't know how to replenish its source.
It dies of blindness and errors and betrayals. It dies of illness and wounds;
it dies of weariness, of witherings, of tarnishings.

ANAÏS NIN

Love is much like a wild rose,
Beautiful and calm,
But willing to draw blood in its defense.

MARK A. OVERBY

When the roses are gone, nothing is left but the thorns.

OVID

Love is the cheapest of religions.

CESARE PAVESE

People who are not in love fail to understand how an intelligent man
can suffer because of a very ordinary woman.
This is like being surprised that anyone should be stricken with cholera
because of a creature so insignificant as the comma bacillus.

MARCEL PROUST

No, this is not a typo (*common* misspelled as *comma*). *Comma bacillus* is
the term for a microscopic, comma-shaped bacteria that causes Asiatic cholera in humans.

Love rules his kingdom without a sword.

ENGLISH PROVERB

Other memorable proverbs on the subject include these:
"Love is the bridge between two hearts." (American)

"Love, and a cough, cannot be hid." (English)
"Love teaches even donkeys to dance." (French)
"The eyes are the doors of love." (German)
"Love is a game in which both players cheat." (Irish)
"Love cures the wound it makes." (Latin)

The lover is a monotheist
who knows that other people worship different gods
but cannot himself imagine that there could be other gods.

THEODOR REIK

Love is like an hourglass, with the heart filling up as the brain empties.

JULES RENARD

Love is the ultimate outlaw. It just won't adhere to any rules.
The most any of us can do is sign on as its accomplice.

TOM ROBBINS

A love song is just a caress set to music.

SIGMUND ROMBERG

Falling in love consists merely in uncorking the imagination
and bottling the common-sense.

HELEN ROWLAND

Love must have wings to fly away from love,
And to fly back again.

EDWIN ARLINGTON ROBINSON

Love should be a tree whose roots are deep in the earth,
but whose branches extend into heaven.

BERTRAND RUSSELL

I know I am but summer to your heart,
And not the full four seasons of the year.

EDNA ST. VINCENT MILLAY

This is from a 1922 sonnet. The passage poignantly describes the feeling of sadness when one's heartfelt love for another is only partially reciprocated.

Love is a cunning weaver of fantasies and fables.

SAPPHO

Perhaps the old monks were right when they tried to root love out;
perhaps the poets are right when they try to water it.
It is a blood-red flower, with the color of sin;
but there is always the scent of a god about it.

OLIVE SCHREINER

To say the truth, reason and love keep little company together now-a-days.

WILLIAM SHAKESPEARE,
from A Midsummer Night's Dream

In his 1636 play *El Cid*, Pierre Corneille has a character say it this way: "Reason and love are sworn enemies."

Love comforteth like sunshine after rain,

SHAKESPEARE,
from Venus and Adonis

There lives within the very flame of love
A kind of wick or snuff that will abate it.

SHAKESPEARE,
from Hamlet

**Therefore is love said to be a child
Because in choice he is so oft beguiled.**

SHAKESPEARE,
from A Midsummer Night's Dream

The child reference here is to Cupid. In the same play, Shakespeare also writes: "Love looks not with the eyes, but with the mind; And therefore is winged Cupid painted blind."

Love is the only disease that makes you feel better.

SAM SHEPARD

**Love is like a game of poker.
The girl, if she wants to win a hand that may affect her whole life,
should be careful not to show her cards before the guy shows his.**

FRANK SINATRA

A very small degree of hope is sufficient to cause the birth of love.

STENDHAL

**Love is a fruit, in season at all times and within the reach of every hand.
Anyone may gather it and no limit is set.**

MOTHER TERESA

Love must be as much a light as a flame.

HENRY DAVID THOREAU

**To say that you can love one person all your life is like
saying that one candle will continue to burn as long as you live.**

LEO TOLSTOY

There is the same difference in a person before and after he is in love
as between an unlighted lamp and one that is burning.
The lamp was there and was a good lamp,
but now it is shedding light, too, and that is its real function.

VINCENT VAN GOGH,
in a letter to brother Theo

To love and be loved is to feel the sun from both sides.

DAVID VISCOTT

Love is a canvas furnished by Nature and embroidered by Imagination.

VOLTAIRE

Love . . . wears a bandage which conceals the faults of the beloved.
He has wings; he comes quickly and flies away the same.

VOLTAIRE

In this passage from the *Philosophical Dictionary* (1764), Voltaire uses the
word *bandage* in a manner that is closer in meaning to the English word
blindfold.

Love is like a cigar.
If it goes out, you can light it again, but it never tastes quite the same.

ARCHIBALD WAVELL

A man in love is like a clipped coupon—it's time to cash in.

MAE WEST

All love that has not friendship for its base,
Is like a mansion built upon the sand.

ELLA WHEELER WILCOX

Love's chemistry thrives best in equal heat.

JOHN WILMOT

That is, one-sided love is a pale imitation of the real thing. If one person heats up and the other doesn't, there can be no chemical reaction.

Wine comes in at the mouth
And love comes in at the eye;
That's all we shall know for truth
Before we grow old and die.

WILLIAM BUTLER YEATS

chapter 9

Marriage Is a Souvenir of Love

Michel de Montaigne was born in 1533 at his family's chateau near Bordeaux, France. The first child of a wealthy Catholic landowner and a mother of Spanish-Jewish descent, he had an unusual upbringing. While he was permitted to speak French when playing outside with friends or interacting with farmhands, in the home he was allowed to communicate only in Latin until he was six years old (a practice his father believed would greatly enhance the youngster's mental development). As part of his grooming process, he was roused from his sleep each morning by the soothing sounds of a small chamber music ensemble and, as the day progressed, he was privately tutored in classical literature. Young Montaigne developed a great love of reading, a passion that continued until his death. Not much else is known about his early years, but he did go on to study law and, for a time, practiced law and dabbled in politics.

In 1570, at age thirty-seven, Montaigne stepped away from public life and retired to his family's chateau. He spent most of his time in a circular tower room—his *Solitarium*—where he was surrounded by over a thousand books, an astonishing number for the time. Of his special room, he wrote,

"I try to keep this corner as a haven against the tempest outside." And of his treasured library, he wrote, "When I am attacked by gloomy thoughts, nothing helps me so much as running to my books. They quickly absorb me and banish the clouds from my mind."

Montaigne broke new ground in the age-old method of introspection with the invention of a whole new literary genre: the essay. When the first two volumes of his work were published in 1580, they were titled *Essais* (in English, *Essays*). Before Montaigne, the word *essay* meant "to try; to attempt." The root meaning was "to examine, to put to a test," similar to the current term *assay*. After Montaigne, the word took on its modern meaning—a short written composition on a subject, usually presenting the personal view of the author.

When readers discover Montaigne for the first time—as I did when I was in college—they are often delighted to find so modern a thinker in someone writing almost 450 years ago. Montaigne was tolerant in an age of bigotry, curious in a time of dogmatism, and focused on self—a truly modern fixation—in an era when few others would admit to such a thing. And unlike anyone else in his time, he wrote in a loose and free-wheeling way, generously quoting ancient thinkers and meandering off the path with delightful digressions. Aldous Huxley once described his method as "free association, artistically controlled."

In addition to writing about himself, Montaigne also wrote with wisdom—and often wit—on many other subjects. A classic is his description of marriage:

It may be compared to a cage,
the birds without despair to get in, and those within despair to get out.

When Montaigne's three-volume collection of essays was translated into English in 1603, it became very popular in London's literary circles (Shakespeare and Ben Jonson both read it with great interest). A few years later, somewhere between 1609 and 1612, John Webster's play titled *The White Devil* featured the following passage, also about marriage:

> 'Tis just like a summer bird-cage in a garden:
> the birds that are without despair to get in, and
> the birds that are within despair . . . for fear they shall never get out.

The wording is so similar to Montaigne's that it seems indisputable that Webster had plagiarized the thought. He also might have been influenced by a 1602 poem by the English poet John Davies:

> Wedlock indeed hath oft compared been
> To public feasts, where meet a public rout;
> Where they that are without would fain go in,
> And they that are within would fain go out.

Throughout history, a wide variety of marital metaphors have been advanced. In his 1693 play *The Old Bachelor*, English playwright William Congreve found an analogy between marriage and the theater:

> Courtship to marriage,
> as a very witty prologue to a very dull play.

A prologue, of course, is an introduction to a literary work. From ancient Greece to the eighteenth century, prologues were commonly used to introduce characters and set the stage for poems as well as plays. Prologues went out of fashion in the nineteenth century and are now rarely seen. But to seventeenth-century theater-goers, the point of Congreve's analogy was clear—compared with the drama of courtship, marriage is boring. A 1714 poem by Alexander Pope changed the metaphor but made the same point:

> They dream in courtship, but in wedlock wake.

In his 1820 book *Lacon*, English writer Charles Caleb Colton echoes the Congreve and Pope sentiments but does so by likening marriage to a meal:

Marriage is a feast where the grace is sometimes better than the dinner.

In Colton's observation, courtship is analogous to grace, and his argument is that both are often better than what is to come after them. This was history's first *marriage as a meal* metaphor, and it may have stimulated two later observations:

Marriage is a meal where the soup is better than the dessert.
AUSTIN O'MALLEY

Marriage is like a dull meal, with the dessert at the beginning.
HENRI DE TOULOUSE-LAUTREC

One fascinating discovery I made while researching this book was seeing how often a theme can be maintained, even though the metaphor changes:

**Marriage is a book in which the first chapter is written in poetry
and the remaining chapters in prose.**
BEVERLEY NICHOLS

**The days just prior to marriage
are like a snappy introduction to a tedious book.**
WILSON MIZNER

Here, the metaphor has been changed to a book, but the message is the same: marriage is good at the beginning and gets worse over time. And in one final example, notice how the same point is made in yet another way in this old German proverb:

**Marriage is fever in reverse;
it starts with heat and ends with cold.**

While many of the observations so far have portrayed matrimony as dull and boring, many marriages are so quarrelsome and contentious they can hardly be called unexciting. These combative marriages represent another common type of marriage, and they require another type of metaphor—*marriage as war*. A perfect illustration is an anonymous saying that goes back many generations:

**Marriage is the only war
where one sleeps with the enemy.**

A more recent example surfaced in pop culture in the early nineties, just after the first Gulf War, when a character on the *Murphy Brown* television sitcom said:

Marriage is the Scud missile of relationships.

Despite the missile reference, this remark was less about war and more about the quality of marital relationships. And when you recall that many of Iraq's Scud missiles were complete duds, the implication is clear.

Perhaps the most famous *marriage as war* metaphor comes from one of history's most famous writers, Robert Louis Stevenson:

**Marriage is like life in this—
that it is a field of battle, and not a bed of roses.**

Stevenson is best known for adventure novels like *Treasure Island*, *Kidnapped*, and *The Strange Case of Dr. Jekyll and Mr. Hyde*, but he was also a poet, children's author, travel writer, and essayist. This observation comes from *Virginibus Puerisque*, an 1881 collection of essays in which he opined on many subjects, including matrimony. On that topic, he also wrote: "Marriage is one long conversation, checkered by disputes."

One would normally think that likening marriage to war is a negative thing, but not necessarily. In her 1968 autobiography *On Reflection*, Helen Hayes wrote:

> **Marriage is like a war.**
> **There are moments of chivalry and gallantry**
> **that attend the victorious advances and strategic retreats,**
> **the birth or death of children, the momentary conquest of loneliness,**
> **the sacrifice that ennobles him who makes it.**
> **But mostly there are the long dull sieges,**
> **the waiting, the terror and boredom.**
> **Women understand this better than men;**
> **they are better able to survive attrition.**

Hayes, called the First Lady of the American Theater, had a career that lasted a full eighty years. She made her first stage appearance in 1905, at age five, and her last in 1985, when she played Miss Marple in a made-for-TV adaptation of an Agatha Christie novel. In the 1920s, she was having a miserable time at a New York party when she was approached by Charles MacArthur, a playwright and journalist from Chicago. He gently placed some salted peanuts into her hand and said, "I wish they were emeralds." She was instantly smitten, and the couple were soon wed. Their marriage saw deep personal fulfillment, great professional success, and a fair amount of tragedy, including the death of their only daughter to polio. By all accounts, the couple had a legendary love affair, and they remained married until his death in 1956.

Of all human institutions, marriage has been one of the most maligned, and many of the characterizations have been metaphorical. Some are centuries old, as when the legendary lover Giacomo Casanova wrote that "Marriage is the tomb of love." Or when Lord Byron wrote "Though women are angels, yet wedlock's the devil." Many more come from recent times:

If variety is the spice of life,
marriage is the big can of leftover Spam.
JOHNNY CARSON

I always compare marriage to communism.
They're both institutions that don't conform to human nature,
so you're going to end up with lying and hypocrisy.
BILL MAHER

Marriage can be viewed as the waiting room for death.
MIKE MYERS

While men have generally led the parade against marriage, women have also contributed many memorable observations:

Love-matches are made by people who are content,
for a month of honey, to condemn themselves to a life of vinegar.
MARGUERITE BLESSINGTON

Marriage is usually considered the grave, and not the cradle of love.
MARY WOLLSTONECRAFT SHELLEY

Conjugality made me think of a three-legged race,
where two people cannot go fast and keep tripping each other
because their two legs are tied together.
BRENDA UELAND

But perhaps my favorite female offering comes from the English writer Marie Corelli, a woman who is now barely remembered, even though she was the best-selling female novelist in England at the turn of the twentieth century. Once described as "the Jacqueline Susann of her time," she wrote melodramatic and highly romanticized novels that were ridiculed by critics but devoured by a fan base that included such elite readers as Queen Victoria and Oscar Wilde. Of the hundreds of thousands of words she penned, the most famous were these:

**I never married because there was no need.
I have three pets at home which answer the same purpose as a husband.
I have a dog which growls every morning,
a parrot which swears all afternoon,
and a cat that comes home late at night.**

So far, we've featured observations strictly about *marriage*. In the rest of the chapter you'll find analogies, metaphors, and similes on such related topics as husbands and wives, giving birth and raising children, divorce and remarriage, parent-child relationships, and a few other aspects of home and family life.

Marriage, in life, is like a duel in the midst of a battle.
EDMOND ABOUT

**A divorce is like an amputation;
you survive, but there's less of you.**
MARGARET ATWOOD

**Wives are young men's mistresses,
companions for middle age, and old men's nurses.**
FRANCIS BACON

**A bachelor's life is a fine breakfast,
a flat lunch, and a miserable dinner.**
FRANCIS BACON

That is, young bachelors have it best, but things get worse as they age, when—recalling the prior Bacon quote—they have nobody to nurse them.

Alimony is like buying oats for a dead horse.

ARTHUR "BUGS" BAER

Baer was a popular sports writer and humorist in the first half of the twentieth century. When Milton Berle needed fresh material, he would take Baer to lunch at Toots Shor's to pick his brain. Baer likely inspired a famous Berle quip: "Alimony is like putting gas into another guy's car."

**When you're the only pea in the pod
your parents are likely to get you confused with the Hope diamond.**

RUSSELL BAKER, *on only children*

**Marriage must constantly fight against
a monster which devours everything: routine.**

HONORÉ DE BALZAC

This comes from Balzac's 1829 *The Physiology of Marriage*, where he also wrote, "The majority of husbands remind me of an orangutan trying to play the violin."

**Divorce is the psychological equivalent
of a triple coronary by-pass.**

MARY KAY BLAKELY

**In a happy marriage,
it is the wife who provides the climate,
the husband the landscape.**

GERALD BRENAN

**The best of all possible marriages is a seesaw
in which first one, then the other partner is dominant.**

DR. JOYCE BROTHERS

Marriage is an adventure, like going to war.

G. K. CHESTERTON

Chesterton viewed the adventure with good humor, once writing: "Variability is one of the virtues of a woman. It avoids the crude requirement of polygamy. So long as you have one good wife you are sure to have a spiritual harem."

A child, like your stomach, doesn't need all you can afford to give it.

FRANK A. CLARK

**Marriage is like a bank account.
You put it in, you take it out, you lose interest.**

PROFESSOR IRWIN COREY

**Raising children is like baking bread;
it has to be a slow process or
you end up with an overdone crust and an underdone interior**

MARCELENE COX

**Marriage is a lottery in which men stake their liberty
and women their happiness.**

VIRGINIE DE RIEUX

Madame de Rieux was a sixteenth-century French noblewoman and writer. Her point is that marriage is a gamble for both men and women, but they risk different things. A century later, Ben Jonson picked up the theme in *A Tale of a Tub* (1692): "I smile to think how like a lottery these weddings are."

Marriage is to courting as humming is to singing.

PETER DE VRIES

De Vries also wrote: "The bonds of matrimony are like any other bonds—they mature slowly."

I . . . have another cup of coffee with my mother.
We get along very well, veterans of a guerrilla war we never understood.

JOAN DIDION

In Amy Tan's *The Kitchen God's Wife* (1991), the character Pearl also describes a complicated mother-daughter relationship: "Whenever I'm with my mother, I feel as though I have to spend the whole time avoiding land mines."

Remarrying a husband you've divorced
is like having your appendix put back in.

PHYLLIS DILLER

Comedian Larry Miller put it this way: "I don't understand couples who break up and get back together, especially couples who divorce and remarry. That's like pouring milk on a bowl of cereal, tasting it, and saying, 'This milk is sour. Well, I'll put it back in the refrigerator; maybe it will be okay tomorrow.'"

The chains of marriage are so heavy
that it takes two to bear them, sometimes three.

ALEXANDRE DUMAS FILS

This is one of history's most famous justifications for a mistress. It comes from the son of a very famous father, Alexandre Dumas *père*, the author of *The Three Musketeers* and *Count of Monte Cristo*. In France, instead of using *Sr.* and *Jr.*, *père* and *fils* are used (from the Latin; *pater*, for "father" and *filius*, for "son").

The father is always a Republican to his son,
and his mother's always a Democrat.

ROBERT FROST

Husbands are like fires.
They go out when unattended.

ZSA ZSA GABOR

You are the bows from which your children
as living arrows are sent forth.

KAHLIL GIBRAN

Children are like wet cement.
Whatever falls on them makes an impression.

HAIM GINOTT

Ginott, an Israeli with a Ph.D. from Columbia University, burst on the cultural scene in 1965 with *Between Parent and Child,* a book on parenting that remained on the best-seller list for more than a year.

When a woman gets married,
it's like jumping into a hole in the ice in the middle of winter;
you do it once and you remember it the rest of your days.

MAXIM GORKY

Childhood is a short season.

HELEN HAYES

The Wedding March always reminds me
of the music played when soldiers go into battle.

HEINRICH HEINE

Matrimony, the high sea for which no compass has yet been invented!

HEINRICH HEINE

The *sea of marriage* is a popular literary metaphor. In Edith Wharton's *The Age of Innocence* (1920), protagonist Newland Archer is looking at a photograph of his betrothed, the innocent and inexperienced May Welland. Just then, his thoughts turn to the exciting and unconventional Countess Ellen Olenska. He feels unsettled. Wharton writes: "The young girl who knew nothing and expected everything, looked back at him like a stranger through May Welland's familiar features; and once more it was borne in on him that marriage was not the safe anchorage he had been taught to think, but a voyage on uncharted seas."

**Marriage is a psychological condition, not a civil contract and a license.
Once a marriage is dead, it is dead,
and it begins to stink even faster than a dead fish.**

ROBERT A. HEINLEIN

The concept of two people living together for twenty-five years without a serious dispute suggests a lack of spirit only to be admired in sheep.

ALAN P. HERBERT

We are all tattooed in our cradles with the beliefs of our tribe.

OLIVER WENDELL HOLMES, SR.

A man who marries a woman to educate her falls victim to the same fallacy as the woman who marries a man to reform him.

ELBERT HUBBARD

Wedlock is like wine—not properly judged of till the second glass.

DOUGLAS JERROLD, *on second marriages*

There is a rhythm to the ending of a marriage
just like the rhythm of a courtship—only backward.
You try to start again but get into blaming over and over.
Finally you are both worn out, exhausted, hopeless.
Then lawyers are called in to pick clean the corpses.
The death occurred much earlier.

ERICA JONG

Marrying a man is like buying something
you've been admiring for a long time in a shop window.
You may love it when you get it home,
but it doesn't always go with everything else in the house.

JEAN KERR

Being divorced is like being hit by a Mack truck.
If you live through it,
you start looking very carefully to the right and to the left.

JEAN KERR

At every step the child should be allowed
to meet the real experience of life;
the thorns should never be plucked from his roses.

ELLEN KEY

I personally am inclined to approach housework
the way governments treat dissent: ignore it until it revolts.

BARBARA KINGSOLVER

Before we can leave our parents, they stuff our heads like the suitcases
which they jam-pack with homemade underwear.

MAXINE HONG KINGSTON

Marriage is very difficult.
Marriage is like a five-thousand-piece jigsaw puzzle, all sky.

CATHY LADMAN

Marriage is not a reform school.

ANN LANDERS

Having a baby is like trying to push a grand piano through a transom.

ALICE ROOSEVELT LONGWORTH

This may be the most famous simile on the subject of birthing (a similar version has also been attributed to Fanny Brice). Another popular one, from Carol Burnett, goes this way: "Giving birth is like taking your lower lip and forcing it over your head."

A man's home may seem to be his castle on the outside;
inside it is more often his nursery.

CLARE BOOTH LUCE

American women expect to find in their husbands
the perfection that English women only hope to find in their butlers.

W. SOMERSET MAUGHAM

A successful marriage is an edifice that must be rebuilt every day.

ANDRÉ MAUROIS

After the chills and fever of love, how nice is the 98.6° of marriage!

MIGNON MCLAUGHLIN

Marrying is like enlisting in a war or being sentenced to a form of
penal servitude that makes the average American husband into a slave.

H. L. MENCKEN

More recently, actor James Garner reflected, "Marriage is a lot like the army; everyone complains, but you'd be surprised at the large number that re-enlist."

If I ever marry, it will be on a sudden impulse—as a man shoots himself.
H. L. MENCKEN

Mencken was one of history's great *misogamists* (marriage haters). He once wrote, "Whenever a husband and a wife begin to discuss their marriage, they are giving evidence at a coroner's inquest." In 1930, he married Sara Haardt, a college professor eighteen years his junior. Given his well-known views, the marriage made headlines. Always ready with a quip, Mencken wrote: "Getting married, like getting hanged, is a great deal less dreadful than it has been made out." Mencken finally found love, but sadly, it was not to last. His wife died of meningitis five years later.

Children are messengers to us from a world we once deeply knew.
ALICE MILLER

The American educator Neil Postman offered a similar thought: "Children are the living messages we send to a time we will not see."

Today, while the titular head of the family may still be the father,
everyone knows that he is little more than chairman,
at most, of the entertainment committee.
ASHLEY MONTAGU

People commonly educate their children as they build their houses,
according to some plan they think beautiful, without considering
whether it is suited to the purposes for which they are designed.
MARY WORTLEY MONTAGU

Marriage is based on the theory that
when a man discovers a particular brand of beer exactly to his taste
he should at once throw up his job and go to work in the brewery.

GEORGE JEAN NATHAN

Anybody can have one kid. But going from one kid to two
is like going from owning a dog to running a zoo.

P. J. O'ROURKE

Quarrels are the dowry which married folk bring one another.

OVID

A dowry is money or personal property brought to a marriage, often in a chest or piece of baggage. This observation from Ovid's *The Art of Love* (first century B.C.) may be history's first metaphor on bringing "emotional baggage" to a marriage. Harriet Lerner said it in another way in *The Dance of Anger* (1985): "Underground issues from one relationship or context invariably fuel our fires in another."

Getting married is a lot like getting into a tub of hot water.
After you get used to it, it ain't so hot.

MINNIE PEARL

Marriage is like paying an endless visit in your worst clothes.

J. B. PRIESTLEY

Alcoholism isn't a spectator sport. Eventually the whole family gets to play.

JOYCE REBETA-BURDITT

Marriage: a souvenir of love.

HELEN ROWLAND

A souvenir is a memento of something in the past, so this is a variation on the theme of marriage being the death of love. It comes from *Reflections of a Bachelor Girl* (1909), which also contains this simile: "Marriage is like twirling a baton, turning a hand spring, or eating with chopsticks; it looks so easy until you try it."

A husband is what is left of a lover,
after the nerve has been extracted.
HELEN ROWLAND

A woman who takes her husband about with her everywhere
is like a cat that goes on playing with a mouse long after she's killed it.
SAKI *(H. H. Munro)*

A baby is God's opinion that the world should go on.
CARL SANDBURG

Parents teach in the toughest school in the world—
The School for Making People.
You are the board of education, the principal, the classroom teacher,
and the janitor.
VIRGINIA SATIR

Marriage is like pantyhose. It all depends on what you put into it.
PHYLLIS SCHLAFLY

Big sisters are the crab grass in the lawn of life.
CHARLES M. SCHULZ, *from Linus,*
in a 1952 Peanuts *cartoon*

Men are April when they woo, December when they wed:

maids are May when they are maids,
but the sky changes when they are wives.
WILLIAM SHAKESPEARE, *in* As You Like It

Combining a calendar and a weather metaphor, Shakespeare describes the changes from courtship to marriage—fresh male fervor begins to cool, and the sunny disposition of women is quickly replaced by cloudy and rainy days. Another popular calendar metaphor is the *May-December marriage,* commonly used to describe an age disparate couple, generally one in which the wife is in the spring of her life and the husband in the winter of his.

A married man forms married habits and becomes dependent on marriage
just as a sailor becomes dependent on the sea.
GEORGE BERNARD SHAW

Home life as we understand it is no more natural to us
than a cage is natural to a cockatoo.
GEORGE BERNARD SHAW

Chains do not hold a marriage together.
It is threads, hundreds of tiny threads,
which sew people together through the years.
SIMONE SIGNORET

To the family—that dear octopus from whose tentacles
we never quite escape nor, in our inmost hearts, ever quite wish to.
DODIE SMITH

This is from Smith's 1938 play *Dear Octopus,* in which the character Nicholas delivers this toast at the golden wedding anniversary of his grandparents.

Marriage resembles a pair of shears,
so joined that they cannot be separated;
often moving in opposite directions,
yet always punishing anyone who comes between them.

SYDNEY SMITH

Children are the anchors that hold a mother to life.

SOPHOCLES

In automobile terms, the child supplies the power
but the parents have to do the steering.

DR. BENJAMIN SPOCK

A good many men still like to think of their wives
as they do of their religion, neglected but always there.

FREYA STARK

The matter between husband and wife
stands much the same as it does between two cocks in the same yard.
The conqueror once is generally the conqueror for ever after.
The prestige of victory is everything.

ANTHONY TROLLOPE

In *Myra Breckinridge*, Gore Vidal described it this way: "That long wrangling for supremacy which is called marriage."

Parents are the bones on which children sharpen their teeth.

PETER USTINOV

Take it from me, marriage is not a word . . . it's a sentence!

KING VIDOR

This is exceptional wordplay—at one level, a simple remark about words and sentences and, at another, a *marriage is a prison* metaphor. The line comes from Vidor's 1928 silent film classic *The Crowd*. It is delivered by the main character, John Sims, who angrily says it to his wife as he storms out the door.

**Every marriage is a battle
between two families struggling to reproduce themselves.**
CARL A. WHITAKER

It is a well-established psychoanalytic notion that six people are present in every bedroom: the couple and both sets of parents. Here, a pioneering figure in the field of family therapy extends the thought by suggesting that, in every marriage, two family traditions war with each other in a battle for survival.

**Twenty years of romance make a woman look like a ruin;
but twenty years of marriage make her something like a public building.**
OSCAR WILDE

Marriage is a bribe to make a housekeeper think she's a householder.
THORNTON WILDER

**Marriage isn't a process of prolonging the life of love,
but of mummifying the corpse.**
P. G. WODEHOUSE

chapter 10

Sex Is an
Emotion in Motion

In 468 B.C., an unknown Greek playwright named Sophocles shocked everyone by winning a national drama competition. On the way to victory, he defeated the reigning champion, a popular writer known as Aeschylus. Dramatic writing competitions were all the rage in Athens—a kind of literary Super Bowl—and almost everyone expected Aeschylus to once again emerge triumphant. The victory proved to be anything but a fluke for the twenty-eight-year-old Sophocles, who continued to compete in subsequent years (in the rest of his career, he won more than any other Greek writer, and never finished lower than second place).

Sophocles, who lived to age ninety, produced more than 120 plays in his career. Only seven complete plays survive today, but they include *Oedipus Rex*, *Antigone*, *Electra*, and other classics of Greek literature. Sophocles, an extremely talented writer, was especially adept at figurative language, creating many metaphors—like *ship of state*—that live on twenty-five hundred years after his death.

A half century after the death of Sophocles, Plato wrote in his *Republic* that he once overheard a student ask the aging Greek writer, "How do you stand in matters of love? Are you still able to have sex with a woman?" Sophocles put his finger to his mouth and said, "Hush! If you please." Then, leaning forward, as if he were revealing a great secret, he said:

**To my great delight, I have escaped from it,
and feel as if I had escaped from a frantic and savage master.**

In his earlier life, Sophocles was typical of Greek noblemen—he had been married twice, enjoyed the services of a concubine, probably had a favorite prostitute, and in all likelihood had more than just a passing acquaintance with a few young boys. If he had framed his answer by means of another literary device—*chiasmus*—he might have said that he didn't possess sexual desire, sexual desire had possessed him. But he chose to express himself in metaphorical terms, becoming the first person in history to describe sexual desire as a ravenous monster.

The metaphor clearly resonated with Plato, who wrote, "I thought then, as I do now, that he spoke wisely. For unquestionably, old age brings us profound repose and freedom from this and other passions." For Plato, as with so many other thinkers after him, the goal of philosophy was to help people gain control of their passions. This has also been the historic goal of religion, as reflected in this metaphorical passage from the Talmud:

**Our passions are like travelers: at first they make a brief stay;
then they are like guests, who visit often;
and then they turn into tyrants, who hold us in their power.**

Despite centuries of philosophizing and religious training, the wild beast of sexual desire has remained largely untamed. History is replete with examples of intelligent and powerful men—and occasionally women—who have risked everything for a moment of sexual pleasure. This reality shows up in one of the most popular pieces of advice that teenage boys get from their fathers, coaches, and other plain-speaking authority figures:

Never let the little head do the thinking for the big head.

The *little head*, of course, is a metaphor for the penis. But because sex is such an emotionally loaded subject, people routinely talk about it in veiled metaphorical references. We don't teach children about sex, after all, we tell them about *the birds and the bees*. And we don't have sex, we *make love*, *go all the way*, *do the nasty*, or simply *do the deed*.

For many centuries, people in the public eye have found ways of communicating in sexual innuendo to people "in the know" without offending those folks—especially those prudish ones—who are not. In the 1983 smash hit *Little Red Corvette*, the artist known as Prince relates a one-night stand in the back seat of a car with a passionate and promiscuous woman. With lyrics like "you had a pocket full of horses" (code for *Trojan* condoms) and "I'm gonna try to tame your little red love machine," the entire song is a huge sexual metaphor (and ever since, the term *little red corvette* has been sexual slang for a woman's vagina).

This tradition of covert communication has always been popular in music, especially in the blues. In the 1930s, the great Bessie Smith wasn't talking about sweeteners and frankfurters when she sang "I need a little sugar in my bowl and a little hot dog between my roll." Even literary greats have joined in the act. The German man of letters, Johann Wolfgang von Goethe, was delicately talking about sexual intercourse when he said:

Women are silver saucers into which we put golden apples.

The great master of sexual allusion, however, has to be William Shakespeare, who was often able to shroud ribald and risqué sentiments in presentable language. In *Venus and Adonis*, he has the provocative Venus say:

I'll be a park, and thou shalt be my deer;
Feed where thou wilt, on mountain or in dale:
Graze on my lips, and if those hills be dry,
Stray lower, where the pleasant fountains lie.

And in *Othello*, after the lovely Desdemona and Othello become an item, the villainous Iago announces to Desdemona's father:

Your daughter and the Moor are now making the beast with two backs.

Many believe the *beast with two backs* expression—a metaphor for sexual intercourse—is yet another one of Shakespeare's verbal inventions, but it first appeared in print more than three decades before Shakespeare's birth. In his classic 1532 *Gargantua and Pantagruel*, François Rabelais creatively combined it with a food metaphor when he wrote:

In the prime of his years he married Gargamelle,
daughter of the king of the Butterflies, a fine, good-looking piece,
and the pair of them often played the two-backed beast,
joyfully rubbing their bacon together.

In the world of metaphor, sex is usually compared to other things, but occasionally we find other things being likened to sex, often in fascinating ways:

Writing is like making love.
Don't worry about the orgasm, just concentrate on the process.
ISABEL ALLENDE

Money, it turned out, was exactly like sex; you thought of nothing else
if you didn't have it and thought of other things if you did.
JAMES BALDWIN

**Physics is like sex. Sure, it may give some practical results,
but that's not why we do it.**

RICHARD P. FEYNMAN

Art is the sex of the imagination.

GEORGE JEAN NATHAN

Hair is another name for sex.

VIDAL SASSOON

**Religion is probably, after sex, the second oldest resource
which human beings have available to them for blowing their minds.**

SUSAN SONTAG

In the rest of the chapter, though, you'll see sex related to dozens of other things. And whether they are done seriously or humorously, the metaphorical observations you will find here may help you look at this age-old phenomenon in new ways.

**Sex is like having dinner—sometimes you joke about the dishes,
sometimes you take the meal seriously.**

WOODY ALLEN

**Erotic literature is closely akin to fairy tales,
because everything one wishes or desires is made available.**

HENRY ANGELINO

Sex is like air—it's not important until you're not getting any.

ANONYMOUS

Other great sex metaphors from anonymous sources include the following:

"Virginity is like a balloon: one prick and it's gone."
"Memory is like an orgasm. It's a lot better if you don't have to fake it."
"Love is a matter of chemistry, but sex is a matter of physics."
"Sex is like snow; you never know how many inches you're going to get or how long it will last."

Sex is just another real good drug . . .
and it can make a junkie out of you.
ELIZABETH ASHLEY

Sex as something beautiful may soon disappear.
Once it was a knife so finely honed the edge was invisible
until it was touched and then it cut deep.
Now it is so blunt that it merely bruises and leaves ugly marks.
MARY ASTOR, *in her 1967 autobiography*
A Life on Film

Woman is a delicious instrument of pleasure,
but one must know the chords, study the pose of it,
the timid keyboard, the changing and capricious fingering.
HONORÉ DE BALZAC

In his 1829 classic, *The Physiology of Marriage*, Balzac also wrote: "No man should marry until he has studied anatomy and dissected at least one woman."

Men read maps better because only a male mind
could conceive of an inch equaling a hundred miles.
ROSEANNE BARR

At the heart of pornography is sexuality haunted by its own disappearance.
JEAN BAUDRILLARD

This captures what is wrong with pornography—it is sex without sexuality.

There is no aphrodisiac like innocence.
JEAN BAUDRILLARD

This may be true for men. For turning on women, though, many would agree with Henry Kissinger's view: "Power is the ultimate aphrodisiac." Graham Greene weighed in with "Fame is a powerful aphrodisiac," and Saul Bellow observed, "All a writer has to do to get a woman is to say he's a writer. It's an aphrodisiac." But P. J. O'Rourke may have said it best: "There are a number of mechanical devices which increase sexual arousal, especially in women. Chief among these is the Mercedes-Benz 3890SL convertible."

Sex is a pleasurable exercise in plumbing, but be careful or you'll get yeast in your drain tap.
RITA MAE BROWN

Sexual intercourse is kicking death in the ass while singing.
CHARLES BUKOWSKI

Sex after ninety is like trying to shoot pool with a rope. Even putting my cigar in its holder is a thrill.
GEORGE BURNS

My mom always said, "Men are like linoleum floors. You lay them right, and you can walk on them for thirty years."
BRETT BUTLER

Male sexual response is far brisker and more automatic. It is triggered easily by things—like putting a quarter in a vending machine.
DR. ALEX COMFORT

Comfort was the author of *The Joy of Sex*, an illustrated 1972 sex manual that was a publishing blockbuster (it spent nearly three months at the top of the *New York Times* bestseller list and almost a year and a half in the top five).

Sex is the great amateur art.

DAVID CORT

**For flavor, Instant Sex will never supersede
the stuff you have to peel and cook.**

QUENTIN CRISP

**Having sex is like playing bridge.
If you don't have a good partner, you'd better have a good hand.**

RODNEY DANGERFIELD

Similar observations have also been attributed to Mae West and Woody Allen.

The act of sex, gratifying as it may be, is God's joke on humanity.

BETTE DAVIS

**Sex pleasure in woman . . . is a kind of magic spell;
it demands complete abandon;
if words or movements oppose the magic of caresses, the spell is broken.**

SIMONE DE BEAUVOIR

**Sex in marriage is like medicine.
Three times a day for the first week.
Then once a day for another week.
Then once every three or four days until the condition clears up.**

PETER DE VRIES

A country without bordellos
is like a house without bathrooms.

MARLENE DIETRICH

Sex is identical to comedy in that it involves timing.

PHYLLIS DILLER

He could handle women as smoothly as operating an elevator.
He knew exactly where to locate the top button.

BRITT EKLUND, *on Warren Beatty*

This is a classic *double entendre* observation. The top button is not only a building floor designation in an elevator, it is also sexual slang for the clitoris. Also on the topic of Beatty's magic touch with women, Woody Allen once quipped, "If I could come back in another life, I want to be Warren Beatty's fingertips."

The sexual embrace, worthily understood,
can only be compared with music and with prayer.

HAVELOCK ELLIS

Men want a woman whom they can turn on and off like a light switch.

IAN FLEMING

For a man, sex is hunger—like eating.
If a man is hungry and can't get to a fancy French restaurant,
he'll go to a hot dog stand.

JOAN FONTAINE

Getting married for sex is like buying a 747 for the free peanuts.

JEFF FOXWORTHY

Men perform oral sex like they drive.
When they get lost, they refuse to ask for directions.

CATHERINE FRANCO

Beauty and folly are old companions.

BENJAMIN FRANKLIN

Over the centuries, great beauty has charmed otherwise smart people into doing many foolish things. On the same subject, the seventeenth-century English naturalist John Ray offered this thought: "Beauty is power; a smile is its sword."

Sexuality is the great field of battle
between biology and society.

NANCY FRIDAY

It is a crossing of a Rubicon in life history.

PAUL H. GEPHARD,
on one's first sexual intercourse

There may be no more significant event in a person's life than losing one's virginity, and Gephard, director of the Kinsey Institute for Sex Research, chose an apt metaphor to describe it. The Rubicon is a river that, in ancient times, divided Italy and Gaul. In 49 B.C., Julius Caesar crossed the river in a military march against Pompey. He acted in defiance of the Roman Senate's orders, saying "the die is cast" as he crossed the river. Ever since, "Crossing the Rubicon," has been a metaphor for taking a step after which there is no turning back.

I think that making love is the best form of exercise.

CARY GRANT

So female orgasm . . . may be thought of as a pleasure prize
that comes with a box of cereal.
It is all to the good if the prize is there
but the cereal is valuable and nourishing if it is not.

MADELINE GRAY

Despite a lifetime of service to the cause of sexual liberation,
I have never caught venereal disease, which makes me feel rather like
an Arctic explorer who has never had frostbite.

GERMAINE GREER

Greer, the Australian author of the feminist classic *The Female Eunuch*
(1970), authored two other metaphorical observations of interest:
"A full bosom is actually a millstone around a woman's neck."
"Conventional sexual intercourse is like squirting jam into a doughnut."

Masturbation is the thinking man's television.

CHRISTOPHER HAMPTON

A woman's chastity consists, like an onion, of a series of coats.

NATHANIEL HAWTHORNE

Playboy exploits sex the way *Sports Illustrated* exploits sports.

HUGH HEFNER

Female passion is to masculine as the epic is to an epigram.

KARL KRAUS

Since an epic contains many thousands of words, and an epigram generally fewer than a dozen, it is clear who has the most passion, according to
this observation.

Sex and beauty are inseparable, like life and consciousness.
D. H. LAWRENCE

And when beauty fades, problems surface for those who have relied heavily on it. On the fading nature of great looks over time, Joan Collins wrote: "The problem with beauty is that it's like being born rich and getting poorer."

As for the topsy-turvy tangle known as *soixante-neuf*,
personally I have always felt it to be madly confusing,
like trying to pat your head and rub your stomach at the same time.
HELEN LAWRENSON

Soixante-neuf is French for the sexual position known in English as *sixty-nine*.

Sex when you're married is like going to a 7-Eleven.
There's not as much variety, but at three in the morning, it's always there.
CAROL LEIFER

I was wondering today what the religion of the country is—
and all I could come up with is sex.
CLARE BOOTH LUCE, *in a 1982 column*

She was our angel . . . and the sugar of sex came up from her
like a resonance of sound in the clearest grain of a violin . . .
a very Stradivarius of sex.
NORMAN MAILER, *on Marilyn Monroe*

In the duel of sex, women fight from a dreadnaught,
and man from an open raft.
H. L. MENCKEN

A dreadnaught is a class of battleship that first appeared in 1906. The ship was so technically advanced and, with its huge guns, so deadly that it immediately made all previous battleships obsolete. A raft, by comparison, is pretty a flimsy craft, so it is clear in Mencken's view who has the upper hand in this duel.

I love the lines men use to get us into bed.
"Please, I'll only put it in for a minute."
What am I, a microwave?

BEVERLY MICKINS

The sex organ has a poetic power, like a comet.

JOAN MIRO

Do they still call it infatuation?
That magic ax that chops away the world in one blow . . .
Whatever they call it, it leaps over anything, takes the biggest chair,
the largest slice, rules the ground wherever it walks . . .
People with no imagination feed it with sex—the clown of love.

TONI MORRISON, *from her 2003 novel* Love

The kiss is a wordless articulation of desire
whose object lies in the future, and somewhat to the south.

LANCE MORROW

Sex has become the religion of the most civilized portions of the earth.
The orgasm has replaced the cross
as the focus of longing and the image of fulfillment.

MALCOLM MUGGERIDGE

Muggeridge, a controversial English journalist, was a self-proclaimed drinker, smoker, and womanizer who also authored another widely quoted

metaphor: "Sex is the *ersatz* or substitute religion of the twentieth century."
In 1968, after meeting Mother Teresa, he brought her work to an English
audience in a television documentary. Meeting her changed him—and the
former agnostic shocked many when he wrote *Jesus Rediscovered* in 1969.

In sex as in banking there is a penalty for early withdrawal.

CYNTHIA NELMS

I like my sex the way I play basketball:
one-on-one with as little dribbling as possible.

LESLIE NIELSON

Sex—the poor man's polo.

CLIFFORD ODETS

A century earlier, Charles Baudelaire wrote in his journal: "Sexuality is
the lyricism of the masses." Both observations were preceded by a centuries-old Italian proverb: "Bed is the poor man's opera."

Sex is power, and all power is inherently aggressive.

CAMILLE PAGLIA

Leaving sex to the feminists
is like letting your dog vacation at the taxidermist.

CAMILLE PAGLIA

What is an orgasm, after all, except laughter of the loins?

MICKEY ROONEY

Sex is like art.
Most of it is pretty bad, and the good stuff is out of your price range.

SCOTT ROEBEN

Sex is currency.
What's the use of being beautiful
if you can't profit from it?

LILI ST. CYR

In the mid-twentieth century, St. Cyr was the best-known striptease dancer in America.

The basic conflict between men and women, sexually,
is that men are like firemen. To men, sex is an emergency,
and no matter what we're doing we can be ready in two minutes.
Women, on the other hand, are like fire. They're very exciting,
but the conditions have to be exactly right for it to occur.

JERRY SEINFELD

I've always felt that foreplay should be like a good meal,
going from soup . . . to nuts.

CYBILL SHEPHERD, *from her 2000*
memoir Cybill Disobedience

Anyone who calls it *sexual intercourse* can't possibly be interested in doing it.
You might as well announce that you're ready for lunch by proclaiming,
"I'd like to do some masticating and enzyme secreting."

ALLEN SHERMAN

The sexual organs are the most sensitive organs of the human being.
The eye or the ear seldom sabotages you.
An eye will not stop seeing if it doesn't like what it sees.
I would say that the sexual organs express the human soul
more than any other part of the body.
They are not diplomats. They tell the truth ruthlessly.

ISAAC BASHEVIS SINGER

Men tend to be like microwave ovens—
instantly ready to be turned on at anytime, day or night . . . .
The average woman, however, is more like a crock-pot.
She needs to warm up to the sexual experience and savor the process.

GARY SMALLEY

In a related metaphor, actress Sandra Bullock agreed: "Women are like ovens. We need fifteen minutes to heat up."

On the level of simple sensation and mood,
making love surely resembles an epileptic fit at least as much as,
if not more than, it does eating a meal or conversing with someone.

SUSAN SONTAG

In the fifth century B.C., the Greek philosopher Democritus said, "Coition is a slight attack of apoplexy." Also on the topic of fitful sex, Sontag wrote, "Sexuality is something, like nuclear energy, which may prove amenable to domestication . . . but then again may not."

Most men approach sex a lot like shooting a game of pinball.
We don't have any idea about the internal workings
or what we should do to win,
we're just gonna try to keep the ball in play as long as possible.

TIM STEEVES

For guys, sex is like going to a restaurant.
No matter what they order off that menu,
they walk out saying, "Damn! That was good!"
For women, it don't work like that. We go to the restaurant;
sometimes it's good, sometimes you got to send it back . . . .
Or you might go, "I think I'm going to cook for myself today."

WANDA SYKES

I have observed on board a steamer,
how men and women easily give way to their instinct for flirtation,
because water has the power of washing away our sense of responsibility,
and those who on land resemble the oak in their firmness
behave like floating seaweed when on the sea.

RABINDRANATH TAGORE

The Fifties was the most sexually frustrated decade: ten years of foreplay.

LILY TOMLIN

Germaine Greer said the same thing: "The 1950s were ten years of fore-play." Jerry Rubin, reflecting on the role the automobile played in the process, observed "The back seat produced the sexual revolution."

The buttocks are the most aesthetically pleasing part of the body . . .
Although they conceal an essential orifice, these pointless globes
are as near the human form can ever come to abstract art.

KENNETH TYNAN

Sex is like money; only too much is enough.

JOHN UPDIKE

History is filled with the sound of
silken slippers going downstairs
and wooden shoes coming up.

VOLTAIRE

Throughout history, the privileged classes have snuck downstairs at night to have sex with servants or slaves—and sometimes those same servants and slaves have trekked upstairs for the same purpose.

Sex and religion are bordering states.
They use the same vocabulary, share like ecstasies,
and often serve as a substitute for one another.

JESSAMYN WEST

An ounce of performance is worth pounds of promise.

MAE WEST

An orgasm is just a reflex, like a sneeze.

DR. RUTH WESTHEIMER

In the 1980s, Dr. Ruth was the world's most famous sex therapist, and this was her attempt to portray the orgasm as a natural bodily function. Mason Cooley may have been inspired by her when he offered this definition: "Orgasm: the genitals sneezing." But a decade before Dr. Ruth, the authors of a 1972 sex manual for children had already discovered the value of the sneeze metaphor in explaining the nature of an orgasm to prepubescent children: "An orgasm is like the tickling feeling you get inside your nose before you sneeze."

Sex is the Tabasco sauce which an adolescent national palate
sprinkles on every course in the menu.

MARY DAY WINN

chapter 11

Old & Young, We Are All on Our Last Cruise

John Quincy Adams became the sixth president of the United States in 1825, the first son of a president to be elected to the nation's highest office. At the end of the campaign, none of the candidates—which included Andrew Jackson and Henry Clay—had garnered enough electoral votes, and the election was decided in the House of Representatives. When the new President Adams went on to appoint Clay as secretary of state, Jackson cried foul and complained of "a corrupt bargain." With serious political opposition from the Jacksonians and a weak political base, the Adams presidency was not a happy—or a particularly distinguished—one.

But Adams was an interesting guy. He often began his day by taking a vigorous early morning swim—often in the nude—in the Potomac River. In a famous anecdote, a female journalist once snatched his clothes from the riverbank and returned them only after Adams agreed to give her an interview. He served one term, defeated in 1828 by his old nemesis, Andrew Jackson. He returned to Massachusetts to lick his political wounds and write his memoirs, but in 1831 he returned to the U. S. Congress, the only former president to do so.

In the middle of an impassioned 1848 speech in Congress, Adams suffered a stroke and fell unconscious to the floor. His health had been failing in recent years, and some previous heart problems had limited him severely. He died two days later, at age eighty.

In a eulogy, Massachusetts Senator Daniel Webster recalled his last meeting with the deceased former President. While visiting Adams at his home in D.C., Webster overheard a man ask the aging politician how he was doing. Adams's voice was weak, but his words reflected a mind that was still strong and vibrant:

> **I inhabit a weak, frail, decayed tenement;**
> **battered by the winds and broken in upon by the storms,**
> **and from all I can learn, the landlord does not intend to repair.**

Webster, one of the great orators of his era, admired eloquence whenever it surfaced, and he was deeply moved by this powerful—and poignant—metaphor. Happily for lovers of language, he recorded Adam's reply for posterity.

Observations about age and aging have appeared with great frequency over the centuries, but until I began work on this book I didn't realize how many of them are metaphorical. Many, like the Adams observation, have come from elderly people contemplating a death that is soon to come. Others have been written by younger people as they begin to imagine death. In 1728, at age twenty-two, Benjamin Franklin began tinkering with a possible epitaph for himself. He went through several possibilities—some serious, some clever—before composing this metaphorical masterpiece:

> **The body of Benjamin Franklin, Printer,**
> **(like the cover of an old book,**
> **its contents torn out and stripped of its lettering and gilding),**

Lies here, food for worms;
But the work shall not be lost, for it will (as he believed)
appear once more in a new and more elegant edition,
revised and corrected by the Author.

Franklin, a printer by trade, was a voracious reader and one of America's
first great bibliophiles. When he died in 1790, at age eighty-four, his personal library had grown to more than four thousand volumes, the largest
private collection in the colonies. Given Franklin's great love of books, it is
not surprising that in his famous epitaph he would liken himself to a worn
and weathered volume destined to be improved in a Second Edition.

Franklin returned to the book analogy in his autobiography, which made
its first appearance in 1791 (in an unauthorized edition and, amazingly, not
in English, but in French). When the first English version appeared a few
years later, the very first page of the book featured a reappearance of the
theme:

If it were left to my choice, I should have no objection
to go over the same life from its beginning to the end:
requesting only the advantage authors have,
of correcting in a second edition the faults of the first.

In the late nineteenth century, Scottish author Robert Louis Stevenson
was one of the world's most famous writers. Best known as the author of
great adventure novels, to literary types he was also an admired essayist. In
his most famous collection of essays, *Virginibus Puerisque* (1881), he wrote
beautifully on a host of subjects. One observation on aging stands out:

For, after a certain distance, every step we take in life
we find the ice growing thinner below our feet,
and all around us and behind us
we see our contemporaries going through.

When I read this for the first time, I had a flashback to something Blaise Pascal once wrote: "Eloquence is a painting of thought." When a writer paints a verbal masterpiece, as Stevenson does here, the result is an unforgettable *mental picture* that lingers in the mind long after the words have been processed by the brain.

The image of people falling through ice also brings to mind the expression *skating on thin ice*, which has been used since colonial times to refer to the act of placing oneself in a potentially dangerous situation. The actual practice of skating on ice that has not frozen to a safe thickness has always had an allure for thrill-seekers. Ralph Waldo Emerson may have even had this risky activity in mind when he wrote: "In skating over thin ice, our safety is in our speed."

Some of the most impressive metaphorical observations on aging aren't about death and dying, but about simply getting older. In his 1992 novel *When Nietzsche Wept*, psychotherapist-turned-novelist Irvin D. Yalom weaves a fascinating fictional account of a relationship that develops between Dr. Josef Breuer, a founder of *the talking cure* that became known as psychoanalysis, and a little-known, poverty-stricken, and suicidally depressed young philosopher named Friedrich Nietzsche. While working in Vienna in 1882, Breuer is persuaded to take on Nietzsche's case. He agrees to do so, despite a major stumbling block—the young philosopher is far too proud to seek help.

Breuer concocts an ingenious ploy to cure Nietzsche without Nietzsche knowing it—he will pose as a person struggling with his own existential problems, and ask the philosopher for help. Nietzsche, of course, is happy to oblige, and the result is a thoroughly engaging yarn. Breuer's ploy is not a complete ruse, however, for he has just turned forty and is in the middle of a full-blown mid-life crisis. At one point, he looks in a mirror and is dismayed by the sight:

He hated the sight of his beard . . .
He hated also the outcropping of gray that had insidiously appeared

in his mustache, on the left side of his chin, and in his sideburns.
These gray bristles were, he knew,
the advance scouts of a relentless, wintry invasion.
And there would be no stopping the march of the hours, the days, the years.

By viewing the emergence of gray hair as the initial foray of an unstoppable army, Breuer experiences the dread that small and vulnerable countries must feel when they are about to be invaded by an invincible enemy. The seventeenth-century poet Thomas Flatman also used a military image to convey this realization:

Age . . . brings along with him
A terrible artillery.

As you peruse the observations in this chapter, you will notice that many—even though expressed cloquently—are sad, poignant, or even a little depressing:

A man in old age is like a sword in a shop window.
HENRY WARD BEECHER

Old age is an island surrounded by death.
JUAN MONTALVO

Old age is an incurable disease.
SENECA

An aged man is but a paltry thing,
A tattered coat upon a stick.
WILLIAM BUTLER YEATS

But you will also find observations from people who approach age, not with dread and a sense of foreboding, but with grace and good humor. In Samuel Butler's 1903 novel *The Way of All Flesh*, a character says:

There's many a good tune played on an old fiddle.

In writing this, Butler may have been influenced by a similar English proverb that was popular at the time. Proverbial wisdom has often celebrated maturity. And in the grand tradition of indirect communication, proverbs often appear to be about other subjects when they are, in fact, observations about age and aging:

**Just because there's snow on the roof,
it doesn't mean the boiler's gone out.**
AMERICAN PROVERB

The older the fiddle, the sweeter the tune.
ENGLISH PROVERB

The oldest trees often bear the sweetest fruit.
GERMAN PROVERB

The afternoon knows what the morning never suspected.
SWEDISH PROVERB

Some people have even viewed the mature years as a liberation from the problems associated with youth. In *Fear of Fifty* (1995), Erica Jong wrote:

**At fifty, the madwoman in the attic breaks loose,
stomps down the stairs, and sets fire to the house.
She won't be imprisoned anymore.**

And speaking of good-humored observations, the British actress Gertrude Lawrence described the stages of a woman's life in a spectacular geographical metaphor:

> **From 16 to 22, like Africa—part virgin, part explored;**
> **23 to 35, like Asia—hot and mysterious;**
> **35 to 45, like the USA—high-toned and technical;**
> **46 to 55, like Europe—quite devastated, but interesting in places.**

Any reasonably complete discussion of age and aging must include descriptions about the youthful years, and you will find many of them in this chapter as well. Perhaps the most famous metaphor about youth comes from Shakespeare's *Antony and Cleopatra*. Cleopatra tries to convince Mark Antony that her love for him is the real thing, and nothing like the youthful and foolish infatuation she had for Julius Caesar. In making her case, she refers to:

> **My salad days, when I was green in judgment.**

Salad days is now a universal metaphor for that period between childhood and adulthood when people are inexperienced—or *green* with youth—and not yet ripened into maturity. Today, thanks to Shakespeare, we still use the word *green* to describe a lack of experience.

As people move from the dawn of their lives and get closer to the twilight, thoughts about aging and death become natural and commonplace. And, as we've already seen with observations about life, love, and so many other aspects of the human condition, many of the most compelling thoughts about the ages and stages of life have been expressed metaphorically.

> **Old minds are like old horses;**
> **you must exercise them if you wish to keep them in working order.**
> JOHN QUINCY ADAMS

A dying man needs to die, as a sleepy man needs to sleep,
and there comes a time when it is wrong, as well as useless, to resist.

STEWART ALSOP

To know how to grow old is the master work of wisdom,
and one of the most difficult chapters in the great art of living.

HENRI-FRÉDÉRIC AMIEL

The older I get, the greater power I seem to have to help the world;
I am like a snowball—the further I am rolled, the more I gain.

SUSAN B. ANTHONY

The timing of death, like the ending of a story,
gives a changed meaning to what preceded it.

MARY CATHERINE BATESON

Youth: The too-brief span wherein
the human chassis is factory fresh, undented, and free of corrosion.

RICK BAYAN

Old age is like climbing a mountain. You climb from ledge to ledge.
The higher you get, the more tired and breathless you become—
but your views become more extensive.

INGRID BERGMAN

As you get older, you find that often the wheat,
disentangling itself from the chaff, comes out to meet you.

GWENDOLYN BROOKS

Separating wheat from the chaff means to separate the valuable from the useless. In ancient times, winnowing was the process of exposing harvested wheat to the blowing air in order to separate the useless *chaff* from the valuable kernels. The metaphor became established after a passage in Luke 3:17 described Jesus as using a winnowing fork to gather the wheat (worthy followers) into his granary (heaven), and leaving the chaff (the unworthy) to the fires of hell.

> Youth is like spring, an overpraised season—
> delightful if it happens to be a favored one,
> but in practice very rarely favored and more remarkable,
> as a general rule, for biting east winds than genial breezes.
> SAMUEL BUTLER

> As a white candle
> In a holy place,
> So is the beauty
> Of an aged face.
>
> JOSEPH CAMPBELL

This is not from the contemporary mythologist of the same name but from an earlier Irish poet who went on to become an Irish nationalist. The passage comes from one of his most famous poems, "Old Woman," written in 1913.

> The dead might as well try to speak to the living as the old to the young.
> WILLA CATHER

> Young men are apt to think themselves wise enough,
> as drunken men are apt to think themselves sober enough.
> LORD CHESTERFIELD
> *(Philip Dormer Stanhope)*

> Old age: the crown of life, our play's last act.
> CICERO

Since the day of my birth, my death began its walk.
It is walking toward me, without hurrying.

JEAN COCTEAU

Cocteau also wrote, "You've never seen death? Look in the mirror every day and you will see it like bees working in a glass hive."

The excesses of our youth are drafts upon our old age,
payable with interest about thirty years after.

CHARLES CALEB COLTON

In another metaphor, on one of life's most painful realities, Colton wrote, "Body and mind, like man and wife, do not always agree to die together."

Age is like love: it cannot be hid.

THOMAS DEKKER

Old age was growing inside me.
It kept catching my eye from the depths of the mirror.
I was paralyzed sometimes as I saw it
making its way toward me so steadily
when nothing inside me was ready for it.

SIMONE DE BEAUVOIR

The loss of friends is a tax on age!

NINON DE LENCLOS

I think of death as a fast approaching end of a journey.

GEORGE ELIOT

Eliot wrote this in an 1861 letter. She would live another fifteen years.

When you live with another person for fifty years,
all of your memories are invested in that person,
like a bank account of shared memories.
It's not that you refer to them constantly.
In fact, for people who do not live in the past,
you almost never say, "Do you remember that night we . . . ?"
But you don't have to. That is the best of all.
You know that the other person does remember.
Thus, the past is part of the present as long as the other person lives.
It is better than any scrapbook,
because you are both living scrapbooks.

FEDERICO FELLINI

We don't grow old in a vacuum, but in a web of relationships with others—and often with one very special person. On October 30, 1943, Fellini and Italian actress Giulietta Masina wed, beginning a romantic and creative partnership that lasted half a century. On October 31, 1993, at 73, Fellini died of a heart attack, one day after the couple's fiftieth wedding anniversary (she died six months later).

At eighteen our convictions are hills from which we look;
at forty-five they are caves in which we hide.

F. SCOTT FITZGERALD

If wrinkles must be written on our brows,
let them not be written upon the heart.
The spirit should never grow old.

JAMES A. GARFIELD

General Douglas MacArthur wrote similarly: "Nobody grows old by merely living a number of years. People grow old by deserting their ideals. Years may wrinkle the skin, but to give up interest wrinkles the soul."

An adult is an obsolete child.

THEODORE GEISEL *(Dr. Seuss)*

Simone de Beauvoir put it this way: "What is an adult? A child blown up by age." And British science fiction writer Brian Aldiss expressed it even more vividly: "When childhood dies, its corpses are called adults."

The abbreviation of time, and the failure of hope,
will always tinge with a browner shade the evening of life.

EDWARD GIBBON

Childhood is a disease—a sickness that you grow out of.

WILLIAM GOLDING

There is always one moment in childhood
when the door opens and lets the future in.

GRAHAM GREENE

I am about to take my last voyage, a great leap in the dark.

THOMAS HOBBES, *his last words*

A man over ninety is a great comfort to all his elderly neighbors:
he is a picket-guard at the extreme outpost:
and the young folks of sixty and seventy feel that the enemy
must get by him before he can come near their camp.

OLIVER WENDELL HOLMES, SR.

The advice of the elders to young men is
very apt to be as unreal as a list of the hundred best books.

OLIVER WENDELL HOLMES, JR.

Fun is like life insurance; the older you get, the more it costs.
ELBERT HUBBARD

**I think middle-age is the best time, if we can escape
the fatty degeneration of the conscience which often sets in at about fifty.**
W. R. INGE

**We cannot live in the afternoon of life
according to the program of life's morning.**
CARL JUNG

This comes from Jung's *Modern Man in Search of a Soul* (1933). Later in the chapter, he continued: "The afternoon of life must also have a significance of its own and cannot be merely a pitiful appendage to life's morning."

**Adolescence is a kind of emotional seasickness.
Both are funny, but only in retrospect.**
ARTHUR KOESTLER

On the *Phil Donahue Show* in 1986, Carol Burnett said, "Adolescence is one big walking pimple." Capturing the prickly aspect of the stage, Anaïs Nin wrote: "Adolescence is like cactus." And Anna Quindlen recalled the stage this way: "I remember adolescence, the years of having the impulse control of a mousetrap, of being as private as a safe-deposit box."

Youth is a perpetual intoxication, a fever of the brain.
FRANÇOIS DE LA ROCHEFOUCAULD

**He was then in his fifty-fourth year, when even in the case of poets,
reason and passion begin to discuss a peace treaty
and usually conclude it not very long afterwards.**
G. C. LICHTENBERG, *on a contemporary*

The struggle between reason and passion is a lifelong battle, with periodic victories for each side, and an uneasy truce holding most of the time. Kahlil Gibran, who reconciled so many contraries in his writing, believed they could be complementary, once writing, "Your soul is oftentimes a battlefield, upon which your reason and your judgment wage war against your passion and your appetite. Rest in reason, but move in passion."

Is it not possible that middle age can be looked upon as a period of second flowering, second growth, even a kind of second adolescence?

ANNE MORROW LINDBERGH

There is a reaper whose name is death.
And with his sickle keen,
He reaps bearded grain at a breath,
And the flowers that grow in between

HENRY WADSWORTH LONGFELLOW,
in "The Reaper and the Flowers" (1839)

This is the first time in history when death was formally personified as a reaper (although Longfellow was probably inspired by Jeremiah 9:22: "The dead bodies of men shall fall . . . like sheaves after the reaper"). Today, death is commonly called *the Grim Reaper* and is usually rendered as a skeleton carrying a scythe. The analogy is that the lives of people are cut off in the same way a reaper harvests grain.

To be seventy years old is like climbing the Alps.
You reach a snow-crowned summit,
and see behind you the deep valley stretching miles and miles away,
and before you other summits higher and whiter,
which you may have strength to climb, or may not.
Then you sit down and meditate and wonder which it will be.

HENRY WADSWORTH LONGFELLOW

Memorial services are the cocktail parties of the geriatric set.

HAROLD MACMILLAN

Youth is a religion from which one always ends up being converted.

ANDRÉ MALRAUX

In an 1886 address at Harvard University, American poet James Russell Lowell said similarly, "If youth be a defect, it is one that we outgrow only too soon."

Old age is like a plane flying through a storm.
Once you're aboard, there's nothing you can do.

GOLDA MEIR

Age imprints more wrinkles in the mind than it does on the face.

MICHEL DE MONTAIGNE

Cherish all your happy moments; they make a fine cushion for your old age.

CHRISTOPHER MORLEY

Teenage boys, goaded by their surging hormones
run in packs like the primal horde.
They have only a brief season of exhilarating liberty
between control by their mothers and control by their wives.

CAMILLE PAGLIA

Youth is the seed time of good habits, as well in nations as in individuals.

THOMAS PAINE

Years are only garments, and you either wear them with style all your life,
or else you go dowdy to the grave.

DOROTHY PARKER

Most men in years, as they are generally discouragers of youth,
are like old trees that, being past bearing themselves,
will suffer no young plants to flourish beneath them.

ALEXANDER POPE

Growing old is like being increasingly penalized
for a crime you haven't committed.

ANTHONY POWELL

It is a mistake to regard age as a downhill grade toward dissolution.
The reverse is true. As one grows older one climbs with surprising strides.

GEORGE SAND

The country of the aged is a land
few people think very hard and seriously about
before the time of life when they sense that they're *arriving* there.

MAGGIE SCARF

The closing years of life are like the end of a masquerade party,
when the masks are dropped.

ARTHUR SCHOPENHAUER

Just as I shall select my ship when I am about to go on a voyage,
or my house when I propose to take a residence,
so I shall choose my death when I am about to depart from life.

SENECA

Love with old men is as the sun upon the snow,
it dazzles more than it warms them.

J. P. SENN

**Don't laugh at a youth for his affectations;
he is only trying on one face after another to find his own**

LOGAN PEARSALL SMITH

**Being over seventy is like being engaged in a war.
All our friends are going or gone and we survive
amongst the dead and dying as on a battlefield.**

MURIEL SPARK

Old and young, we are all on our last cruise.

ROBERT LOUIS STEVENSON

Stevenson also compared the sweetness of youth with the bitter reality of old age in a memorable meal metaphor: "There is only one difference between a long life and a good dinner: that, in the dinner, the sweets come last."

**Childhood is the Last Chance Gulch for happiness.
After that, you know too much.**

TOM STOPPARD

**For the unlearned, old age is winter;
for the learned, it is the season of the harvest.**

THE TALMUD

**His cousin was now of more than middle age . . .
She was lean, and yellow, and long in the tooth;
all the red and white in all the toy-shops in London
could not make a beauty of her.**

WILLIAM MAKEPEACE THACKERAY

This passage, from Thackeray's 1852 novel *The History of Henry Esmond*,

Esq., contains the earliest appearance in English of the expression *long in the tooth*, now a popular metaphor for aging. A horse's teeth become longer with age, as they are pushed out of the gums. Since ancient times, a person buying a horse has examined the teeth to estimate the animal's age. With humans, teeth don't grow, but the gums recede over time, giving the appearance of longer teeth.

> With sixty staring me in the face,
> I have developed inflammation of the sentence structure
> and definite hardening of the paragraphs.
>
> JAMES THURBER

> It's true, some wine improves with age.
> But only if the grapes were good in the first place.
>
> ABIGAIL VAN BUREN *("Dear Abby")*

In the early 1960s, Pope John XXIII offered a similar observation: "Men are like wine; some turn to vinegar, but the best improve with age."

> Boyhood, like measles, is one of those complaints
> which a man should catch young and have done with,
> for when it comes in middle life it is apt to be serious.
>
> P. G. WODEHOUSE

> Like our shadows,
> Our wishes lengthen as our sun declines.
>
> EDWARD YOUNG

chapter 12

An Actor
Is a God in Captivity

One of the most popular actors on the American stage in the nineteenth century was Edwin Booth (his statue stands today in Gramercy Park, near his Manhattan mansion). Born into a prominent acting family, Edwin and his two brothers carried on the family tradition. One of those brothers was John Wilkes Booth (yes, *that* John Wilkes Booth). After the Lincoln assassination in 1865, a cloud of infamy settled over the entire Booth family, and Edwin was forced for a time to abandon the stage.

Edwin, a handsome man with dark piercing eyes, was often described as "the American Hamlet," and many still consider him one of America's greatest actors. Like so many actors of his era, he had an elegant air and a great facility with words, once saying:

An actor is a sculptor who carves in snow.

In this observation, offered many decades before technological advances made it possible to preserve stage performances on film, Booth describes the world of the nineteenth-century actor. Unlike other artists, they worked in an ephemeral medium—their creations melting away as soon as they were created. In 1962, Shelley Winters updated the idea:

Acting is like painting pictures on bathroom tissues.

Metaphorical observations about actors and acting are very common, and they often help us look at this ancient profession in a new way:

Acting is like prizefighting.
The downtown gyms are smelly,
but that's where the champions are.

KIRK DOUGLAS

Acting is like making love.
It's better if your partner is good.

JEREMY IRONS

Acting is like letting your pants down; you're exposed.

PAUL NEWMAN

Actors are the jockeys of literature.
Others supply the horses, the plays, and we simply make them run.

RALPH RICHARDSON

Directors have also offered intriguing analogical observations about the theatrical life. The Swedish director Ingmar Bergman, who won three Academy Awards and was nominated for six more, was often asked about how he approached the myriad of decisions he had to make as a director. While he usually said he favored intuition over intellect, he once offered a fascinating description of how both were at work in his decision-making process:

I make all my decisions on intuition. I throw a spear into the darkness.
That is intuition.
Then I must send an army into the darkness to find the spear.
That is intellect.

The relationship between director and actor has also been described in metaphorical ways. Billy Wilder, winner of six Academy Awards and the first person to win three Oscars in a single night (as director, producer, and cowriter of the screenplay for the 1960 film *The Apartment*), explained it this way:

A director must be a policeman, a midwife,
a psychoanalyst, a sycophant, and a bastard.

A few years later, the French film director Jean Renoir picked up on the midwife theme and took it to a completely new level. Writing in his 1974 autobiography *My Life and My Films*, he offered one of the film world's most famous quotations:

A film director is not a creator, but a midwife.
His business is to deliver the actor of a child
that he did not know he had within him.

Kirk Douglas once said that movie making is a collaborative art, and the proof of his observation is evident whenever we see screen credits roll. In addition to actors, directors, and producers, hundreds of other professionals are involved in the making of a film—screenwriters, film editors, camera people, composers, musicians, sound technicians, wardrobe and set designers, and many others (including, of course, those mysterious *grips* and *best boys*). By contrast, writing is one of history's most solitary activities. When novels get turned into films, these two very different worlds intersect, and sometimes collide.

In 2001, the forty-nine-year-old Douglas Adams died of a sudden heart attack while working out in a gym in Santa Barbara, California. He had recently moved to California to complete a movie deal for *The Hitchhiker's Guide to the Galaxy*. Adams, initially excited over the prospect of seeing his work adapted to film, became increasingly frustrated over what seemed like pointless meetings with endless numbers of people. The inordinate delays finally got to him, causing him to write:

> **Getting a movie made in Hollywood is like**
> **trying to grill a steak by having a succession of people**
> **coming into the room and breathing on it.**

Adams never lived to see his work brought to the big screen—which might not have been such a bad thing if you listen to the experience of some other writers. John Le Carré, author of such famous spy novels as *The Spy Who Came in from the Cold*, once summarized his Hollywood experiences this way:

> **Having your book turned into a movie**
> **is like seeing your oxen turned into bouillon cubes.**

Not all writers have problems when their novels are turned into films, however, and the secret has something to do with the way the whole process is viewed. Rather than see the transaction as a precious transfer of artistic ownership, it might be better thought of as a simple property purchase. Rita Mae Brown recommended the latter approach:

> **You sell a screenplay like you sell a car.**
> **If someone drives it off a cliff, that's it.**

No discussion of acting and screen life would be complete without some mention of television, which has become so central to the lives of people that the veteran newsman Daniel Schorr once described it as "a nightly national séance." But perhaps the most famous observation on the small screen came in 1955, when the American critic John Mason Brown said in an interview that he had recently overheard a noteworthy remark from one of his son's friends:

Television is chewing gum for the eyes.

A year later, in another interview, Brown said, "So much of television is chewing gum for the eyes," this time without mentioning the original author. As the years passed, the remark has been repeated innumerable times, sometimes as "Television is chewing gum for the mind." Variations have been attributed to many others, including Fred Allen, Aldous Huxley, and Frank Lloyd Wright. But no matter who the line is attributed to, I've always found it fascinating that the original author of the observation—in my view, the most memorable words ever offered on the subject—was not some celebrated writer or wordsmith, but a simple schoolboy who in a momentary muse happened to notice a connection between two of his favorite activities, watching television and chewing gum.

In the remainder of the chapter, I'll present many more metaphorical musings for your enjoyment—all having to do with the world of stage and screen.

You can take all the sincerity in Hollywood,
place it in the navel of a fruit fly, and still have room enough
for three caraway seeds and a producer's heart.
FRED ALLEN

Comedy just pokes at problems, rarely confronts them squarely.
Drama is like a plate of meat and potatoes.
Comedy is rather like a dessert; a bit like meringue.
WOODY ALLEN

I feel like a father towards my old films.
You bring children into the world,
then they grow up and go off on their own.
From time to time you get together,
but it isn't always a pleasure to see them again.

MICHELANGELO ANTONIONI

What Einstein was to physics, what Babe Ruth was to home runs,
what Emily Post was to table manners . . .
that's what Edward G. Robinson was to dying like a dirty rat.

RUSSELL BAKER

Here, a house without a pool is like a neck with no diamond necklace;
a swimming pool is like jewelry for your house.

DREW BARRYMORE, *on life in Hollywood*

There is as much difference between the stage and the films
as between a piano and a violin.
Normally you can't become a virtuoso in both.

ETHEL BARRYMORE

For an actress to be a success she must have the face of Venus,
the brains of Minerva, the grace of Terpsichore, the memory of Macaulay,
the figure of Juno, and the hide of a rhinoceros.

ETHEL BARRYMORE

No form of art goes beyond ordinary consciousness as film does,
straight to our emotions, deep into the twilight room of the soul.

INGMAR BERGMAN

Being a screenwriter in Hollywood is like being a eunuch at an orgy.
Worse, actually; at least the eunuch is allowed to watch.

ALBERT BROOKS

Brooks, never a great fan of Hollywood's decision-makers, also observed: "Ten years ago, the studio heads thought the audiences were sheep. Now, they think they're snails with Down's Syndrome."

A play is like a cigar.
If it is a failure no amount of puffing will make it draw.
If it is a success everyone wants a box.

HENRY F. BRYAN

Be like a duck. Calm on the surface,
but always paddling like the dickens underneath.

MICHAEL CAINE

Some are able and humane men and some are low-grade individuals
with the morals of a goat, the artistic integrity of a slot machine,
and the manners of a floorwalker with delusions of grandeur.

RAYMOND CHANDLER,
on Hollywood producers

Chandler created one of America's best-known fictional characters, the hard-boiled private eye Philip Marlowe. Many of his novels and short stories were made into films, including the *film noir* classic *The Big Sleep*. He also wrote screenplays for many films, including *Double Indemnity* and *The Blue Dahlia*. He once said, "If my books had been any worse, I should not have been invited to Hollywood, and . . . if they had been any better, I should not have come."

The movie actor, like the sacred king of primitive tribes, is a god in captivity.

ALEXANDER CHASE

The point is that members of the public worship actors but often feel as if they own them as well. The ancient gods of captivity—who were nothing special outside their little universe—were in some ways less important to the tribe than the tribe was to them. Today, many actors become like deities imprisoned in golden cells.

A film is a petrified fountain of thought.

JEAN COCTEAU

Hollywood grew to be the most flourishing factory of popular mythology since the Greeks.

ALISTAIR COOKE

Film music is like a small lamp that you place below the screen to warm it.

AARON COPLAND

This intriguing image of a film score warming the screen comes from one of America's great composers. He also did the musical scores for dozens of Hollywood films, including *Of Mice and Men*, *Our Town*, *The Red Pony*, and *The Heiress*, for which he won an Oscar. Two other composers added these thoughts:

"A film musician is like a mortician—he can't bring the body back to life, but he's expected to make it look better." *Adolph Deutsch*

"Film music should have the same relationship to the film drama that somebody's piano-playing in my living room has on the book I'm reading." *Igor Stravinsky*

Some young Hollywood starlets remind me of my grandmother's old farmhouse— all painted up nice on the front side, a big swing on the backside, and nothing whatsoever in the attic.

BETTE DAVIS

The real actor—like any real artist—has a direct line to the collective heart.

BETTE DAVIS

When I talk to him, I feel like a plant that's been watered.

MARLENE DIETRICH, *on Orson Welles*

The relationship between the make-up man and the film actor
is one of accomplices in crime.

MARLENE DIETRICH

Hollywood is the gold cap on a tooth
that should have been pulled out years ago.

W. C. FIELDS

Filmmaking has now reached the same stage as sex—
it's all technique and no feeling.

PENELOPE GILLIATT

Modesty is the artifice of actors, similar to passion in call-girls.

JACKIE GLEASON

Gleason's point is that any demonstration of modesty from an actor is likely to be insincere. The notion has been advanced by others, but never so well.

The cinema is truth twenty-four times a second.

JEAN-LUC GODARD

This may be history's most famous description of cinema. The allusion is to the speed with which the individual frames on a roll of 35-millimeter film pass through a movie camera. In another memorable metaphorical observation on his craft, Godard said, "A film is the world in an hour and a half."

That's the way with these directors,
they're always biting the hand that lays the golden egg.

SAMUEL GOLDWYN

Technically, this is a *mixed metaphor*; but when a metaphor is badly mixed—a Sam Goldwyn specialty—it is often called a *mangled metaphor*.

Movies are just another form of merchandising—
we have our factory, which is called a stage;
we make a product, we color it, we title it, and we ship it out in cans.

CARY GRANT

I felt like a raisin in a gigantic fruit salad.

MARK HAMILL, *on acting in* Star Wars

Lana Turner is to an evening gown
what Frank Lloyd Wright is to a pile of lumber.

REX HARRISON

A movie without music is a little bit like an aeroplane without fuel.
However beautifully the job is done,
we are still on the ground and in a world of reality.
Your music has lifted us all up and sent us soaring.
Everything we cannot say with words or show with action
you have expressed for us.

AUDREY HEPBURN, *to Henry Mancini*

This came in a 1961 letter Hepburn wrote to Mancini, composer of the score for *Breakfast at Tiffany's*. The movie, adapted from a Truman Capote novella, stars Hepburn as Holly Golightly, a glamorous New Yorker who is working as a high-priced escort. Her goal is to meet and marry a wealthy older man, but she becomes attracted to a handsome and struggling young writer (George Peppard), who moves into her apartment building (he, in turn, is being kept by a wealthy older woman). Of the seven Oscar nominations the film received, Mancini took home two, one for the sound track and one (with Johnny Mercer) for the song "Moon River."

> **The stage is actors' country.**
> **You have to get your passport stamped every so often**
> **or they take away your citizenship.**
> CHARLTON HESTON

This was Heston's way of saying that film stars needed to occasionally appear on the live theatrical stage, even though stage roles are far less lucrative.

> **Drama is life with the dull bits cut out.**
> ALFRED HITCHCOCK

> **For me the cinema is not a slice of life, but a piece of cake.**
> ALFRED HITCHCOCK

> **A good review from the critics is just another stay of execution.**
> DUSTIN HOFFMAN

Also employing an executioner's analogy, Eli Wallach famously observed: "Having the critics praise you is like having the hangman say you've got a pretty neck." Tyne Daly changed the metaphor, but made the same point: "A critic is someone who never actually goes to battle, yet who afterwards comes out shooting the wounded."

> **Academy awards are like orgasms—**
> **only a few of us know the feeling of having had multiple ones.**
> JOHN HUSTON

Huston was nominated for ten Academy Awards, winning two. He had his multiple orgasms in 1948, when he took home the Best Director and the Best Screenplay Oscars for *The Treasure of the Sierra Madre*.

The cinema, like the detective story, makes it possible to experience without danger all the excitement, passion, and desirousness which must be suppressed in a humanitarian ordering of society.

CARL JUNG

Glamour is just sex that got civilized.

DOROTHY LAMOUR

Producing is like pushing Jell-O up a hill on a hot day.

LUCY LIU

This is a variation on the metaphor *nailing Jell-O to the wall*, which describes a task that is virtually impossible. The expression originated in 1903 when Theodore Roosevelt was trying to finalize an agreement with the Columbian government to build a canal in (at the time) their province of Panama. Roosevelt was so frustrated with Columbian officials that he bellowed, "Negotiating with those pirates is like trying to nail currant jelly to the wall."

Being a writer in Hollywood is like going into Hitler's Eagle's Nest with a great idea for a bar mitzvah.

DAVID MAMET

Mamet's dim view of Hollywood was also reflected in his 1988 play *Speed the Plow*, where a character says, "Life in the movie business is like the beginning of a new love affair: it's full of surprises and you're constantly getting fucked."

A trip through a sewer in a glass-bottom boat.

WILSON MIZNER, *on his years in Hollywood*

Mizner was one of Hollywood's most colorful characters (Anita Loos called him "America's most fascinating outlaw"). He and brother Addison were the inspiration for Stephen Sondheim's 2003 musical, *Bounce*. Like David Mamet earlier, Mizner also had a dim view of his bosses: "Working for Warner Brothers is like fucking a porcupine; it's a hundred pricks against one."

Hollywood is high school with money.

MARTIN MULL

If they tell you that she died of sleeping pills you must know
that she died of a wasting grief, of a slow bleeding at the soul.

CLIFFORD ODETS, *on Marilyn Monroe*

This appeared in a tribute Odets wrote a month after Monroe's August 1962 death by an overdose of sleeping pills (it was ruled a probable suicide). In predicting that a legend would spring up around the blonde sex symbol, Odets quoted a magnificent metaphorical line from the poet William Butler Yeats: "The tree has to die before it can be made into a cross."

The difference between being a director and being an actor is
the difference between being
the carpenter banging the nails into the wood,
and being the piece of wood the nails are being banged into.

SEAN PENN

Working with Julie Andrews
is like getting hit over the head with a valentine.

CHRISTOPHER PLUMMER,
Andrews's Sound of Music *co-star*

Bond smoked like Peter Lorre, drank like Humphrey Bogart,

ate like Sydney Greenstreet, used up girls like Errol Flynn—
then went to a steam bath and came out looking like Clark Gable.

HARRY REASONER,
on Sean Connery's James Bond

It's hard to act in the morning. The muse isn't even awake.

KEANU REEVES

Every playwright should try acting, just as every judge should
spend some weeks in jail to find out what he is handing out to others.

ERICH MARIA REMARQUE

The camera is a little like the surgeon's knife.

JEAN RENOIR

Being given good material is like being assigned to bake a cake
and having the batter made for you.

ROSALIND RUSSELL

My native habitat is the theatre. In it, I toil not, neither do I spin.
I am a critic and commentator.
I am essential to the theatre—as ants to a picnic,
as the boll weevil to a cotton field.

GEORGE SANDERS

This is a classic line in cinema history, delivered by Sanders in the role
of critic Addison de Witt in the 1950 film *All About Eve* (screenplay by Joseph L. Mankiewicz). The line captures how critics have been viewed by
playwrights and actors (and writers as well, as you will see in the upcoming
literary life chapter). The most colorful remark about critics from a stage
performer, though, comes from George Burns, who said, "Critics are eunuchs at a gang-bang."

**Acting is like roller skating.
Once you know how to do it, it is neither stimulating nor exciting.**

GEORGE SANDERS

**Making a film is like going down a mine—
once you've started, you bid a metaphorical goodbye
to the daylight and the outside world for the duration.**

JOHN SCHLESINGER

**A fellow with the inventiveness of Albert Einstein
but with the attention span of Daffy Duck.**

TOM SHALES,
on Robin Williams

Another well-known attention span comparison was Robert Redford's light-hearted jab at Paul Newman: "He has the attention span of a lightning bolt."

**Going to Hollywood to talk about menopause
was a little like going to Las Vegas to sell savings accounts.**

GAIL SHEEHY

This was Sheehy's explanation for the lack of interest Hollywood producers showed when she pitched them on doing a film adaptation of *The Silent Passage* (1992).

**The body of an actor is like a well in which
experiences are stored, then tapped when needed.**

SIMONE SIGNORET

**Careers, like rockets, don't always take off on time.
The trick is to always keep the engine running.**

GARY SINISE

This is great advice for anyone, but especially for people in an occupation with long periods of inactivity between gigs and even longer odds against success.

> **In the creative process there is the father, the author of the play;**
> **the mother, the actor pregnant with the part;**
> **and the child, the role to be born.**
>
> KONSTANTIN STANISLAVSKY

> **Remember this practical piece of advice:**
> **Never come into the theatre with mud on your feet.**
> **Leave your dust and dirt outside.**
> **Check your little worries, squabbles, petty difficulties**
> **with your outside clothing—all the things that ruin your life**
> **and draw your attention away from your art—at the door.**
>
> KONSTANTIN STANISLAVSKY,
> *advice to actors*

> **Directing is like being a father on a set; comedy is like being a kid.**
>
> DAVID STEINBERG

Steinberg was one of the best-known comics in the 1970s (he appeared on *The Tonight Show* 130 times and was the youngest person ever to guest-host the show). He went on to achieve great success behind the camera, directing such TV sitcoms as *Seinfeld, Mad About You*, and *Designing Women*. In 2005, he returned to the front of the camera with his TV Land talk show *Sit Down Comedy*.

> **It's a little like wrestling a gorilla.**
> **You don't quit when you're tired, you quit when the gorilla is tired.**
>
> ROBERT STRAUSS,
> *on acting careers*

**A film is a boat which is always on the point of sinking—
it always tends to break up as you go along and drag you under with it.**
FRANÇOIS TRUFFAUT

**By increasing the size of the keyhole,
today's playwrights are in danger of doing away with the whole door.**
PETER USTINOV

The reference here is to the increased appearance of gratuitous sex in modern plays. Ustinov, a talented writer as well as a great actor, was suggesting that what used to be peeked at through keyholes was now in plain view.

Choice is to the cable monopoly what sunlight is to the vampire.
JACK VALENTI

Valenti said this in 1987, as president of the Motion Picture Association of America. At the time, five companies controlled over 40 percent of cable-TV subscriptions and dictated what viewers would get to watch on television.

A film is never really good unless the camera is an eye in the head of a poet.
ORSON WELLES

In 1938, Welles achieved national notoriety and everlasting fame when his *War of the Worlds* radio broadcast created a panic on the East Coast. Two years later, the twenty-five-year-old Welles was lured to Hollywood by RKO studio executives. In 1941, he came out with *Citizen Kane*, often hailed as America's greatest film. Welles once described the RKO lot as "The biggest electric train set any boy ever had."

**I hate television. I hate it as much as peanuts.
But I can't stop eating peanuts.**
ORSON WELLES

This observation, made in 1956, nicely communicates the ambivalence so many people feel about television. More recently, Dennis Miller made a similar point: "Bad television is three things: a bullet train to a morally bankrupt youth, a slow spiral into an intellectual void, and of course, a complete blast to watch."

Making movies is a little like walking into a dark room.
Some people stumble across furniture, others break their legs,
but some of us see better in the dark than others.

BILLY WILDER

Many plays, certainly mine, are like blank checks.
The actors and directors put their own signatures on them.

THORNTON WILDER

Wilder's plays may have been blank checks, but the plays of many other playwrights are written for very precise amounts. Using two different similes, Vivien Leigh compared two famous playwrights this way: "Shaw is like a train. One just speaks the words and sits in one's place. But Shakespeare is like bathing in the sea—one swims where one wants."

A movie without sex would be like a candy bar without nuts.

EARL WILSON

chapter 13

Washington, D.C., Is to Lying What Wisconsin Is to Cheese

O n September 17, 1787, the men responsible for drafting a constitution for the new American nation walked out of Independence Hall in Philadelphia. They had labored for nearly four months, first attempting a simple revision of the Articles of Confederation, and in the end drafting an entirely new document. It had been an unusually hot summer, and the framers of the constitution had sweltered inside the great hall with the windows closed to the throng of curious onlookers who had gathered outside to witness history in the making.

The Constitutional Convention, as it came to be called, was chaired by George Washington, who represented his home state of Virginia. Washington had planned to retire when the Revolutionary War ended in 1783, but his sense of duty took him to Philadelphia instead. His status as a war hero made him an obvious choice as chairman of the gathering. But many other luminaries were in attendance as well, including James Madison and Alexander Hamilton (Thomas Jefferson and John Adams were in Europe and did not attend). To the gathering crowd, though, the most familiar face was that of the eighty-one-year-old Benjamin Franklin, an original signer of the Declaration of Independence eleven years earlier and a resident of Philadelphia since he was seventeen. As the men descended the stairs, many people in the crowd shouted out questions about the nature of the new government. One female voice shouted at Franklin, "Well, Doctor, what have we got, a republic or a monarchy?" The Grand Old Man replied, "A republic, if you can keep it."

In the years that followed, a lively debate ensued over whether a republican form of government was indeed the best model for America. As the new nation struggled to get established, there were a predictable number of second-guessers, and many even suggested a return to a monarchical form of government.

In a 1795 debate in Congress, this issue surfaced yet again. Fisher Ames, a congressman from Massachusetts, rose to speak in favor of the republican model. Ames, who would later become president of Harvard University, was one of the great orators of the era. And in one of the most memorable metaphors ever offered in a Congressional debate, he compared the competing forms of government to two very different types of eighteenth-century maritime vessels:

A monarchy is a merchantman, which sails well,
but will sometimes strike on a rock, and go to the bottom;
whilst a republic is a raft which would never sink,
but then your feet are always in the water.

As often happens with particularly apt metaphors, the remark helped put things into perspective for new Americans, reminding them that their fledgling government had a plain and simple seaworthiness that was far preferable to the elegant fragility of European governments. The image was so compelling, it had tremendous staying power. Two hundred years later, the sentiment showed up in an observation from Louisiana senator Russell B. Long:

Democracy is like a raft.
It won't sink, but you'll always have your feet wet.

With the Constitutional Convention over, George Washington left Philadelphia and headed back to Mount Vernon. He was fully expecting—at long last—to spend the remainder of his life pursuing his many interests and avocations. But private life was not in his future.

In 1788, after the Constitution was formally ratified by the states, a new entity called the electoral college selected Washington as the first United States president. Once again, the hero of the Revolutionary War struggled to reconcile his personal desires with his sense of duty. He had always harbored a deep disdain for politics, and even worried that the formation of political parties would deeply—and dangerously—divide the country. He finally accepted the nomination, but he approached the new role with great trepidation. In a letter he wrote to a friend on April 1, 1789, less than a month before his inauguration, he confessed:

My movements to the chair of Government
will be accompanied by feelings not unlike those of
a culprit who is going to the place of his execution.

Figurative language has had a long history in political life. In the sixth century B.C., the legendary Athenian lawmaker Solon embarked on a series of political reforms that repealed the harsh laws of the Emperor Draco (of *draconian* fame) and established the foundation for the world's first democracy. In the early days of Solon's reign, a bearded stranger showed up at his door and identified himself as Anacharsis, a prince from the distant Northern kingdom of Scythia (modern-day Ukraine). With his rustic appearance and well-worn clothing, Anacharsis was not exactly a regal sight, but he proved to be a man of uncommon wisdom, penetrating insight, and refreshing frankness. Within a short time, this curious man won over the citizens of Athens, much like Benjamin Franklin did in the 1770s when, as America's first ambassador to France, he captivated the French people.

Anacharsis became a trusted advisor to Solon and was the first outsider to be made an Athenian citizen (he, along with Solon, went on to achieve immortality when ancient historians included them among the legendary Seven Wise Men of Greece). One day, in a show of confidence in his new confidante, Solon revealed his plans for a wholesale revision of laws governing the Athenian people. Expecting support for his great dream, the emperor was shocked when Anacharsis laughed at the idea. When pressed for an explanation, Anacharsis explained that it was impossible to restrain the vices of people by statute. And then he added:

> **Written laws are like spiders' webs,**
> **and will, like them, only entangle and hold the poor and weak,**
> **while the rich and powerful will easily break through them.**

This fascinating anecdote was passed along by word of mouth for centuries before the Greek historian Plutarch recorded it for posterity. Today, twenty-five hundred years after Anacharsis offered his analogy, it is routinely cited in discussions about the lack of justice in judicial systems all around the world. His observation also simulated many spin-offs, including this from a 1707 essay by Jonathan Swift:

> **Laws are like cobwebs, which may catch small flies,**
> **but let wasps and hornets break through.**

Metaphorical language goes back to antiquity and continues with force today. When politicians describe a campaign as *a marathon and not a sprint,* we all know what they mean. And when we say an issue is *a red herring* or describe a candidate as *a dark horse* or *a loose cannon,* we're speaking metaphorically, even if we're unaware of the origins of such expressions.

One of the most famous contemporary political metaphors emerged in

1962, when Jesse Unruh, Speaker of the California State Assembly, said in an interview in *Look* magazine:

Money is the mother's milk of politics.

At the time, Unruh was one of the state's most flamboyant politicians (he was nicknamed *Big Daddy* by Raquel Welch). The remark, which vividly captured the role of Big Money in the political process, immediately took hold, and went on to become one of history's best-known political quotations. By the 1990s, as Unruh's observation began to suffer from overexposure, another colorful politician—Jim Hightower of Texas—stepped up to the plate with an updated version:

Money is the crack cocaine of politics.

Out of the thousands of new metaphors that appear every year, most have only a limited shelf life. But every now and then a great one appears and goes on to become an integral part of the cultural vocabulary. During the Reagan presidency, many Democrats were frustrated by the President's ability to remain unscathed despite a variety of mistakes and blunders made during his administration. On an August morning in 1983, as Colorado Congresswoman Patricia Schroeder was cooking breakfast for her children, she had a flash of inspiration. "He's just like a Teflon frying pan," she thought, "Nothing sticks to him." Later that day, in an address in Congress, she unveiled the image:

Mr. Speaker, after carefully watching Ronald Reagan,
he is attempting a great breakthrough in political technology—
he has been perfecting the Teflon-coated presidency . . .
Harry Truman had a sign on his desk
emblazoned with his motto: "The Buck Stops Here."
It has obviously been removed and Reagan's desk has been Teflon-coated.

Schroeder's colleagues in Congress seized on the concept, and soon people all around the country were repeating it. Within a week, the *New York Times* helped make it a permanent part of the political lexicon with an article head-lined "The Teflon Presidency." Nobody before Schroeder had ever likened a politician to a non-stick frying pan. But the Teflon metaphor was so brilliant that—there is no better way to describe what happened—it stuck.

Continuing with the adhesion theme, here's hoping that you find a few more metaphorical observations with sticking power in the remainder of the chapter.

Patriotism is in political life what faith is in religion.

LORD ACTON *(John Dahlberg)*

Lord Acton, a nineteenth-century British historian, is best known for the dictum, "Power tends to corrupt, and absolute power corrupts absolutely." Also on the subject of power, John Adams painted this vivid verbal picture in 1765: "The jaws of power are always opened to devour, and her arm is always stretched out, if possible, to destroy the freedom of thinking, speaking, and writing."

Gratitude, like love, is never a dependable international emotion.

JOSEPH W. ALSOP, JR.

Man is by nature a political animal.

ARISTOTLE

A group of politicians deciding to dump a President because his morals are bad is like the Mafia getting together to bump off the Godfather for not going to church on Sunday.

RUSSELL BAKER

You might think this is about the attempt to impeach Bill Clinton in

1998, but it came in 1974 in response to calls to impeach Richard Nixon over Watergate.

**The president of the United States bears about as much relationship
to the real business of running America
as does Colonel Sanders to the business of frying chicken.**
J. G. BALLARD

In the 1990s, South Carolina congressman Bob Inglis also employed a memorable KFC metaphor: "Asking an incumbent member of Congress to vote for term limits is a bit like asking a chicken to vote for Colonel Sanders."

Bureaucracy is a giant mechanism operated by pygmies.
HONORÉ DE BALZAC

As long as there have been governments, people have derided bureaucracies. In 1868, Russian writer Alexander Ostrovsky wrote in *The Diary of a Scoundrel*: "It's all papers and forms; the entire Civil Service is like a fortress, made of papers, forms, and red tape." Since the early 1800s, *red tape* has been a metaphor for complicated and time-consuming procedures. The expression comes from a centuries-old practice of tying official government documents in red ribbon.

Laws are like sausages. It's better not to see them being made.
OTTO VON BISMARCK

**Here's a Washington political riddle where you fill in the blanks:
"As Alberto Gonzales is to the Republicans,
_____ _____ is to the Democrats—
a continuing embarrassment thanks to his amateurish performance."**
DAVID BRODER

This is how Broder began his syndicated column in April 2007. Analogies have long been a part of the school curriculum, so it was appropriate for Broder to add: "If you answered Sen. Harry Reid, give yourself an A." The column came a week after Attorney General Gonzalez's inept performance before senators investigating the controversial firing of eight U. S. attorneys. In the column, Broder also surveyed a variety of Reid's verbal gaffes, including his 2005 comment that Alan Greenspan was "one of the biggest political hacks" in Washington.

We don't just have egg on our face. We have omelette all over our suits.

TOM BROKAW

Brokaw placed all the news networks into the same red-faced category when he made this comment on the premature—and ultimately wrong—announcement that Al Gore had carried Florida in the 2000 presidential election. *Egg on your face* is an American expression that means to have embarrassed oneself through a foolish action.

The government is becoming the family of last resort.

JERRY BROWN

**"My country, right or wrong" is a thing that no patriot
would think of saying except in a desperate case.
It is like saying, "My mother, drunk or sober."**

G. K. CHESTERTON

**Meeting Franklin Roosevelt
was like opening your first bottle of champagne;
knowing him was like drinking it.**

WINSTON CHURCHILL

This is one of the great compliments in world history. Churchill, who once wrote that "Apt analogies are among the most formidable weapons of the rhetorician," sprinkled his speeches and writings with examples. Here are a few more:

"Hatred plays the same part in government as acid in chemistry."

"An appeaser is one who feeds a crocodile—hoping it will eat him last."

"What the horn is to the rhinoceros, what the sting is to the wasp, the Mohammadan faith is to the Arabs."

"We contend that for a nation to try to tax itself into prosperity is like a man standing in a bucket and trying to lift himself up by the handle."

Politics is the womb in which war develops.

KARL VON CLAUSEWITZ

Clausewitz, a nineteenth-century Prussian general and military theorist, offered this in his 1832 classic *On War*. The book also contains his most famous observation: "War is merely the continuation of political intercourse by other means."

The art of taxation consists in so plucking the goose as to obtain the largest amount of feathers with the least amount of hissing.

JEAN-BAPTISTE COLBERT

In the seventeenth century, Colbert was Louis XIV's tax collector. In the eighteenth century, Edmund Burke said on the same subject, "To tax and to please, no more than to love and to be wise, is not given to men." And recently, the American economist Donald J. Boudreaux observed: "Tax hikes are to markets what bacon grease is to human arteries."

Power will intoxicate the best hearts, as wine the strongest heads.

CHARLES CALEB COLTON

You campaign in poetry. You govern in prose.

MARIO CUOMO

This famous line, from a 1985 *New Republic* article, masterfully contrasts the excitement of campaigning with the reality of governing. The underlying sentiment is not original to Cuomo. In a 1718 poem, Matthew Prior wrote:

> **I court others in verse; but I love thee in prose:**
> **And they have my whimsies, but thou hast my heart.**

> **Treaties are like roses and young girls—they last while they last.**
> CHARLES DE GAULLE

> **In Mexico, an air conditioner is called a "politician,"**
> **because it makes a lot of noise but doesn't work very well.**
> LEN DEIGHTON

> **Nationalism is an infantile disease. It is the measles of mankind.**
> ALBERT EINSTEIN

English writer Richard Aldington agreed, writing: "Patriotism is a lively sense of collective responsibility. Nationalism is a silly cock crowing on its own dunghill." Nationalism, it seems fair to conclude, is a corruption of patriotism.

> **Farming looks mighty easy when your plow is a pencil,**
> **and you're a thousand miles from the corn field.**
> DWIGHT D. EISENHOWER

> **An election is coming. Universal peace is declared,**
> **and the foxes have a sincere interest in prolonging the lives of the poultry.**
> GEORGE ELIOT

Great political metaphors sometimes come from fictional characters.

This cynical one comes from the protagonist in George Eliot's 1866 novel *Felix Holt, The Radical.* In another popular animal metaphor, English theologian W. R. Inge wrote in a 1919 essay: "It is useless for the sheep to pass resolutions in favor of vegetarianism while the wolf remains of a different opinion."

> **Politicians, like prostitutes, are held in contempt.**
> **But what man does not run to them when he needs their services?**
> BRENDAN FRANCIS
> *(pen name of Edward F. Murphy)*

> **For George Bush to fire Karl Rove**
> **would be like Charlie McCarthy firing Edgar Bergen.**
> AL FRANKEN

When critics began calling for the head of Karl Rove, George W. Bush's controversial political adviser, Franken said it wasn't likely to happen. Picking up on the notion that Rove was "Bush's Brain," he argues here that Rove was like ventriloquist Edgar Bergen and Bush was like the dummy Charlie McCarthy. It was a sophisticated jab, suggesting that Bush could speak only the words Rove was putting into his mouth. Rove did resign near the end of Bush's second term, but there was never any danger of his being fired. In 1975, David Steinberg applied the same ventriloquist metaphor to Gerald Ford: "He looks and talks like he just fell off Edgar Bergen's lap."

> **Trickle-down theory—the less than elegant metaphor**
> **that if one feeds the horse enough oats,**
> **some will pass through to the road for the sparrows.**
> JOHN KENNETH GALBRAITH

Molly Ivins put it this way: "We've had trickle-down economics in the country for ten years now, and most of us aren't even damp yet."

**In politics, as on the sickbed, people toss from side to side,
thinking they will be more comfortable.**

JOHANN WOLFGANG VON GOETHE

**When religion and politics travel in the same cart,
the riders believe nothing can stand in their way.**

FRANK HERBERT

**Politics is a choice of enemas.
You're gonna get it up the ass, no matter what you do.**

GEORGE V. HIGGINS

The metaphor may be coarse, but not many would quibble with its accuracy. The words come from the character Ed Cobb in Higgins's 1991 novel *Victories.*

**I hold it that a little rebellion, now and then, is a good thing,
and as necessary in the political world as storms in the physical.
It is a medicine necessary for the sound health of government.**

THOMAS JEFFERSON

Jefferson also famously wrote: "The tree of liberty must be refreshed from time to time with the blood of patriots and tyrants. It is its natural manure."

**A prince without letters is a pilot without eyes.
All his government is groping.**

BEN JONSON

This analogy about a leader with inadequate learning has a timeless quality—and clear contemporary relevance. It comes from a commonplace book kept by Jonson and published posthumously in 1641. Commonplace books go back to antiquity but became widespread in the fifteenth century as paper became more affordable. Essentially, they were loosely organized scrapbooks containing literary excerpts and other information of interest. Compilers also commonly recorded their own thoughts and reflections, as Jonson did in his book.

> **There's an old saying that victory has a hundred fathers
> and defeat is an orphan.**
>
> JOHN F. KENNEDY

If JFK had known more, he might not have used this metaphor in a 1961 address about the Bay of Pigs fiasco. In 1942, Mussolini's foreign minister, Galeazzo Ciasno, wrote, "As always, victory finds a hundred fathers, but defeat is an orphan." The saying became popular with many Italian and German officers. In his 2007 book *No Excuses,* political strategist Bob Schrum updated the thought: "If victory has a hundred fathers, it also brings forth a hundred advisors."

> **Washington is like a Roman arena.
> Gladiators do battle, and the spectators determine who survives
> by giving the appropriate signal, just as in the Coliseum.**
>
> HENRY A. KISSINGER

> **The sound bite is to politics what the aphorism is to exposition:
> the art of saying much with little.**
>
> CHARLES KRAUTHAMMER

In his 1997 *Time* magazine piece, he added: "The sound bite is the ultimate in making every word tell. It is the very soul of compactness. Brevity is not enough. You need weight. Hence some sound bites qualify for greatness: FDR's 'The only thing we have to fear is fear itself' or Reagan's 'Tear down this wall.'"

The great nations have always acted like gangsters,
and the small nations like prostitutes.

STANLEY KUBRICK

Politicians are like monkeys.
The higher they climb, the more revolting are the parts they expose.

GWILYM LLOYD GEORGE
(son of David Lloyd George)

The average man . . . regards government as a sort of great milk cow,
with its head in the clouds eating air,
and growing a full teat for everybody on earth.

CLARENCE MANION

Manion, Dean of the Notre Dame law school in the mid–1900s, might have been inspired by a somewhat similar metaphor from Winston Churchill: "Some see private enterprise as the predatory target to be shot, others as a cow to be milked, but few are those who see it as the sturdy horse pulling the wagon."

The Vice-President of the United States is like a man in a cataleptic state:
he cannot speak; he cannot move; he suffers no pain;
and yet he is perfectly conscious of everything that is going on about him.

THOMAS R. MARSHALL

Marshall was Woodrow Wilson's vice president. John Nance Garner, FDR's vice president, offered an even more famous line: "The vice-presidency isn't worth a pitcher of warm piss."

Scooter is to Cheney as Cheney is to Bush.

MARY MATALIN

I. Lewis "Scooter" Libby was Vice President Dick Cheney's chief of staff when CIA operative Valerie Plame was "outed" in 2005. After a special prosecutor investigation, Libby was indicted on charges of perjury and obstruction of justice, and was ultimately convicted in March 2007 (President Bush later commuted the sentence but let the conviction stand). In this analogy, Matalin was saying that Libby—who was known as "Cheney's Cheney" to Washington insiders—was as important to Cheney as the vice president was to President George W. Bush.

> **Being in politics is like being a football coach.**
> **You have to be smart enough to understand the game**
> **and dumb enough to think it's important.**
> EUGENE MCCARTHY

> **Washington, D.C. is to lying what Wisconsin is to cheese.**
> DENNIS MILLER

> **Political image is like mixing cement.**
> **When it's wet, you can move it around and shape it,**
> **but at some point it hardens**
> **and there's almost nothing you can do to reshape it.**
> WALTER MONDALE

> **Ideas are like great arrows, but there has to be a bow.**
> **And politics is the bow of idealism.**
> BILL MOYERS

This is the idealistic view. A cynical one comes from Aldous Huxley: "Idealism is the noble toga that political gentlemen drape over their will to power."

> **Old politicians, like old actors, revive in the limelight.**
> MALCOLM MUGGERIDGE

The politician is . . . trained in the art of inexactitude.
His words tend to be blunt or rounded because
if they have a cutting edge they may later return to wound him.

EDWARD R. MURROW

The battle for the mind of Ronald Reagan
was like the trench warfare of World War I:
never have so many fought so hard for such barren terrain.

PEGGY NOONAN

This is from *What I Saw at the Revolution* (1990) by a key Reagan speechwriter. Often misinterpreted as a swipe at Reagan's intelligence, it was really a comment on his disinterest in and detachment from the details of governance.

Everybody knows politics is a contact sport.

BARACK OBAMA

In *The Audacity of Hope* (2007), Obama offered another interesting metaphor: "Maybe the trivialization of politics has reached a point of no return, so that most people see it as just one more diversion, a sport, with politicians our paunch-bellied gladiators and those who bother to pay attention just fans on the sidelines. We paint our faces red or blue and cheer our side and boo their side, and if it takes a late hit or cheap shot to beat the other team, so be it, for winning is all that matters. But I don't think so."

The American political system is like fast food—
mushy, insipid, made out of disgusting parts of things,
and everybody wants some.

P. J. O'ROURKE

Monarchy is the gold filling in a mouth of decay.

JOHN OSBORNE

On the same subject, George Orwell concurred, writing, "England resembles a family, a family with the wrong members in control." Also on the English monarchy, Nancy Mitford observed: "An aristocracy in a republic is like a chicken whose head has been cut off; it may run about in a lively way, but in fact it is dead."

Politics is supposed to be the second oldest profession.
I have come to realize that it bears a very close resemblance to the first.
RONALD REAGAN, *comparing*
politicians to prostitutes

Government is like a baby.
An alimentary canal with a big appetite at one end
and no sense of responsibility at the other.
RONALD REAGAN

Like many of Reagan's lines, this one was borrowed and adapted from someone else. The twentieth-century English clergyman Ronald Knox defined a baby as "A loud noise at one end and no sense of responsibility at the other."

A government is the only known vessel that leaks from the top.
JAMES RESTON

The man who loves other countries as much as his own
stands on a level with the man
who loves other women as much as he loves his own wife.
THEODORE ROOSEVELT

Power is apt to be so insolent and Liberty to be so saucy,
that they are very seldom upon good terms.
GEORGE SAVILE *(Lord Halifax)*

Freedom of the press is to the machinery of the state
what the safety valve is to the steam engine.

ARTHUR SCHOPENHAUER

Politics in the middle of things that concern the imagination
is like a pistol-shot in the middle of a concert.

STENDHAL

This observation comes to mind whenever I see an entertainer or celebrity make a political statement at a concert, awards ceremony, or other cultural event.

Politics is the gizzard of society, full of gut and gravel.

HENRY DAVID THOREAU

Criticizing a political satirist for being unfair
is like criticizing a nose guard for being physical.

GARRY TRUDEAU, *creator of* Doonesbury

Within the first few months I discovered
that being a president is like riding a tiger.
A man has to keep on riding or be swallowed.

HARRY S TRUMAN

These are the opening words of Truman's 1956 *Memoirs*, echoing the words of an ancient Eastern proverb: "Whoever mounts a tiger can never again dismount." Truman, who often expressed himself in vivid metaphorical ways, also wrote: "The White House is the finest jail in the world."

A prince who writes against flattery
is as strange as a pope who writes against infallibility.

VOLTAIRE

The implication is clear—powerful people who say they're immune from flattery are only fooling themselves. Benjamin Disraeli, who served Queen Victoria for many years, expressed it best: "Everyone likes flattery; and when you come to Royalty, you should lay it on with a trowel."

Government is not reason and it is not eloquence. It is force!
Like fire, it is a dangerous servant and a fearful master.
Never for a moment should it be left to irresponsible action.
GEORGE WASHINGTON, *attributed*

This popular quotation appears in many quotation anthologies, and even shows up on a Department of Justice web site. It ostensibly comes from Washington's farewell address, but has never been found in that speech, or anywhere else. It's now regarded as apocryphal.

Politics in America is the binding secular religion.
THEODORE H. WHITE

Politicians are like diapers.
They should be changed frequently, and for the same reason.
ROBIN WILLIAMS

In the 2006 film *Man of the Year*, Williams plays Tom Dobbs, a TV comedian who is persuaded by his fans to run for president. Written and directed by Barry Levinson, the film raises an intriguing question—could a Jon Stewart-like TV star actually become president? It's not a great film, but it does contain this spectacular simile.

The Labor Party is like a stage-coach.
If you rattle along at great speed, everybody inside is too exhilarated
or too seasick to cause any trouble.
But if you stop, everybody gets out and argues about where to go next.
HAROLD WILSON

The seed of revolution is repression.

WOODROW WILSON

The point is that the seed of revolution doesn't germinate in free societies but in oppressive ones. In *The Female Eunuch* (1971), Germaine Greer put it this way: "Revolution is the festival of the oppressed." However, the best line on the subject comes from John Kenneth Galbraith: "All successful revolutions are the kicking in of a rotten door."

Every man who takes office in Washington either grows or swells,
and when I give a man an office,
I watch him carefully to see whether he is swelling or growing.

WOODROW WILSON

chapter 14

Sports Is the
Toy Department of Life

I have two distinct memories of my life as an eighth-grade student at St. Nicholas Elementary School in Garrison, North Dakota, in the mid–1950s. The first was memorizing "Paul Revere's Ride" and then reciting the entire poem without error at a school assembly. I had never read a poem before, much less memorized one, and I still recall the feeling of apprehension when I first committed to the effort, and the ultimate thrill when I finally achieved the goal.

The second memory involves *getting to second base* with a certain female classmate in a darkened cloak room just off an empty classroom. I had never advanced that far before, even though it was something I'd dreamed about for quite some time. Out of a sense of decorum, I won't go into any more detail here. But I will say the experience was quite delightful and exceeded all my expectations.

In the sport of baseball, *getting to first base* is the first step players take as they round the bases on the way to their ultimate goal—scoring a run. In everyday life, the expression is used metaphorically to mean getting off to a good start—or to indicate no progress at all, as when people say "I didn't even make it to first base." In sexual slang, gradations in petting have long been described by this *rounding the bases* analogy, with the final step of sexual intercourse most commonly called *scoring*. Many readers will remember Meat Loaf's *Paradise by the Dashboard Light*, a 1977 rock & roll classic about a couple of teenagers making out inside a parked car, their amorous actions illuminated by the light of the dashboard. The song cleverly blends music and lyrics with the play-by-play voice of the legendary Phil Rizutto, who at the climax of the evening announces in his trademark way: "Holy cow, I think he's gonna make it!"

When people use sports analogies and metaphors, they use concepts from the athletic arena to better understand or describe things in other aspects of life:

You can't steal second base while keeping your foot on first.

This statement, literally true about baseball and metaphorically true about life, advances the notion that life involves risk, and overly cautious people won't get very far.

Sports metaphors show up in all aspects of life, but they are especially prevalent in the business world. Every day, in conference rooms all around the world, people talk about *hitting the bull's-eye, going for the Gold*, or *putting on a full-court press*. The boxing world alone has provided such expressions as *being on the ropes, going down for the count, throwing in the towel*, and *delivering a knock-out blow*. Managers in almost every industry believe it is their job to *pump-up* employees with such exhortations as *be a good team player* or *keep your eye on the ball*.

Who among us doesn't know that we must *learn the playbook* and *stick to the game plan?* And then, if we can *go with the flow* and *sprint to the finish*, we might be able to *win one for the Gipper* (that is, as long as we don't *drop the ball* or somebody doesn't *move the goalposts*).

Politicians rival business people in their fondness for sports metaphors.

An electoral contest is called a *race*, after all, and in all political races at least one candidate trots out the hackneyed notion that an election is a marathon and not a sprint. During an election year, nightly newscasts routinely talk about contests that are *dead heats*, and about candidates who are *gaining ground*, *losing momentum*, or *choking under pressure*. Football metaphors are especially common in politics. Theodore Roosevelt, our earliest sports-minded president, once said:

> **In life, as in a football game,**
> **the principle to follow is: hit the line hard.**

A half century later, John F. Kennedy, another sports-oriented president, said:

> **Politics is like football.**
> **If you see daylight, go through the hole.**

Basketball metaphors are also used with frequency by politicians, some quite famously. In his 2004 best-seller *Plan of Attack*, Pulitzer Prize-winning journalist Bob Woodward provided a behind-the-scenes glimpse into the events leading to the invasion of Iraq in 2003. The book is filled with many tidbits, but none was more interesting than his report of a briefing in the Oval Office on December 21, 2002. Flanking President Bush at that meeting were many high-ranking officials, including Vice President Dick Cheney, National Security Advisor Condoleezza Rice, and CIA Director George Tenet. The purpose of the meeting was to review the evidence for the existence of weapons of mass destruction (WMD) in Iraq. After an initial presentation by CIA intelligence experts, Bush was not overwhelmed. He even made a comment that, on the basis of what had been presented so far, Joe Public would not be convinced. Then, referring specifically to the presence of WMDs, he turned to Tenet and asked, "George, how confident are you?" According to Woodward, the CIA director replied:

Don't worry, it's a slam-dunk!

Tenet, a Georgetown University graduate and a fan of the Georgetown Hoyas basketball team, was using a popular basketball metaphor for *a sure thing*. His meaning appeared unmistakable—WMDs were almost certainly present in Iraq. As all basketball fans know, however, a player will occasionally soar high above the rim on the way to a glorious slam-dunk—and then blow it. A spectacular miss is a huge embarrassment to ballplayers, and Tenet's inapt—or maybe inept—metaphor ultimately became a huge embarrassment for the CIA and the Bush administration. In his 2007 memoir, Tenet downplayed the significance of the remark and even gave it a slightly different interpretation, but he never denied making the metaphorical comment that will forever be part of his legacy.

Just as everyday life is filled with sports metaphors, so the sports world is filled with metaphors from everyday life. Each year, at the beginning of the NCAA basketball tournament, sports analysts wonder who will be this year's *Cinderella team*. On the football gridiron, every weekend from September to January there is at least one quarterback who throws *A Hail Mary*, a long pass thrown into the end zone at the end of regulation time. The underlying analogy is that such passes are desperate prayers, hoping to be answered by the football gods (this notion also shows up in the expression *he threw up a prayer*, which is used in both football and basketball).

In the eighteenth century, English writer Jonathan Swift noticed that popular games often had an aggressive, war-like quality. In a 1711 essay he wrote:

Most sorts of diversion in men, children, and other animals, are an imitation of fighting.

In the essay, Swift planted a *sport-as-fighting* seed that would later blossom into a full-blown *sport-as-war* metaphor. And the most famous observation advancing this notion came in a 1945 essay "The Sporting Spirit," by George Orwell:

**Serious sport has nothing to do with fair play.
It is bound up with hatred, jealousy, boastfulness,
disregard of all rules, and sadistic pleasure in witnessing violence.
In other words, it is war minus the shooting.**

This may be history's finest observation on the subject, but it's certainly not the only one. In a 1988 interview, Berkeley sociology professor and sports consultant Harry Edwards picked up on the theme when he said:

**Football is about as close as you can get to war
and still remain civilized.**

And in a 1960 *Sports Illustrated* article, Frank Gifford, the star running back for the New York Giants, was quoted as saying:

**Pro football is like nuclear warfare.
There are no winners, only survivors.**

At first, this looks like hyperbole—and technically, I guess it is. But in this case, we might forgive the exaggeration. Readers of a certain age remember Gifford as one of the great football players of his era. An All-American at USC before being selected by the Giants in 1952, he took the team to five NFL championship games and was league MVP in 1956. In 1960, he suffered one of the most brutal hits in NFL history when Chuck Bednarik of the Philadelphia Eagles blindsided him, knocking him out and causing a serious head injury. The play—legal at the time, but not allowed today—looked like a career-ender, as Gifford announced his retirement a short while later. Incredibly, though, he returned to the game in 1962—this time as a wide receiver—and performed so effectively that the very next year he was selected to the Pro Bowl, his seventh and final appearance.

When most Americans think of sports analogies, they tend to think of the major sports, like baseball, basketball, football, golf, tennis, and soccer. But almost every sport played by human beings has stimulated—or been described by—metaphorical observations. In a 1987 article on the sport of croquet, a writer for London's *Sunday Times* observed:

> **The clunk of the ball against mallet is a lovely sound,**
> **just like ice cubes in a gin and tonic.**

And here's a metaphorical sampler on some other not-so-common sports:

Yachting is like standing in a cold shower and tearing up hundred-dollar bills.
> ANONYMOUS

Squash is boxing with racquets.
> JONAH BARRINGTON, *English squash player*

It is like balancing an egg on a spoon while shooting the rapids.
> GRAHAM HILL, *on Formula One racing*

Whoever called snooker "chess with balls" was rude, but right.
> CLIVE JAMES

Fencing is like playing chess with a sword in your hand.
> VALENTINA SIDOROVA,
> *Soviet fencer & 1976 Olympic gold medalist*

Playing polo is like trying to play golf during an earthquake.
> SYLVESTER STALLONE, *actor & polo player*

Cricket is baseball on Valium.
ROBIN WILLIAMS

Whether you prefer major sports or the more esoteric ones, here's hoping you enjoy the rest of the metaphorical observations in the remainder of this chapter.

I never thought home runs were all that exciting.
I still think the triple is the most exciting thing in baseball.
To me, a triple is like a guy taking the ball on his one-yard line
and running ninety-nine yards for a touchdown.
HENRY "HANK" AARON

Float like a butterfly, sting like a bee.
The hand can't hit what the eye can't see.
MUHAMMAD ALI

This was Ali's legendary description of his boxing style, probably inspired by a remark from his cornerman, Drew "Bundini" Brown. From a technical point of view, Ali's talent as a poet lagged far behind his pugilistic skills. Norman Mailer described it all in a memorable analogy: "For Ali to compose a few words of real poetry would be equal to an intellectual throwing a good punch."

Your body is like a bar of soap.
The more you use it, the more it wears down.
DICK ALLEN

In America, it is sport that is the opiate of the masses.
RUSSELL BAKER

This line, from a 1967 *New York Times* article, alters Karl Marx's famous metaphor about religion being the opiate of the people.

**Playing for Yogi is like playing for your father;
playing for Billy is like playing for your father-in-law.**

DON BAYLOR

Here, the popular *New York Yankees* ballplayer colorfully contrasts two of the club's best-known managers, Yogi Berra and Billy Martin.

**A catcher and his body are like the outlaw and his horse.
He's got to ride that nag till it drops.**

JOHNNY BENCH

**Bodie was out trying to steal second.
His head was full of larceny, but his feet were honest.**

ARTHUR "BUGS" BAER,
on Yankees ballplayer "Ping" Bodie

This is a classic line in the history of sports journalism, written in 1920 by a master of the craft. Baer, who created the nickname "The Sultan of Swat" for Babe Ruth, was widely admired for his wit and ability to turn a phrase.

If fishing is a religion, fly-fishing is high church.

TOM BROKAW

Fly-fishing fanatics approach their sport with religious fervor. Robert Traver (the pen name of Michigan Supreme Court Judge John D. Voelker) was the author of the 1958 novel *Anatomy of a Murder* and an avid fly-fisherman. He said: "Deep down I've always known fly fishing is to the rest of fishing what high seduction is to rape." And more recently, American sportswriter Howell Raines wrote: "Fly-fishing is to fishing as ballet is to walking."

Boxing's just show business with blood.

FRANK BRUNO

For those of us who are baseball fans and agnostics,
the Hall of Fame is as close to a religious experience as we may ever get.

BILL BRYSON

It's like a woman concentrating on intricate sewing.
If she pricked her finger she'd hardly notice it and just carry on.

JOE BUGNER

This was Bugner's description of how a good boxer absorbs blows from an opponent. Bugner was a British boxer who won the British and European heavyweight title in 1971. He went on to fight Muhammad Ali in 1973 and Joe Frazier in 1974, going the distance in both fights, but in each case losing on points. He had a defensive boxing style that most fans considered dull (one writer said he had "the physique of a Greek statue, but fewer moves").

My back swing off the first tee had put him in mind
of an elderly woman of dubious morals trying to
struggle out of a dress too tight around the shoulders.

PATRICK CAMPBELL

I call tennis the McDonald's of sport—you go in,
they make a quick buck out of you, and you're out.

PAT CASH

To be an American and unable to play baseball
is comparable to being a Polynesian and unable to swim.

JOHN CHEEVER

New Yorkers love it when you spill your guts out there.
Spill your guts at Wimbledon and they make you stop and clean it up.

JIMMY CONNORS

Sports is the toy department of life.
HOWARD COSELL

On his favorite sport, Cosell wrote that "Boxing is drama on its grandest scale."

Golf is like a love affair.
If you don't take it seriously, it's no fun;
if you do take it seriously, it breaks your heart.
ARNOLD DALY

A tie is like kissing your sister.
HUGH "DUFFY" DAUGHERTY

In 1966, Coach Daugherty's Michigan State University Spartans, with nine wins and no losses (and second in the national rankings) played unbeaten Notre Dame, ranked number one. Dubbed "the Game of the Century," it ended in a 10–10 tie, and both teams shared the national championship at season's end. Tie games have always been unsatisfying, but nobody had ever described that feeling better, making Daugherty's quip an instant classic. In 1986, George Brett of the Kansas City Royals updated the thought: "If a tie is like kissing your sister, losing is like kissing your grandmother with her teeth out."

Golf and sex are the only things you can enjoy without being good at them.
JIMMY DEMARET

Skating was the vessel into which I could pour my heart and soul.
PEGGY FLEMING

The triple is the most exciting play of the game.
A triple is like meeting a woman who excites you,

spending the evening talking and getting more excited, then taking her home.
It drags on and on. You're never sure how it's going to turn out.

GEORGE FOSTER

Kill the body and the head will die.

JOE FRAZIER,
on his boxing strategy

Golf balls are attracted to water as unerringly
as the eye of a middle-aged man to a female bosom.

MICHAEL GREEN

A muscle is like a car.
If you want it to run well early in the morning, you have to warm it up.

FLORENCE GRIFFITH-JOYNER

The most beautiful fighting machine I have ever seen.

ERNEST HEMINGWAY, *on Joe Louis*

All fighters are prostitutes and all promoters are pimps.

LARRY HOLMES

College football is a sport that bears the same relation to education
that bullfighting does to agriculture.

ELBERT HUBBARD

Like a Volvo, Borg is rugged, has a good after-sales service, and is very dull.

CLIVE JAMES, *on Björn Borg*

James wrote this in 1980, at the end of a decade in which Borg dominated
the tennis world. Borg's tennis demeanor contrasted starkly with the passionate play of Americans like Jimmy Connors and John McEnroe, leading

James to liken the Swedish Borg to the vehicles manufactured in his native country.

Competitive golf is played mainly on a five-and-a-half-inch course: the space between your ears.

BOBBY JONES

Football players, like prostitutes, are in the business of ruining their bodies for the pleasure of strangers.

MERLE KESSLER

A boxing match is like a cowboy movie. There's got to be good guys and there's got to be bad guys. And that's what people pay for—to see the bad guys get beat.

SONNY LISTON

Throwing people out of a game is like learning to ride a bicycle— once you get the hang of it, it can be a lot of fun.

RON LUCIANO,
on being a baseball umpire

Many baseball fans look upon an umpire as a sort of necessary evil to the luxury of baseball, like the odor that follows an automobile.

CHRISTY MATHEWSON

Baseball is a game, yes. It is also a business. But what it most truly is, is disguised combat. For all its gentility, its almost leisurely pace, baseball is violence under wraps.

WILLIE MAYS

A pool player in a tuxedo is like whipped cream on a hot dog.

MINNESOTA FATS *(Rudolf Wanderone)*

**Bobby admits he has "a temper problem"—
which is like Jeffrey Dahmer saying that he suffers from an eating disorder.**

LANCE MORROW, *on Bobby Knight*

Dahmer, of course, was the American serial killer who became infamous in the early 1990s for the gruesome way he dismembered and cannibalized his victims. This observation from Morrow appeared in a 2000 *Time* magazine article. Knight, at the time the head basketball coach at Indiana University, was notorious for his courtside eruptions. After formally investigating Knight's "pattern of inappropriate behavior," the school suspended the volatile coach for three games and fined him $30,000. It was the first step on the way out for Knight, who went on to become the head basketball coach at Texas Tech.

**Most riders beat horses as if they were guards in slave-labor camps.
Shoe treated them as if he were asking them to dance.**

JIM MURRAY,
on jockey Willie Shoemaker

**Boxing is a celebration of the lost religion of masculinity,
all the more trenchant for its being lost.**

JOYCE CAROL OATES

This is from Oates's 1987 book *On Boxing*. As a child she was introduced by her father to "the sweet science" (an increasingly controversial metaphor). A lifelong fan, she also wrote that "Boxing has become America's tragic theater."

**I'm like the Pythagorean theorem.
Not too many people know the answer to my game.**

SHAQUILLE O'NEAL, *in a rare
example of metaphorical boasting*

What other people may find in poetry, I find in the flight of a good drive.

ARNOLD PALMER

Golf is a puzzle without an answer.

GARY PLAYER

The basketball is a tool that the Black man has now,
same as maybe once he had a plow.

WILLIS REED

Luck is the residue of design.

BRANCH RICKEY

Rickey is best known for signing Jackie Robinson to a contract with the Brooklyn Dodgers in 1945, but he also contributed some famous quotations—like this classic metaphor on luck and the immortal "Baseball is a game of inches."

Baseball is like a poker game.
Nobody wants to quit when he's losing;
nobody wants you to quit when you're ahead.

JACKIE ROBINSON

What they call a baseball "glove"
bears as much resemblance to a human hand
as snowshoes bear to a man's feet.
It's not a glove; it's a leather basket.

ANDY ROONEY

I threw the kitchen sink at him, but he went to the bathroom and got his tub.

ANDY RODDICK,
on Roger Federer

This was Roddick's assessment after losing to Federer in the Wimbledon Finals in 2004.

> **Athletic proficiency is a mighty good servant,**
> **and like so many other good servants, a mighty bad master.**
> THEODORE ROOSEVELT

Roosevelt wrote this in a 1903 letter to his son Ted. The thought was preceded by these words: "I am delighted to have you play football. I believe in rough, manly sports. But I do not believe in them if they degenerate into the sole end of any one's existence. I don't want you to sacrifice standing well in your studies to any over-athleticism; and I need not tell you that character counts for a great deal more than either intellect or body in winning success in life."

> **Hating the New York Yankees is as American as apple pie,**
> **unwed mothers, and cheating on your income tax.**
> MIKE ROYKO

> **Making love is like hitting a baseball;**
> **you just gotta relax and concentrate.**
> SUSAN SARANDON

These words were delivered by Sarandon in the opening narration of the 1988 film *Bull Durham* (screenplay by Ron Shelton). Sarandon plays Annie Savoy, a sexy baseball fan who each year selects a minor league player as a lover and then puts the athlete through her own version of a player development project.

> **Football is to baseball as blackjack is to bridge.**
> **One is the quick jolt; the other the deliberate, slow-paced game of skill.**
> VIN SCULLY

**Statistics are used by baseball fans
in much the same way that a drunk leans against a street lamp;
it's there more for support than enlightenment.**

VIN SCULLY

This analogy was inspired by a famous remark from the nineteenth-century Scottish writer Andrew Lang, who said of a contemporary: "He uses statistics as a drunken man uses lamp-posts—for support rather than illumination." On the same subject, an anonymous wag once said, "Baseball is an island of activity amidst a sea of statistics." And CBS newsman Harry Reasoner agreed, once observing: "Statistics are to baseball what a flaky crust is to Mom's apple pie."

Bridge is a sport of the mind.

OMAR SHARIF

**Trying to sneak a fastball past Henry Aaron
was like trying to sneak the sun past a rooster.**

CURT SIMMONS

It was like watching an autopsy performed on a live person.

SYLVESTER STALLONE

This was Stallone's graphic assessment of the 1980 Larry Holmes–Muhammad Ali heavyweight championship fight, when the aging Ali, at age thirty-eight, was no match for his youthful opponent. It was a vicious beating—stopped after ten rounds—and some analysts wondered how Ali had even survived the fight.

**Angling may be said to be so like the mathematics
that it can never be fully learnt.**

IZAAK WALTON

This comes from *The Compleat Angler*, a 1653 treatise on fishing that was interspersed with maxims, verse, and reflections on life. Walton had only a few years of schooling, but after apprenticing with a London ironmonger, he acquired a small shop of his own and began to prosper. With more leisure, he read widely and began to associate with men of learning, including John Donne, who became his friend and fishing companion. His famous book also contained this analogy: "As no man is born an artist, so no man is born an angler."

**My golf swing is like ironing a shirt. You get one side smoothed out,
turn it over and there is a big wrinkle on the other side.
You iron that side, turn it over and there's another wrinkle.**

TOM WATSON

Baseball is like church. Many attend, but few understand.

WES WESTRUM

Ernie Harwell, a veteran sportscaster, offered a related observation: "Opening day . . . is to baseball what Easter is to church. The faithful come out, but a lot of once-a-year attendees are there too." And in a 2004 column, respected baseball scholar John Thorn continued the church analogy when he wrote: "At a ballgame, as in a place of worship, no one is alone in the crowd."

**Super Bowl Sunday is to the compulsive gambler
what New Year's Eve is to the alcoholic.**

ARNIE WEXLER

When he said this in 1994, Wexler was executive director of New Jersey's Council on Compulsive Gambling.

It has been said that baseball is to the United States
what revolutions are to Latin America,
a safety valve for letting off steam.

GEORGE WILL

Football combines the two worst features of modern American life.
It's violence punctuated by committee meetings.

GEORGE WILL

Will has offered several variations of this remark over the years, but the first came in his *Newsweek* column in 1976. It's possible that he was inspired by a somewhat similar comment Winston Churchill made when he attended his first American football game: "Actually, it is somewhat like rugby. But why do they have to have all those committee meetings?"

Stealing bases is like jumping out of a car
that's going twenty miles per hour.

WILLIE WILSON

Running is the greatest metaphor for life,
because you get out of it what you put into it.

OPRAH WINFREY

chapter 15

Writing Is the Manual Labor of the Mind

Writers are commonly called *wordsmiths*, but it might be more accurate to call them *ideasmiths*, for they live in a world of *ideas* as much as of *words*. In 1890, French writer Paul Bourget expressed the importance of ideas in an analogy:

Ideas are to literature what light is to painting.

For many creative people, ideas are like a flash flood, arriving without advance warning and carrying everything along with it. It can be a frenzied process, and there is always the danger that the torrent will engulf a writer, who is trying to put the key elements of the idea into words before it exits the mind. This may have been what F. Scott Fitzgerald had in mind when he once wrote in a letter to his daughter:

All good writing is swimming under water and holding your breath.

At one time or another, all writers have tried to describe the process of transforming ideas into words on a page. But nobody has ever captured the drama better than Honoré de Balzac:

> **Ideas quick-march into motion like battalions of a grand army**
> **to its legendary fighting ground, and the battle rages.**
> **Memories charge in, bright flags on high;**
> **the cavalry of metaphor deploys with a magnificent gallop;**
> **the artillery of logic rushes up with clattering wagons and cartridges;**
> **flashes of wit pop up like sharpshooters;**
> **forms and shapes and characters rear up;**
> **the paper is spread with ink.**

Many writers subscribe to the theory that ideas come with the charge of an explosive. In an 1857 letter to a friend, Henry David Thoreau wrote:

> **New ideas come into this world somewhat like falling meteors,**
> **with a flash and an explosion,**
> **and perhaps somebody's castle-roof perforated.**

And in his 1902 classic, *The Varieties of Religious Experience*, William James wrote:

> **An idea, to be suggestive, must come**
> **to the individual with the force of revelation.**

While some ideas arrive with the power of a thunderbolt, others announce themselves in a soft whisper, barely able to be heard. Still others resemble a seed that must be nurtured before it germinates. This more subtle and tender process was described by Ernest Hemingway in a 1929 conversation with Gertrude Stein and F. Scott Fitzgerald:

> **When I have an idea, I turn down the flame,**
> **as if it were a little alcohol stove, as low as it will go.**
> **Then it explodes and that is my idea.**

In yet another variation, ideas sometimes multiply rapidly:

> **Ideas are like rabbits. You get a couple and learn how to handle them,**
> **and pretty soon you have a dozen.**
> JOHN STEINBECK

And sometimes they need to be coaxed before they give up their secrets:

> **An idea, like a ghost . . . must be spoken to a little before it will explain itself.**
> CHARLES DICKENS

While some writers struggle with the problem of too many ideas, others despair over having too few. In a 1752 letter to a friend, Horace Walpole put it this way:

> **Every drop of ink in my pen ran cold.**

Every writer has experienced a literary drought—most commonly called *a writer's block*—and almost all have tried to describe it. But few descriptions of the phenomenon can rival a passage that appears on the very first page of William Styron's 1979 novel, *Sophie's Choice*. The words come from Stingo, the protagonist, who has recently lost his job as a manuscript reader at McGraw-Hill. It is 1947, and Stingo, two years out of the military, has moved from Virginia to New York to pursue a writing career. Now, living in a Brooklyn rooming house, he is out of work, almost out of money, and in the middle of serious dry spell—a condition he describes masterfully:

At twenty-two, struggling to become some kind of writer,
I found that the creative heat which at eighteen
had nearly consumed me with its gorgeous, relentless flame
had flickered out to a dim pilot light
registering little more than a token glow in my breast,
or wherever my hungriest aspirations once resided.
It was not that I no longer wanted to write,
I still yearned passionately to produce the novel
which had been for so long captive in my brain.
It was only that, having written down the first few fine paragraphs,
I could not produce any others, or—to approximate Gertrude Stein's
remark about a lesser writer of the Lost Generation—
I had the syrup but it wouldn't pour.

When you are trying to generate ideas with traction for a mind that has been spinning its wheels, there are few better methods than walking away from your writing table, picking up a book from a favorite author, reading for a while, and then reflecting on what you've read. It's like priming a pump. You pour a little water in, begin pumping on the handle like mad, and the water often starts gushing out. Of course, by reading the works of other writers, you always run the risk of inadvertently pilfering a phrase or two, but it's probably a risk worth taking. And if you're ever accused of leaning on others for your ideas, my recommendation is to plead guilty. It might be called the Thornton Wilder Defense after his remark:

I do borrow from other writers, shamelessly! I can only say in my defense,
like the woman brought before the judge on a charge of kleptomania,
"I do steal, but, your Honor, only from the very best stores."

Another remedy for those who are having trouble writing is to begin talking. There's something about *thinking out loud*—whether done to a friend, aloud to oneself, or into a tape recorder—that gets the juices flowing again. Robert Frost said it this way:

Talking is a hydrant in the yard and writing is a faucet upstairs in the house. Opening the first takes all the pressure off the second.

No matter how ideas come—by flash, incubation, larceny, or pressure release— they must be turned into words before they can be turned into literature. This is where the actual task of writing begins. And as long as there have been writers, there have been people advising them how to do it. The first great writing advice book was *The Elements of Style*, a 1918 guide by William Strunk, Jr., a professor of English at Cornell University. Strunk, who believed that writers used too many words to express their ideas, advocated an economy of style. "Omit needless words," he advised. "Vigorous writing is concise." And then he wrote:

A sentence should contain no unnecessary words,
a paragraph no unnecessary sentences,
for the same reason that a drawing should have no unnecessary lines
and a machine no unnecessary parts.
This requires not that the writer make all his sentences short,
or that he avoid all detail . . . but that every word tell.

In 1959, E. B. White of *The New Yorker* magazine—and a student of Professor Strunk's forty years earlier—came out with a revised and updated edition of *The Elements of Style*. The writing world, hungry for a new style guide, gobbled up over ten million copies of *Strunk & White*—as it was called—over the next forty years. In the new edition, White continued the tradition of phrasing prescriptive writing advice in dramatic metaphorical ways:

Avoid the use of qualifiers. *Rather, very, little, pretty*—
these are the leeches that infest the pond of prose, sucking the blood of words.

Strunk and White were not the first people in history to use fanciful metaphorical imagery while providing writing advice. The nineteenth-century English poet Robert Southey was a critic of elaborate writing and the champion of a lean, vigorous style. He wrote:

**If you would be pungent, be brief; for it is with words as with sunbeams—
the more they are condensed, the deeper they burn.**

While there are wide differences of opinion as to the role of ideas in writing—or even what constitutes good writing—a definite consensus has emerged among writers when it comes to critics and reviewers. In his 1930 book *On Literature*, Maxim Gorky provides an extraordinary passage from Anton Chekhov, who begins with a simple but spectacular simile:

Critics are like horse-flies which hinder the horses in their plowing of the soil.

But then Chekhov takes off on an unexpected, but equally spectacular, flight of fancy. It's a bit lengthy, but I think you'll enjoy the full passage:

**The muscles of the horse are as taut as fiddle-strings,
and suddenly a horse-fly alights on its croup, buzzing and stinging.
The horse's skin quivers, it waves its tail.
What is the fly buzzing about? It probably doesn't know itself.
It simply has a restless nature and wants to make itself felt—
"I'm alive, too, you know!" it seems to say.
"Look, I know how to buzz, there's nothing I can't buzz about!"
I've been reading reviews of my stories for twenty-five years, and
can't remember a single useful point in any of them, or the slightest good advice.
The only reviewer who ever made an impression on me was Skabichevsky,
who prophesied that I would die drunk in the bottom of a ditch.**

Henry Wadsworth Longfellow didn't take such a harsh view of critics, once even calling them "sentinels in the grand army of letters, stationed at the corners of newspapers and reviews, to challenge every new author." But he didn't view them all favorably:

Some critics are like chimneysweepers;
they put out the fire below, and frighten the swallows from the nests above;
they scrape a long time in the chimney, cover themselves with soot,
and bring nothing away but a bag of cinders,
and then sing out from the top of the house, as if they had built it.

At the end of this chapter, I will provide a compilation titled "Writers on Critics & Reviewers: A Metaphorical Potpourri." In that section you will find a few dozen additional things writers have said about critics—all negative, and all metaphorical.

Before we get to that, though, let's begin this final chapter of the book by featuring more analogies, metaphors, and similes about the literary life.

The career of a writer is comparable to that of a woman of easy virtue.
You write first for pleasure, later for the pleasure of others, and finally for money.
MARCEL ACHARD

Achard was a French writer whose play *The Idiot* was made into the Hollywood film *A Shot in the Dark* (with Peter Sellers as Inspector Clouseau). A similar observation has been attributed to Moliére: "Writing is like prostitution. First you do it for love, and then for a few close friends, and then for money."

Talent is like a faucet, while it is open, one must write.
JEAN ANOUILH

It is easy to write a check if you have enough money in the bank,
and writing comes more easily if you have something to say.
SHOLEM ASCH

Writing, to me, is simply thinking through my fingers.
ISAAC ASIMOV

Asimov was one of history's most prolific authors, with over five hundred books to his credit. He once wrote, "I write for the same reason I breathe—because if I didn't, I would die."

Old books that have ceased to be of service should no more be abandoned than should old friends who have ceased to give pleasure.
BERNARD BARUCH

Fitting people with books is about as difficult as fitting them with shoes.
SYLVIA BEACH

Just as there is nothing between the admirable omelette and the intolerable, so with autobiography.
HILAIRE BELLOC

That is, with omelettes and autobiographies, either they're great, or they stink.

With a novelist, like a surgeon, you have to get a feeling that you've fallen into good hands— someone from whom you can accept the anesthetic with confidence.
SAUL BELLOW

Conversation is the legs on which thought walks; and writing, the wings by which it flies.
MARGUERITE BLESSINGTON

I go to books and to nature as a bee goes to the flower, for a nectar that I can make into my own honey.
JOHN BURROUGHS

In 1842, Nathaniel Hawthorne used the same metaphor to make a slightly different point: "Bees are sometimes drowned (or suffocated) in the honey which they collect. So some writers are lost in their collected learning."

To read without reflecting is like eating without digesting.
EDMUND BURKE

Translations (like wives) are seldom faithful if they are in the least attractive.
ROY CAMPBELL

A novel is never anything but a philosophy put into images.
ALBERT CAMUS

Writing has laws of perspective, of light and shade,
just as painting does, or music.
If you are born knowing them, fine. If not, learn them.
Then rearrange the rules to suit yourself.
TRUMAN CAPOTE

The American writer B. J. (Beatrice Joy) Chute, who taught creative writing at Barnard College for many years, wrote similarly: "Grammar is to a writer what anatomy is to a sculptor, or the scales to a musician. You may loathe it, it may bore you, but nothing will replace it, and once mastered it will support you like a rock."

Writing is to descend like a miner to the depths of the mine
with a lamp on your forehead,
a light whose dubious brightness falsifies everything,
whose wick is in permanent danger of explosion,
whose blinking illumination in the coal dust exhausts and corrodes your eyes.
BLAISE CENDRARS

Anaïs Nin agreed: "To write is to descend, to excavate, to go underground." And James Baldwin put it this way: "The responsibility of a writer is to excavate the experience of the people who produced him."

After the writer's death, reading his journal is like receiving a long letter.

JEAN COCTEAU

Authors are sometimes like tomcats:
they distrust all the other toms, but they are kind to kittens.

MALCOLM COWLEY

An autobiography is an obituary in serial form with the last installment missing.

QUENTIN CRISP

I think of an author as somebody who goes into the marketplace
and puts down his rug and says, "I will tell you a story,"
and then he passes the hat.

ROBERTSON DAVIES

A truly great book should be read in youth, again in maturity,
and once more in old age, as a fine building should be seen
by morning light, at noon, and by moonlight.

ROBERTSON DAVIES

The author who speaks about his own books is almost as bad
as a mother who talks about her own children.

BENJAMIN DISRAELI

Employing a similar metaphor, Alex Haley of *Roots* fame wrote: "I look at my books the way parents look at their children. The fact that one becomes more successful than the others doesn't make me love the less successful one any less."

Writing is like driving at night in the fog.
You can only see as far as your headlights,
but you can make the whole trip that way.

E. L. DOCTOROW

Writing is a socially acceptable form of schizophrenia.

E. L. DOCTOROW

Is writing a disease, or a cure? Graham Greene wrote, "Writing is a form of therapy; sometimes I wonder how all those who do not write, compose, or paint can manage to escape the madness . . . which is inherent in a human situation."

It is with publishers as with wives: one always wants somebody else's.

NORMAN DOUGLAS

Writing is manual labor of the mind: a job, like laying pipe.

JOHN GREGORY DUNNE

Cut out all those exclamation marks.
An exclamation mark is like laughing at your own joke.

F. SCOTT FITZGERALD

This is the most famous simile on the subject of exclamation marks, but it's not the only one. In a 1976 *Punch* article, Miles Kingston wrote, "So far as good writing goes, the use of the exclamation mark is a sign of failure. It is the literary equivalent of a man holding up a card reading LAUGHTER to a studio audience."

It's splendid to be a great writer, to put men into
the frying pan of your imagination and make them pop like chestnuts.

GUSTAVE FLAUBERT

I am irritated by my writing. I am like a violinist whose ear is true,
but whose fingers refuse to reproduce precisely the sounds he hears within.

GUSTAVE FLAUBERT

This is from an 1845 letter Flaubert wrote to his mistress, Louise Colet. In another letter to her, he wrote: "I love my work with a frenetic and perverse love, as an ascetic loves the hair shirt which scratches his belly."

Word carpentry is like any other kind of carpentry:
you must join your sentences smoothly.

ANATOLE FRANCE

The most technologically efficient machine
that man has ever invented is the book.

NORTHROP FRYE

Prose books are the show dogs I breed and sell to support my cat.

ROBERT GRAVES

Graves, a celebrated poet, wrote novels and non-fiction works to finance the publication of his poetry, an arrangement he expresses so exquisitely here.

Biography is a very definite region bounded on the north by history,
on the south by fiction, on the east by obituary, and on the west by tedium.

PHILIP GUEDALLA

Guedalla, an English barrister who gave up a legal career in 1913 to pursue his interest in history and biography, went on to write more than thirty books. He also wrote: "Biography, like big game hunting, is one of the recognized forms of sport, and it is as unfair as only sport can be."

Prose is architecture, not interior decoration.
ERNEST HEMINGWAY

I started out very quietly and I beat Mr. Turgenev.
Then I trained hard and I beat Mr. de Maupassant.
I've fought two draws with Mr. Stendhal,
and I think I had the edge in the last one.
But nobody's going to get me in any ring with Mr. Tolstoy
unless I'm crazy or I keep getting better.
ERNEST HEMINGWAY

This well-known boxing analogy appeared in a 1950 *New Yorker* profile that Lillian Ross did on Hemingway. The comment was not well received by critics, who viewed it as grandiose. In the interview, Hemingway also used a few baseball metaphors. He said, "I learned my knuckle-ball" from Baudelaire and he added that Flaubert "always threw them perfectly straight, hard, high, and inside." He also compared a writer to a starting baseball pitcher, saying a novelist "has to go the full nine, even if it kills him."

The most foolish kind of a book is a kind of leaky boat on the sea of wisdom;
some of the wisdom will get in anyhow.
OLIVER WENDELL HOLMES, SR.

Writing a novel, like making chicken soup or making love,
is an idiosyncratic occupation; probably no two people do it the same way.
SUSAN ISAACS

Footnotes—little dogs yapping at the heels of the text.
WILLIAM JAMES

This may be the best thing ever written about footnotes; but a serious rival comes from Nöel Coward: "Having to read a footnote resembles having to go downstairs to answer the door while in the midst of making love."

Being a writer is like having homework every night for the rest of your life.
LAWRENCE KASDAN

My imagination is a monastery and I am its monk.
JOHN KEATS

**Liking a writer and then meeting the writer
is like liking goose liver and then meeting the goose.**
ARTHUR KOESTLER

**I'm like a big old hen.
I can't cluck too long about the egg I've just laid
because I've got five more inside me pushing to get out.**
LOUIS L'AMOUR

L'Amour also wrote, "A writer's brain is like a magician's hat. If you're going to get anything out of it, you have to put something in it first."

**Magazines all too frequently lead to books
and should be regarded as the heavy petting of literature.**
FRAN LEBOWITZ

Writing books is the closest men ever come to childbearing.
NORMAN MAILER

The writer Walker Percy might have been thinking about Mailer's observation when he wrote: "Somebody compared novel-writing to having a baby, but for me it is the conception which is painful and the delivery which is easy."

In literature as in love we are astonished at what is chosen by others.
ANDRÉ MAUROIS

You expect far too much of a first sentence.
Think of it as analogous to a good country breakfast:
what we want is something simple, but nourishing to the imagination.
Hold the philosophy, hold the adjectives, just give us a plain subject and verb
and perhaps a wholesome, nonfattening adverb or two.
LARRY MCMURTRY

I write in order to attain that feeling of tension relieved
and function achieved which a cow enjoys on giving milk.
H.L. MENCKEN

Mencken realized that not all authors viewed the process of writing in this way. He once wrote, "The art of writing, like the art of love, runs all the way from a kind of routine hard to distinguish from piling bricks to a kind of frenzy closely related to delirium tremens."

The structure of a play is always
the story of how the birds came home to roost.
ARTHUR MILLER

The more familiar metaphor is *chickens coming home to roost*, but it means the same thing—our deeds and choices come back to haunt us, like chickens returning to the henhouse each night. The idea was first expressed in 1810 by English poet Robert Southey: "Curses are like young chickens, they always come home to roost." It's also what Robert Louis Stevenson had in mind in his famous "banquet of consequences" line, which we examined earlier.

Writing a book is a long, exhausting struggle,
like a long bout of some painful illness.

One would never undertake such a thing if one were not driven
by some demon whom one can neither resist nor understand.

GEORGE ORWELL

True ease in writing comes from Art, not chance,
As those move easiest who have learned to dance.

ALEXANDER POPE

Long sentences in a short composition are like large rooms in a little house.

WILLIAM SHENSTONE

Writing is easy. You just sit down at the typewriter,
open up a vein, and bleed it out drop by drop.

WALTER "RED" SMITH

This is the best known of the analogies that view writing as a kind of
blood-letting. The first articulation of the idea came from Sydney Smith,
who said of the nineteenth-century English politician Henry Fox: "Fox
wrote drop by drop." A popular variation on the theme comes from the
American screenwriter Gene Fowler: "Writing is easy. All you do is stare at
a blank sheet of paper until drops of blood form on your forehead."

A great writer is, so to speak, a second government in his country.
And for that reason, no regime has ever loved great writers, only minor ones.

ALEXANDER SOLZHENITSYN

A novel is a mirror which passes over a highway.
Sometimes it reflects to your eyes the blue of the skies,
at others the churned-up mud of the road.

STENDHAL

Writing, when properly managed, is but a different name for conversation.

LAURENCE STERNE

Authors are actors, books are theaters.

WALLACE STEVENS

Along the same lines, Rod Serling wrote, "Every writer is a frustrated actor who recites his lines in the hidden auditorium of his skull."

Fiction is to the grown man what play is to the child.

ROBERT LOUIS STEVENSON

Write while the heat is in you.
The writer who postpones the recording of his thoughts
uses an iron which has cooled to burn a hole with.
He cannot inflame the minds of his audience.

HENRY DAVID THOREAU

A sentence should read as if its author,
had he held a plough instead of a pen,
could have drawn a furrow deep and straight to the end.

HENRY DAVID THOREAU

A writer judging his own work is like a deceived husband—
he is frequently the last person to appreciate the true state of affairs.

ROBERT TRAVER

Robert Traver is the pen name of John D. Voelker, a Michigan lawyer who was a prosecuting attorney before becoming a Michigan Supreme Court Justice. He wrote many books reflecting his two passions—the law and fly-fishing—but is best remembered for the 1958 book *Anatomy of a Murder*.

Show me a congenital eavesdropper with the instincts of a Peeping Tom
and I will show you the makings of a dramatist.

KENNETH TYNAN

High and fine literature is wine, and mine is only water;
but everybody likes water.

MARK TWAIN

Twain wrote this in an 1887 letter to a friend, but the idea first occurred to him two years earlier. An 1885 journal entry, written exactly this way, went as follows: "My books are water; those of the great geniuses is wine. Everybody drinks water."

The instruction we find in books is like fire.
We fetch it from our neighbors, kindle it at home,
communicate it to others, and it becomes the property of all.

VOLTAIRE

It is with books as with men;
a very small number play a great part; the rest are lost in the multitude.

VOLTAIRE

On the books that have played a great part, the American poet and writer Thomas Bailey Aldrich observed: "Books that have become classics—books that have had their day and now get more praise than perusal—always remind me of retired colonels and majors and captains who, having reached the age limit, find themselves retired on half pay."

I can never understand how two men can write a book together;
to me that's like three people getting together to have a baby.

EVELYN WAUGH

Delay is natural to a writer. He is like a surfer—
he bides his time, waits for the perfect wave on which to ride in.
Delay is instinctive with him.
He waits for the surge . . . that will carry him along.

E. B. WHITE

Fiction is like a spider's web, attached ever so lightly perhaps, but still attached to life at all four corners.

VIRGINIA WOOLF

Writing a novel is like building a wall brick by brick; only amateurs believe in inspiration.

FRANK YERBY

Edna Ferber said similarly: "Only amateurs say that they write for their own amusement. Writing is not an amusing occupation. It is a combination of ditch-digging, mountain-climbing, treadmill, and childbirth. Writing may be interesting, absorbing, exhilarating, racking, relieving. But amusing? Never!"

Writing is thinking on paper.

WILLIAM ZINSSER

WRITERS ON CRITICS & REVIEWERS:
A METAPHORICAL POTPOURRI

The poison pens of writers have been directed at many targets over the years, but never more venomously than when aimed at critics and reviewers. A sampling of the best appear below.

American critics are like American universities.
They both have dull and half-dead faculties.

EDWARD ALBEE

Reviewers are, as Coleridge declared,
a species of maggots, inferior to bookworms,
living on the delicious brains of real genius.

WALTER BAGEHOT

A critic is a bundle of biases held
loosely together by a sense of taste.

WHITNEY BALLIETT

Critics are like eunuchs in a harem. They're there every night,
they see how it should be done every night,
but they can't do it themselves.

BRENDAN BEHAN

A good writer is not, per se, a good book critic.
No more than a good drunk is automatically a good bartender.

JIM BISHOP

And, of course, with the birth of the artist
came the inevitable afterbirth—the critic.

MEL BROOKS, *from*
History of the World, Part I

Critics . . .
Those cut-throat bandits in the paths of fame.

ROBERT BURNS

The critic roams through culture, looking for prey.

MASON COOLEY

Critics . . . are of two sorts:
those who merely relieve themselves against the flower of beauty,
and those, less continent, who afterwards scratch it up.

WILLIAM EMPSON

A man is a critic when he cannot be an artist,
in the same way that a man becomes an informer
when he cannot be a soldier.

GUSTAVE FLAUBERT

Don't be dismayed by
the opinions of editors, or critics.
They are only the traffic cops of the arts.

GENE FOWLER

Critical lice are like body lice,
which desert corpses to seek the living.

THÉOPHILE GAUTIER

What a blessed thing it is that nature,
when she invented, manufactured, and patented her authors,
contrived to make critics out of the chips that were left.

OLIVER WENDELL HOLMES, SR.

A critic is a gong at a railroad crossing
clanging loudly and vainly as the train goes by.

CHRISTOPHER MORLEY

Insects sting, not from malice, but because they want to live.
It is the same with critics—
they desire our blood, not our pain.

FRIEDRICH NIETZSCHE

Critics are a dissembling, dishonest, contemptible race of men.
Asking a working writer what he thinks about critics
is like asking a lamppost what it feels about dogs.

JOHN OSBORNE, *quoted in*
Time *magazine, October 31, 1977*

Reviewers, with some rare exceptions,
are a most stupid and malignant race.
As a bankrupt thief turns thief-taker in despair,
so an unsuccessful author turns critic.

PERCY BYSSHE SHELLEY

A poet that fails in writing becomes often a morose critic;
the weak and insipid white wine makes at length excellent vinegar.

WILLIAM SHENSTONE

A bad review is like baking a cake
with all the best ingredients
and having someone sit on it.

DANIELLE STEELE

The critic's symbol should be the tumble-bug; he deposits his egg
in somebody else's dung, otherwise he could not hatch it.

MARK TWAIN

A critic is a man who knows
the way but can't drive the car.

KENNETH TYNAN

Critics are like pigs at the pastry cart.

JOHN UPDIKE

Writing criticism is to writing fiction and poetry
as hugging the shore is to sailing in the open sea.

JOHN UPDIKE

I have long felt that any reviewer
who expresses rage and loathing for a novel is preposterous.
He or she is like a person who has just put on full armor
and attacked a hot fudge sundae or banana split.

KURT VONNEGUT, JR.

Critics are like the brushers of noblemen's clothes.

HENRY WOTTON

acknowledgments

When I began working on this book, I wasn't sure what to title it, so I put the question to the people who subscribe to my weekly e-news-letter (*Dr. Mardy's Quotes of the Week*). Out of the hundreds of suggestions received, the one I finally selected was independently suggested by five separate people. I was aware of the saying—a clever alteration of a famous remark from Will Rogers—but for some reason hadn't chosen it. A special thanks to the following people:

Maya DeBus, Don Groves, Sam Hanson, Don Hauptman, and Stan Laite

My deepest gratitude goes to my wife, Katherine Robinson, who is a partner in every aspect of my life, including my book-writing efforts.

I would also like to thank my agent, George Greenfield of *Creative Well, Inc.*, and my HarperCollins editor, Phil Friedman, for their invaluable help.

Many hundreds of subscribers to my newsletter—far too numerous to list here—have provided me with quotations, many of which have found their way into this book. My heartfelt thanks to all. The contributions of the following people, however, deserve special mention: Don Hauptman for his regular *donvelopes,* Carolanne Reynolds for her helpful feedback, Terry Coleman for her knowledge of all things canine and equine, and finally to the following people for their long-standing interest in, and support of, my efforts: Karé Anderson, Amy Brennan, Pam Bruce, Jerry Caplin, Linnda Durré, Loren Ekroth, Howard Eskin, Carl Faith, Anu Garg, Fran Hamilton, Dan and Linda Hart, David Hartson, Blair Hawley,

Art Haykin, Chuck Jambotkar, Norman and Gary Kaplan, Derm Keohane, Bob Kelly, Amit Kothari, Julius La Rosa, Richard Lederer, Milton Lewin, Marlene and Barney Ovrut, Kalman Packhous, Richard Raymond III, Dennis Ridley, Don Ruhl, Lee Sechrest, Ed Sizemore, Ed Schneider, Art Tugman, G. Armour Van Horn, and Joseph Woods.

index